# Leadership in English Language Teaching and Learning

Christine Coombe
Mary Lou McCloskey
Lauren Stephenson
Neil J. Anderson

Editors

Preface by Jun Liu

Ann Arbor
THE UNIVERSITY OF MICHIGAN PRESS

# PREFACE

"How did you become TESOL President as a nonnative speaker of English?" I have been asked the same question again and again by news reporters, colleagues, and students over the years, but my answer is always the same: "Everyone has the potential to be a leader, but not everyone can be a leader. The secret is that you must desire to be a leader for a good cause first. Leadership is not developed in a day. It evolves on a daily basis over a period of time."

Not until I stepped into my first leadership position as a Nonnative English Speakers in TESOL (NNEST) Caucus chair in 1999 did I realize how important leadership is for the TESOL profession. (I was a TESOL board member in 2001 and became TESOL president in 2006.) I believe that success is within the reach of just about everyone. Although it's true that some people are born with greater natural gifts than others, the ability to lead is really a collection of skills, nearly all of which can be learned and improved. But that process doesn't happen overnight.

Leadership is complex. It has many facets: respect, experience, emotional strength, people skills, discipline, vision, momentum, timing, and so on. For the most part, extraordinary people, teams, and associations are simply ordinary people doing extraordinary things that matter to them.

TESOL matters to us because we care about the TESOL profession. For this global association to move to the next level of excellence, each and every TESOL member should take an active role in a variety of capacities and contribute to this great association. If you see changes that should be made, remember that you, as a member, are in a position to make them.

I believe that personal success without leadership ability brings only limited effectiveness. A person's impact is only a fraction of what it could be with good leadership skills. Leadership skills are indispensable in virtually all fields. But in language teaching and learning, leadership plays a role that will directly affect the quality of language education and the soundness of a program, as well as the satisfaction level of both teachers and students in their language classrooms and beyond.

As you can see, many factors that come into play in leadership are intangible. That's why leaders require so much seasoning to be effective. It was around the time I began my presidential year that I truly began to understand the many aspects of leadership in TESOL with clarity and began to appreciate how much time and energy leaders have to invest in various entities of the association we are so proud of. It is for this very reason that TESOL leaders Christine Coombe, Mary Lou McCloskey, Lauren Stephenson, and Neil J. Anderson edited this volume about leadership skill enhancement and strategies development. The contributors to this volume are an impressive line-up of leaders who have contributed to the TESOL profession in a variety of capacities.

Over the past few years, I have come a long way in honing my own leadership skills. It has truly been a learning experience. Had I had a book like this to guide me in my journey to leadership excellence, I would have saved myself a lot of time and some fumbling in the dark. As such, I am grateful that the editors have put together this wonderful volume for the many ELT professionals who desire to become future leaders in our profession.

**Jun Liu, TESOL President (2006–2007)**

# CONTENTS

# ACKNOWLEDGMENTS

This book resulted from our personal reflections as foreign/second language teachers and leaders over the past 27 years. However, it would not have been possible without the help and guidance of many leaders we have encountered along the way.

In particular we would like to acknowledge specific individuals who have encouraged and influenced our leadership. Susanne McMahon, Norm Gray, Dr. Bill Vega, Dr. Tayeb Kamali, and His Excellency Sheikh Nahayan Murbarak Al Nahayan (Christine); D. Scott Enright, Joan Morley, Loreen Pilcher, and Lydia Stack (Mary Lou); UAE Vice President, Prime Minister, and Ruler of Dubai, His Highness Sheikh Mohammed bin Rashid Al Maktoum, and his wife Princess Haya bint Al Hussein (Lauren); and Harold S. Madsen (Neil).

We also want to thank Kelly Sippell, Editor at University of Michigan Press, for her encouragement that we edit this volume and her leadership in ELT publishing.

*Grateful acknowledgment is given to the following authors, publishers, and individuals for permission to reprint previously published material.*

Gwinnett County Public Schools (Georgia) for use of graphs in Chapter 18.

John Wiley & Sons for figure from *Handbook of Leadership Development, 2d ed.*, by E. Van Veslor and C. D. McCauley, 2004.

Rose Management and Amy Schlessman for RAP Sheet.

*Every effort has been made to contact the copyright holders for permission to reprint borrowed material. We regret any oversights that may have occurred and will rectify them in future printings of this book.*

# INTRODUCTION

ELT professionals often find themselves thrust into leadership positions before they feel ready to cope with these new expanded roles. More often than not they have had little or no formal leadership training. We believe that leadership is a learnable skill. In the ELT professional literature, however, there is a dearth of material on the theory and practical application of leadership development skills.

Our decision to put this book together stemmed from the lack of material written for language educators on leadership development. We have each been in leadership positions in the field of TESOL, in our institutions, and with professional associations like TESOL, IATEFL, and local TESOL affiliates. Like many of our colleagues, we have learned much from experience and reflective practice in the field and have in many instances learned through our mistakes. This book addresses current leadership issues drawing on best practices, current leadership research, and the wider literature.

We sincerely hope that this volume—edited by two former TESOL Presidents, three former TESOL Convention Chairs, and an educational leadership specialist—will facilitate the reader's journey to leadership excellence. Contributors, all well-known leaders in the ELT profession, were selected based on their areas of expertise in the field.

This volume is intended for three groups of ELT professionals: (1) language profession leaders (i.e., elected leaders of professional organizations; university or institute leaders; or school administrators who want to learn, develop, and/or hone leadership skills and tools they will need for their professions); (2) language professionals at various levels of the profession who want to prepare themselves to take on leadership roles (i.e., initiating research, grants, and other projects; being productive team members/team leaders; leading learners effectively); and (3) language teachers who are interested in personal development and self-improvement.

## Part One: Theoretical Underpinnings

Because leadership is learnable, skills have been identified and theories have been explored that establish what we can do to develop and improve as leaders. Part One of this book provides the theoretical underpinnings of leadership development.

## Part 1: Theoretical Underpinnings

Leadership is a learnable skill. ELT professionals often find themselves in a leadership position with little or no formal leadership training. Because leadership is learnable, skills have been identified and theories have been explored that establish what we can do to develop and improve as leaders. Section One of this book provides the theoretical underpinnings of leadership development.

**Stephenson** outlines a comparison and contrast of major theories as well as a suggestion that distributed leadership is a perspective that will lead to the development of strong ELT teachers and leaders.

**Anderson** encourages leaders to view leadership through four different scopes: the telescope, the microscope, the gyroscope, and the kaleidoscope. Each provides a different view of leadership and different tools can be used to improve leadership within an ELT context.

## Part 2: Interpersonal and Communication Strategies

To encourage is to "inspire with courage, spirit or confidence, to stimulate by assistance, approval...to promote, advance or foster." Encouragement isn't always considered an essential leadership skill, but **Bailey**, with persuasive arguments and examples, argues for a central role for encouragement in teaching and leading. Bailey concludes her chapter by offering recommendations for practicing both personal encouragement and institutional encouragement.

This chapter describes **Kamhi-Stein and de Oliveira's** successful mentor-mentee relationship. They discuss the factors that contributed to their developing relationship: their values and beliefs, experiences as former international students with very limited support systems in the United States, background as South American women, status as NNES professionals, and willingness and openness to learn from each other.

The role of presentation skills in the development of leaders cannot be underestimated. **Coombe, England, and Schmidt** address the myth that educators have an advantage when it comes to public speaking because they are "in front of an audience" regularly. The authors offer background and rationale for developing one's public speaking abilities and strategies for honing these skills. The authors offer encouragement and recommendations for professionals to be lifelong students of public speaking skills, who are ever growing and improving

Effective meetings are an essential element of leadership no matter what philosophy or approach is taken. Yet many professionals are not satisfied with meeting experiences and do not find them a valuable use of their time. **McCloskey's** article provides principles and recommendations for deciding when meetings are needed, preparing for meetings, carrying out leadership roles during meetings, and meeting follow-up.

## Part 3: Personal Organization Skills and Strategies

**Murphey and Brogan** offer effective time management as a means to make leaders more relaxed and happy, accomplish more, and feel better organized. Time management is a balancing/learning act that must be developed and fine-tuned throughout professional careers. The authors offer a model for time management that includes "Nine –ates" – nine strategies for time management.

In their chapter, **Taylor, Sobel, and Al-Hamly** illuminate a path for excelling at the tenure process. This chapter provides principles and recommendations from the literature and their own successful tenure journeys on how highly qualified faculty members successfully maneuver the rigorous process of tenure and successfully balance and excel at the conflicting demands of teaching, research, and professional service.

**Algren, Dwyer, Eggington, and Witt** are four enthusiastic former convention chairs who inform readers that conferences are worth organizing, that they are unpredictable, and that delegating responsibilities is a highly effective way in managing the task. After discussing why educators attend conferences and the value of the networking that occurs there, the authors address the many considerations in preparing for a conference: choosing venues, planning concurrent sessions, selecting and inviting speakers, working with exhibitors, and publicizing the conference.

### Part 4: Program Organizational Skills and Strategies

**Curtis's** article presents seven practical principles to keep in mind when creating a professional development program. These principles are designed to overlap and complement each other and are primarily derived from the author's years as the executive director of an EAP/IEP school of English at a Canadian university.

Strategic planning is the process that determines where an entity (program, unit, department, association, etc.) wants to be at a set point in the future. Successful programs, schools, departments, companies share two qualities, argue **Christison and Murray.** First, they have an organized strategic plan and work consistently to implement it. Second, they have identified leaders who understand the processes of strategic planning and have the skills and process to carry out the plan. The authors define strategic planning, describe the role of strategic planning in business and English language programs, and describe a flexible process of strategic planning.

The ELT profession is all about communication, and the field of technology plays a big role in how we communicate as professionals. In their chapter, **Siskin and Reynolds** stress that leaders have varying degrees of technological expertise. Regardless of their own situation or approach and their level of expertise, the authors point out that a leader sets the tone for technology use among faculty. Siskin and Reynolds provide helpful information on what technological skills and abilities they feel ELT educators need to have and where and how to acquire these skills.

**Brady** believes that giving to organizations that represent one's profession is an important part of professional engagement as fundraising is vital to our personal development as teachers and researchers. In his chapter, the author defines fundraising and why ELT professionals need to engage in this important activity. His article provides several useful techniques on how to get involved in fundraising activities for your institution.

In their chapter, **Currie and Gilroy** discuss the fact that traditionally many TESOL leaders have arrived at their positions with little formal management training, particularly in the area of recruitment. They feel that the lack of professionally trained recruiters is a key issue facing the TESOL profession. Their chapter helps guide leaders as they build their skills and knowledge to become more effective recruiters of quality language teachers, and future teacher leaders.

**Panferov** tackles another area where she feels that English language program leaders lack knowledge—that of program promotion. In this chapter, the author introduces some current methods of promotion and suggests steps for establishing a promotional plan for a typical intensive university English as a Second Language program. She feels that as program leaders, it is beneficial to have a fundamental understanding of the promotional process.

This chapter presents **Quirke and Allison's** model of DREAM management which was conceived by the authors with the realization that there ought to be some way of defining best ELT leadership practices employed at their institution. By focusing on the issues and feedback received from their college community, they implemented a recognized approach to teacher development and involvement at all levels of the college community.

**Part 5: ELT Leadership Issues in U.S. Public Schools**
Demographic and work trends in the United States have brought new immigrants into rural communities that have never dealt with them before, and offer new demands for leadership. Often ESOL teachers play key roles in assuring that students receive an equitable and effective education. **Carnuccio, Huffman, O'Loughlin, and Rosenthal**, three educators and a lawyer, provide information and guidelines to see that the ESOL leaders in these situations are well-prepared.

**Arnow and Webbert's** article describes the successes of the Gwinnett County Public Schools system. Based on the premise that instructional leadership is key in educational reform, superintendents use their positions in the organization to improve instruction through staff selection, principal supervision, instructional goal-setting and monitoring, financial planning, and consultative management practices.

# PART 1

# Theoretical Underpinnings

Part 1 is designed to present readers with a theoretical background of the leadership literature and how it pertains to the English language teaching field.

**Lauren Stephenson** points out that to meet changing contemporary imperatives, responsibility for leadership is required of all English language teachers in the profession. This chapter discusses individual and collective learning in the context of the learning organization, compares and contrasts major leadership theories, and suggests a distributed leadership perspective as a means for developing ELT leaders and teachers.

**Neil J. Anderson** believes that effective leadership is essential to the success of any organization, especially among professionals in educational contexts. The focus of this chapter is to explore four tools or scopes that leaders can use for effective development of themselves and their educational contexts.

# Chapter 1

## Leadership Theories, Educational Change, and Developing a Learning Organization: An English Language Teaching (ELT) Perspective

Lauren Stephenson

The demand for English language teaching and learning is increasing. Teachers' work has become more complex, and the nature of ELT curricular, materials, and professional teacher learning is changing to ensure quality and best practice in such rapidly changing times. To meet changing contemporary imperatives (Portin, 1995), responsibility for leadership is required of all English language teachers in the profession. The same issues that are making principalship more complicated apply to ELT professionals. All necessitate a different set of skills. Change begins with the individual and requires developing the leadership skills of everyone. Learning and change in an organization are interactive social processes (Stephenson, 2004). This individual and collective learning inspires reform and provides ELT teachers with the necessary skills and knowledge to adapt to multiple changes. This chapter discusses individual and collective learning in the context of the learning organization, compares and contrasts major leadership theories, and suggests a distributed leadership perspective as a means for developing ELT leaders and teachers.

In recent years there has been an ever-increasing emphasis on the importance of leadership in ELT. As evidence of this, consider the numerous TESOL workshops on leadership, symposiums such as the TESOL Symposium on Leadership held in January 2005 in Bangkok, Thailand, and the launch of the TESOL Leadership Development Certificate Program. Such professional learning opportunities provide participants with pertinent research and insights on the important topic of leadership in ELT today. Anderson's (2005) paper from the TESOL Symposium on Leadership in Thailand focuses on thinking about leadership as the responsibility of all, suggests five core skills for ELT teachers to "serve as leaders" (2005, p. 17), and espouses a "leading from behind" perspective that considers all ELT professionals as leaders.

Murray (2005) explores "the ecology of leadership" and adopts a situational leadership perspective by evoking an image of leadership in ELT that is context sensitive. She suggests that the challenge of constant change in ELT and the "intercultural" nature of ELT is what makes leaders work in the profession. Change and the intercultural nature of ELT must be built into English language educational institutions. Murray (p. 31) suggests a transformational leadership model to direct TESOL's future that is flexible enough to allow participative and more directive leadership styles.

In this chapter, I suggest a multidimensional perspective, which means being able to adapt to rapid and continuous change and argue that a distributed leadership perspective provides a possible framework for teacher leaders in ELT (see Stephenson & McNally, 2006).

## DEVELOPING A LEARNING ORGANIZATION

The new view of leadership in learning organizations centers on creating positive change and as such must address subtle and important tasks. Change in English language education and schooling may be a part of such elements as curriculum, assessment, administration, teaching strategies, facilities, and student enrolment. In a learning organization, leaders are facilitators of change. That is, they are responsible for learning. They are designers, stewards, and teachers responsible for building organizations where people continually expand their capabilities to understand complexity, clarify vision, and improve shared mental models (Senge 1991, p. 1).

In their book *The Dance of Change,* Senge, Kleiner, Roberts, Ross, Roth, and Smith (1999) argue that a learning organization continually assesses experience, and transforms that experience into relevant knowledge, which is accessible to the whole organization. Organizational learning involves developing tangible activities: new governing ideas, innovations in the infrastructure, and new management methods and tools for changing the way people conduct their work (Senge et al., 1999, p. 33). The authors believe that when people are given the opportunity to engage in these new activities they develop the capacity to cope with change. This enduring capability for change means they are able to contribute to the organization with greater levels of commitment, talent, and diversity.

Peter Senge's (1990) book, *The Fifth Discipline,* which popularized the term *learning organization*, unites systems thinking with organizational adaptation and the realization of human potential. Senge's normative perspective of organizational learning describes learning organizations as:

> places where people continually expand their capacity to create the results they truly desire; where new and expansive patterns of thinking are nurtured, where collective aspirations are set free, and where people are continually learning how to learn together. (p. 1).

Senge's five disciplines of the learning organization include personal mastery, mental models, shared vision, team learning, and systems thinking. Senge's systems thinking view (the fifth discipline) integrates the other disciplines.

Developing an understanding of the interdependent nature of individual, team, and organizational learning clarifies how individuals and teams participate in and contribute to organizational change and continuous learning.

> The learning organization is an organization that learns continually and has the capacity to transform itself. It does this through alignment and the collective capacity to sense and interpret a changing environment; to generate new knowledge through continuous learning and change; to embed this knowledge in systems and practices; and to transform this knowledge into new products and services. (Watkins & Marsick, 1999, p. 81).

Watkins and Marsick's model identifies three levels of interrelated learning: individual learning, team learning, and organizational learning built around seven "action imperatives":

1. Create continuous learning opportunities.
2. Promote inquiry and dialogue.
3. Encourage collaboration and team learning.
4. Create systems to capture and share learning.
5. Empower people toward a collective vision.
6. Connect the organization to its environment.
7. Provide strategic leadership for learning.

These seven action imperatives can be interpreted in terms of what must change to help individuals learn and organizations become learning communities. The first three imperatives address how individuals need to change as they learn and work collectively with others to share knowledge and its application. The remaining imperatives address the way an organization needs to change as a social unit so that learning is shared and used for positive change and improvement. Learning becomes more complex as individuals interact with increasingly larger social units. That is, "individuals learn first as individuals, but as they join together in organizational change, they learn as clusters, teams, networks, and increasingly larger units" (p. 82). Individual learning is defined as "the way in which people make meaning of situations they encounter, and the way in which they acquire and apply the knowledge, attitudes, and skills they need to act in new ways." Team learning is "the way in which groups of people work and learn collaboratively and, as a result, create new knowledge together as well as the capacity for collaborative action." And organization learning is defined as "shared thinking and the capacity of a system that is embodied in systems, procedures, artefacts, and mental models" (p. 81).

Watkins and Marsick identify two action imperatives that must be in place to support learning at the individual level: the creation of continuous learning incorporating Senge's five disciplines of a learning organization (Bencivenga, 1995). This social learning extends the potential of individuals, groups, teams, the organization, and the cultures of which we are a part (Senge, 1990).

According to Flood (1999), problems, solutions and the normalization of organizational life are challenged by systemic ways of coping with social settings. People, purposes, and issues interrelate and interact in emerging cooperation and/or conflict. Systems thinking helps individuals address complexity by identifying patterns and creating the ability to change these patterns when needed. As such, systemic thinking helps an individual understand organizational cultural agents and their impact in order to develop plans for the future.

Learning and change in an organization are interactive social processes (Stephenson, 2004). Thus, within a cultural background, at the individual and group level, people judge the change process (Stephenson, 2004). Learning, therefore, is both an individual and a collective experience that links the individual to the social world (Mullins, 1996). Individuals experience the change process in their own unique ways and interpret the learning process differently from each other, and leadership shapes this change and individual and collective learning.

## LEADERSHIP THEORIES

The early leadership literature focuses on leadership traits and differentiating between leaders and nonleaders. However, recent literature addresses leadership challenges (Kouzes & Posner, 1995) and advocates a multidimensional approach toward leadership (Hooijberg, 1996). The leadership literature can be divided into universalist, behavioral, and situational approaches. Universalist approaches include great person theories, personality theories, psychoanalytic theories, and visionary leadership models such as transactional, charismatic, and transformational theories, whereas, behavioral and situational models include shared leadership approaches such as distributed leadership and focus on the differences between effective and less effective leadership. In contrast to behavioral and visionary leadership models, situational approaches are based on the idea that different styles of leadership occur in different real-life contexts.

Transactional leadership involves an exchange of valued things. Transactional leadership is based on a contractual exchange of rewards and punishments between follower and leader. These exchanges for the achievement of desired results are often implicit and based on intangibles such as feelings, social acknowledgments, and appreciation (Khunert & Lewis, 1987). Transactional leaders influence others by deriving power using rewards and punishments (Atwater & Wright, 1996). Transactional leaders use reward in exchange for performance and monitor for deviation from the rules. In addition, they use avoiding strategies such as abdicating responsibility and avoiding decision-making and situations of conflict (Hellriegel, Slocum, & Woodman, 1998).

In contrast to transactional leaders, charismatic leaders are able to create visions that align with their followers' emotional engagement (Conger & Kanungo, 1987). Charismatic leaders focus on creating a vision of what could be, identify opportunities, and increase organizational members' desire to control their behaviors. Charismatic leaders are able to change the needs and aspirations of their followers to agree with their own requirements (Heller, 1997). In this manner, followers of charismatic leaders are inspired by the hope that they will find success and power by following the leader (Conger & Kanungo, 1994; Hellriegel et al., 1998). According to Hellriegel et al., charismatic leaders are able to take complex ideas and simplify them into effective communications. They embrace risk and put themselves wholeheartedly into the leadership role.

Transformational leadership is similar to charismatic leadership. Charisma, inspiration, intellectual stimulation, and individualized consideration are key characteristics of a transformational leader (Atwater & Wright, 1996). However, in contrast to transactional leaders, transformational leaders influence their followers as a result of the followers' acceptance of certain values that the leader espouses (Wofford, Whittington, & Goodwin, 2001). Just as charismatic leaders do, transformational leaders transform followers' thoughts and attitudes motivating them to perform beyond expectations. According to Hellriegel et al. (1998), transformational leaders create a vision, frame their vision of the future, and use strategies designed to enhance their attractiveness to others. For this reason, transformational leadership is more appropriate in environments of change and ambiguity (Stephenson, 2004).

The transformational leadership model emphasises that when followers identify with a leader and the leader's vision, they feel a sense of empowerment and work together to achieve the vision. As a result, organizational change may occur, organizational members are more satisfied, and group cohesiveness improves. Furthermore, transformational leaders have the ability to turn their followers into self-directed leaders (Atwater & Wright, 1996). They take risks, build confidence in their followers by believing in their abilities, and encourage others to collaborate with them toward shared goals.

However, it is important to remember that transformational leadership is not ideal in all situations. A transformational leader's appeal to followers' emotions can lead to inappropriate, overzealous behavior by organizational members. This style has also been criticized for its lack of focus on communication and impression management skills. Furthermore, transformational leaders have come under attack for their autocratic management style (Hellriegel et al., 1998).

Situational leadership theories identify certain leadership characteristics that match the complexities of real-life. Situational approaches have dominated the study of leadership for the past three decades. Hersey and Blanchard's (1993) model for situational leadership suggests that there is no one best leadership style for all situations. They argue that a manager's leadership style must be flexible in order to meet the changing needs of organizational members and the situation. Their framework is based on the amount of relationship and task behavior that a leader provides in a given situation. At the same time, the amount of either relationship or task behavior is dependent on the readiness of the follower. Task behaviour refers to the control and supervision a leader uses with his or her followers. Relationship behavior refers to a leader's listening skills (Morrison, 1994), the support he or she provides followers, and the extent to which followers are involved in decision-making. Follower readiness refers to the followers' willingness and ability to perform tasks.

The most recent educational leadership literature distinguishes between leading as the quality of one person, the appointed leaders, and leadership as a collective phenomenon referred to as distributed leadership. Distributed leadership is a way of thinking about leadership where leadership is a collective phenomenon that empowers individuals to make their work more meaningful and effective. Thus, leadership is seen as the professional work of everyone; that is, everyone is responsible and accountable for leadership within his or her area. Individuals who share a common purpose, engage in teamwork, and mutually respect one another cooperate together to create change.

Distributed leadership for change takes a systems view and considers inter- acting elements of change. Sergiovanni's (1994, 1996) systems view of change suggests four interacting units of change: the individual, the school, the workflow, and the political system. Many school leaders tend to focus only on workflow (changing targets, establishing steps to create change, curriculum, materials and teaching units, and professional development) to bring about change. However, for change to be effective and learning to occur, individual needs, interests, and relationships must be considered, along with the nature of the school climate and its culture and the political system in which the school operates.

Change is often hindered by the failure to recognize that change is usually gradual, messy, complex, and difficult. Change is not readily accepted especially when the change is not recognized as holding great promise for the individual. In such cases extra effort is required, particularly in the early phases of the change process, to create a shared vision. The change process brings a certain amount of anxiety and can be threatening for individuals. As such, teachers and others require regular feedback on the effects of their efforts.

Successful leaders are those who distribute leadership, understand relation- ships, and recognize the importance of reciprocal learning processes that lead to shared purposes (Harris, 2005). Leaders who draw on distributed leadership models are more connected to people than those holding the traditional forms of leadership.

> Much of the school leadership literature has tended to concern itself with the traits and characteristics of principals instead of probing the nature of the relationship between leadership and organizational change and development... (Harris, 2005).

Effective leadership in ELT requires a multidimensional perspective, which means being able to adapt to rapid and continuous change. Transformational and distributed leadership theories can create change, facilitate learning, and improve school effectiveness (Stephenson & McNally, 2006). Similarly to Harris (2005), I believe more research is required regarding effective distributed leadership practice, its relationship to improved student outcomes, and how it can be nurtured, supported, and developed. It is this research base that will move distributed leadership from a way of analyzing leadership to a way of describing leadership practice for positive change and improved learning in ELT.

---

### Discussion Questions

1. This chapter discussed transactional, charismatic, transformational, situational, and distributed leadership perspectives. What do you understand about the phrase "leadership in ELT"? What is your leadership philosophy/approach?
2. Who are your leadership models, and how do you perceive that these models affect the decisions you make?
3. Discuss whether leadership in ELT is merely a matter of style and matching that style to the needs of a school.
4. What leadership practices might contribute to developing and sustaining distributed leadership? Give examples.
5. What sources of change are most likely to generate transformational or distributed leadership? Give examples.

---

## REFERENCES

Anderson, N. (2005). Leadership is not about position: Leading from behind. Paper presented at the *TESOL Symposium on Leadership: Initiating and Managing Changes in English Language Teaching*, Bangkok, Thailand.

Argyris, C., & Schon, D. (1978). *Organizational learning: A theory of action perspective.* San Francisco: Jossey-Bass.

Atwater, L. E., & Wright, W. J. (1996). Power and transformational and transactional leadership in public and private organizations. [Electronic version]. *International Journal of Public Administration, 19*(6), 963–990. Retrieved June 17, 1999, from http://proquest.umi.com/pqdweb

Bencivenga, D. (1995). Learning organizations evolve. *New Directions, HR Magazine, 40*(10), 69–73.

Berryman, R. (1995). *Systems thinking and organizations: An initial inquiry into the subject.* CSWT Papers. Retrieved July 8, 1999, from http://www.workteams.unt.edu/reports/rberyman.htm

Conger, J. A., & Kanungo, R. (1987). Toward a behavioral theory of charismatic leadership on organizational settings. *Academy of Management Review, 12*(4), 637–647. Retrieved May 1, 2000, from http://proquest.umi.com/pqdweb?Did=000000000141907&Fmt=6&Deli=1&Mtd=1&Idx=2&Sid=1&RQT=309

Conger, J. A., & Kanungo, R. N. (1994). Charismatic leadership in organizations: Perceived behavioural attributes and their measurement. *Journal of Organizational Behavior, 15,* 439–452.

Flood, R. L. (1999). *Rethinking the fifth discipline: Learning within the unknowable.* London: Routledge.

Gamson, Z. (1994). Collaborative learning comes of age. [Electronic version]. *Change, 26*(5), 44–50. Retrieved May 15, 1999, from http://proquest.umi.com/pqdweb?Did=000000035494376&Fmt=1&Deli=1&Mtd=1&Idx=1&Sid=5&RQT=309

Harris, A. (2005). Leading or misleading? Distributed leadership and school improvement. Retrieved September 7, 2006, from http://faculty.ed.uiuc.edu/westbury/JCS/Vol37/harris.htm

Hellriegel, D., Slocum, J. W., & Woodman, R. W. (1998). *Organizational behavior* (8th ed.). Cincinnati, OH: South-Western College Publishing.

Hersey, P., & Blanchard, K. H. (1993). *Management of organizational behaviour: Utilizing human resources.* Englewood Cliffs, NJ: Prentice Hall.

Hooijberg, R. (1996). A multidirectional approach toward leadership: An extension of the concept of behavioral complexity. *Human Relations, 49*(7), 918–948.

Khunert, R., & Lewis, G. (1987). Transactional leadership and transformational leadership: A constructive/developmental analysis. *Academy of Management Review, 12*(4), 648–657.

Kouzes, J. M., & Posner, B. Z. (1995). *The leadership challenge.* San Francisco: Jossey Bass.

Morrison, K. E. (1994). *Leadership skills.* Tuscon, AZ: Fisher Books.

Mullins, L. J. (1996). *Management and organizational behaviour.* (4th ed.). London: Pitman.

Murray, D. E. (2005). The ecology of leadership. Paper presented at the *TESOL Symposium on Leadership: Initiating and Managing Changes in English Language Teaching,* Bangkok, Thailand.

Portin, B. (1995) Primary headship in a time of systemic change: Conceptions of leadership. Case studies of three Oxfordshire primary headteachers. Unpublished doctoral dissertation, Oxford University, United Kingdom.

Senge, P. M. (1990). *The fifth discipline.* New York: Doubleday.

———. (1991). Learning organizations. [Electronic version]. *Executive Excellence, 8*(9) 7–9. Retrieved July 14, 1998, from http://proquest.umi.com/pqdweb?Did=000000000393373&Fmt=3&Deli=1&Mtd=1&Idx=1&Sid=103&RQT=309

———. (1992). Building learning organizations. [Electronic version]. *The Journal for Quality and Participation, 15*(2) 30–39. Retrieved July 14, 1998, from http://proquest.umi.com/pqdweb?Did=000000008948489&Fmt=3&Deli =1&Mtd=1&Idx=5&Sid=104&RQT=309

———. (1997). *Slow threats.* Society for Organizational Learning. Retrieved March 15, 1997, from http://learning.mit.edu/res/kr/slowthreats.html

Senge, P., Kleiner, A., Roberts, C., Ross, R., Roth, G., & Smith, B., (1999). *The dance of change.* New York: Doubleday.

Sergiovanni, T. J. (1994). Organizations or communities? Changing the metaphor changes the theory. *Educational Administration Quarterly, 30,* 214–226.

———. (1996). *Leadership for the schoolhouse: How is it different? Why is it important?* San Francisco: Jossey-Bass.

Stephenson, L. T. (2004). Individual learning within an organization: An autoethnographic learning journey. Unpublished doctoral dissertation, University of Sydney, Australia.

Stephenson, L., & McNally, P. (2006). Creating teacher leaders: Site-based professional development in the UAE. Paper presented at the ASCD Conference, Chicago, IL.

Watkins, K. E., & Marsick, V. J. (1999). Sculpting the learning community: New forms of working and organizing. [Electronic version]. *NASSP Bulletin, 83*(604), 78–87. Retrieved June 21, 2001, from http://proquest.umi.com/pqdweb?Did=000000038788444&Fmt=3&Deli=1&Mtd=1&Idx=1&Sid=0&RQT=309&LDid=000000038793695&LSid=8&L=1

Wofford, J. C., Whittington, J. L., & Goodwin, V. L. (2001). Follower motive patterns as situational moderators for transformational leadership effectiveness. [Electronic version]. *Journal of Managerial Issues, 13*(20), 196–211.

# Chapter 2

## The Four Scopes of Effective Leadership Development

Neil J. Anderson

During a trip to Yemen, I visited one of the oldest secondary schools in the country, The Cultural Center for Educational and Developmental Activities, in Hadhramaut, Yemen. On the outside of the school is an inscription in both English and Arabic: "He who wants to be a leader, Let him be a bridge." This statement has provided inspiration for me as a leader in the English language teaching profession. It has helped me understand that I can serve as a bridge for other leaders. It has helped me to articulate how I believe leadership development happens.

Effective leadership is essential to the success of any organization, especially among professionals in educational contexts. Within educational contexts, most leaders began their careers as teachers and then moved into leadership roles. I believe that it is important for teachers and leaders of teachers to gain a better understanding of leadership development so that greater success can be achieved in the educational settings in which we work. The focus of this chapter is to explore four tools that leaders can use for effective development of themselves and their educational contexts.

Van Veslor and McCauley (2004, p. 2) define leader development as the expansion of a person's capacity to be effective in leadership roles and processes. Leadership roles and processes are those that facilitate setting direction, creating alignment, and maintaining commitment in groups of people who share common work.

Van Veslor and McCauley (p. 4) outline a two-part leader development model. Figure 1 illustrates their model. Note that in Part (a) developmental experiences must take place in order to lead to Part (b), the development process. Assessment, challenge, and support are essential ingredients to developmental experiences. The context of the organization is central to the development process. The context includes interaction between a variety of developmental experiences and the ability of the individual to learn, and both lead to leader development.

opportunities and the promotion of dialogue and inquiry. They claim that for ongoing learning to occur it should grow out of everyday work activity and be used strategically to improve work processes and, as a result, learning. They suggest ways that school administrators and teachers can take advantage of learning opportunities through self-reflection, the use of mentors and coaches for staff members, and integrating technology to better help individuals gain new skills and resources for continuing education and professional development. They state dialogue and inquiry can create a culture in which people feel that they are in a safe environment to ask questions and discuss difficult issues. They further state that all levels of the organization need to be open to giving and receiving feedback.

Their action imperatives at the team learning level are focused on creating a culture in which people feel they are all part of the same team with a common purpose and shared vision. Collaboration is an essential skill required in effective teamwork and team learning (Gamson, 1994). Watkins and Marsick state that group work that includes students, faculty, staff, administrators, and parents encourages collaborative efforts within schools.

According to Watkins and Marsick (p. 83) organizational learning occurs when "improvements are made in standard operating procedures, policies, the culture, work processes, and the information systems that maintain the memory of the organization." They claim such learning in schools might result in curriculum renewal and reform, team teaching, innovative ways of organizing teaching, learning and assessment, or a changed vision for the school. However, rather than focusing on the development of strategies and systems, the majority of organizations concentrate on individual and team level learning (Watkins & Marsick, 1999). They claim that establishing systems to capture and share learning, and empowering people toward a collective vision, are the two critical action imperatives at the organizational level.

Just as Watkins and Marsick focus on the interconnectedness of clusters of individuals across an organization, so too does Senge in his approach that combines systems dynamics with Argyris and Schon's (1978) theory-of-action perspective. Senge's fifth discipline, systems thinking, integrates his four other disciplines of a learning organization: personal mastery, mental models, team learning, and shared vision. Systems thinking means understanding the internal and external relationships that govern the system and subsystems in which an individual or group are operating. Individuals tend to focus on isolated parts of the systems instead of on the whole. Systems thinking clarifies the "big picture" and assists in understanding the patterns of interrelationships. It refers to the system within a team, its relationships with other systems and teams, and its relationship with the organization and other organizations (Berryman, 1995).

Systems thinking suggests that the self is always in the process of transformation and is never a "given" (Senge, 1997). Transformation, which involves learning and change, occurs when organizational members interact with other individuals,

**Figure 1:**   Leader Development Model

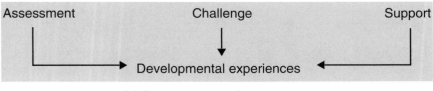

(a) Developmental Experiences

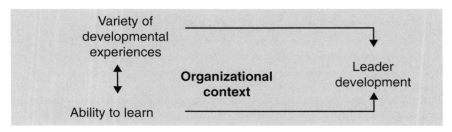

(b) The Development Process

Source: Van Veslor & McCauley 2004.

In order for the leadership development process to move forward, I suggest that we need useful tools to see ourselves and those with whom we work. The Greek root *scope* means to watch, to look at, to gaze. Good leaders *look at* themselves and *watch* those whom they lead as well as the contexts in which they lead. Four scopes serve as useful tools to watch, to look at, or to gaze at ourselves as leaders and at those we lead. We will add prefixes to this root to get a different view of leadership and how we can develop as leaders.

In his great work, *Les Miserables*, Victor Hugo wrote in 1862, "Where the telescope ends, the microscope begins. Which of the two has the grander view?" We will use the metaphor of the telescope and the microscope to look at the concept of leadership. We will also add the views to this important concept from the perspective of the gyroscope and the kaleidoscope. Together we will examine how these four scopes serve as useful metaphors for leaders as they develop themselves and lead in their programs. Unlike Hugo, I will not consider which scope has the grander view, but rather I will argue that leaders in our profession require the use of all four scopes.

## PREFIX #1: *TELE*

The Greek prefix *tele-* means distant or far off. The telescope allows us to view a setting that is in the distance or is far off. As we view the object from a distance, we are able to see the context or complete setting of the object as we use the lens of the telescope to move in on it. Leaders must keep the big picture in mind. Do not forget that you need to see the entire field in which you are leading.

One useful activity that I have regularly used to give me the big picture view of an organizational context in education is called an historical sign-in. An historical sign-in provides leaders with a perspective of an organization's history. I have participated in historical sign-in activities where a very long piece of paper is placed on the wall with key dates identified across the paper. A set of questions is then asked, and individuals *sign in* by recording their name on the time line at the appropriate date. An example of the kinds of questions that could be asked include:

- When were you first aware of the organization?
- When and how did you first become involved?
- When did you become a *trustee*?
- What was the image of the organization at that time?
- What was happening in the external world (local, national, international) at that time? How was the organization affected by those events?
- What was happening in the internal world (inside your organization)?
- What key individuals have shaped your organization? What role did they play in influencing and shaping the life of the organization?
- What groups or individuals does your organization most want to influence? Why?

Once you have a visual perspective on the answers to these questions, you begin to get historical information about why certain decisions and/or policies have been made within an organization. Perhaps you have often wondered why certain things happen the way they do in your program. By participating in an historical sign-in activity, you can get an historical overview that will answer your questions. This big-picture overview is made possible because of telescopic view.

Refer back to Figure 1 on page 18. The organizational context is dependent on a variety of developmental experiences. Van Velsor and McCauley use this model to discuss the development of leaders. But I believe we can also use the model to examine the development process of an organization. The historical sign-in begins to give us insight into the variety of events and activities that have shaped the formation of the educational context in which we lead.

## PREFIX #2: *MICRO*

Microscopes are instruments consisting of a combination of lenses for enlarging images of minute objects. With a microscope we can examine small details that have an impact on our development as leaders as well as the small details that shape our contexts.

The National High Magnetic Field Laboratory in Tallahassee, Florida, has an interesting feature on its website known as *The Power of 10* sequence. The sequence begins 10 million light years away from the Earth in the Milky Way. The sequence moves "through space towards the Earth in successive orders of magnitude until we reach a tall oak tree just outside the buildings of the National High Magnetic Field Laboratory in Tallahassee, Florida. After that, we begin to move from the actual size of a leaf into a microscopic world that reveals leaf cell walls, the cell nucleus, chromatin, DNA and finally, into the subatomic universe of electrons and protons." (Molecular Expressions, n.d)

This visual image is one of the most powerful examples I am aware of that gives us both a telescopic and a microscopic view. We see the power of viewing the Earth within its context in the universe as well as the detailed view of a cell, the cell nucleus, DNA, electrons, and protons. The level of detail gives us a view we otherwise would not have.

Colin Powell (1995) emphasized the importance of attending to the small things as a leader. He outlined 13 rules (p. 613) that highlight the importance of paying attention to the microscopic view of leadership. Note how Powell's 13 rules give importance to things that may seem insignificant in the big picture but that enhance your leadership. He states:

1. It ain't as bad as you think. It will look better in the morning.
2. Get mad, then get over it.
3. Avoid having your ego so close to your position that when your position falls, your ego goes with it.
4. It can be done!
5. Be careful what you choose. You may get it.
6. Don't let adverse facts stand in the way of a good decision.
7. You can't make someone else's choices. You shouldn't let someone else make yours.
8. Check small things.
9. Share credit.
10. Remain calm. Be kind.
11. Have a vision. Be demanding.
12. Don't take counsel of your fears or naysayers.
13. Perpetual optimism is a course multiplier.

One exercise that I have participated in many times with different groups of leaders in order to get a microscopic view in an educational context is one called a SWOT analysis. A SWOT analysis allows leaders and organizations to examine **S**trengths, **W**eaknesses, **O**pportunities, and **T**hreats. In the process of completing a SWOT analysis, details emerge that provide valuable assessment that in turn leads to developmental experiences for both leaders and organizations.

I encourage leaders to conduct a personal SWOT analysis. Find a time when you can be uninterrupted for at least an hour. Identify your strengths. What is it that motivates you to do what you do? What skills do you have to be an effective leader? What would your organization lose if you were not the leader? By answering these detailed, microscopic questions, leaders gain insights into themselves. Next, what weaknesses do you have that you need to be very aware of? What causes you to be less effective than you should be? What changes do you feel you need to make to be a more effective leader? An honest look at one's weaknesses provides useful insights into leadership.

If you are having difficulties identifying your weaknesses, find two to three trusted colleagues. Explain to them that you are conducting a personal SWOT analysis and that you want them to be brutally honest in identifying one to two weaknesses that they see in you. As you listen, do not get defensive. Simply listen. If more than one of these trusted colleagues mentions the same weakness, this is something that you should clearly pay attention to.

Then examine the opportunities that you have both for growth as a leader in your current position as well as opportunities for additional leadership. Finally, examine the threats that exist that prevent you from accomplishing all that you desire to accomplish as a leader. A thorough SWOT analysis can give you a view similar to that of a microscope into yourself as a leader.

Next, complete a SWOT analysis for the educational organization that you lead. This SWOT analysis is most effective when as many people as possible in the organization can participate. List the major strengths of your organization as it faces the next three to five years. What value does your organization make to society as a whole? Then list the major weaknesses of your organization as it faces the next three to five years. What changes need to happen in the organization in order for everyone to be more effective? Next, list the major opportunities that you believe your organization will face in the next three to five years that will determine whether it succeeds or fails. Finally, list the major threats that you believe your organization will face in the next three to five years that will determine whether it succeeds or fails.

Our effectiveness as leaders can be enhanced as we carefully assess the strengths, weaknesses, opportunities, and threats that we individually face as well as those that face our organizations. As pointed out in Figure 1 from Van Veslor and McCauley, assessment leads to developmental experiences that help you develop as a leader. The SWOT analysis serves as one such assessment experience. Good leaders will do all that they can to use the view of a microscope to assist themselves and their organizations.

## PREFIX #3: *GYRO*

A gyroscope is a disk mounted to spin rapidly about an axis. Gyroscopes serve three primary functions. First, gyroscopes serve as a compass. This shows that the direction of gravitation will not change when there is no outside power involved. This is the principle of the gyrocompass. Second, gyroscopes serve as a stabilizer. To keep stability on ships, heavy weights are installed on the bottom. In this way a ship, will keep its stability above the water line on the upper part of the ship. In the case of passenger ships, the gyrostabilizer is used to stabilize and eliminate rolling, allowing the ship to float with a lower water line. Finally, gyroscopes serve as an auto pilot. After an airplane reaches a certain height and direction, it can fly automatically to its destination with the use of an autopilot. When the wind changes the direction of an airplane to the right or left, it will cause the rudder to work automatically and puts the plane back on course.

Covey (2004, p. 100) emphasizes that "literally hundreds of books and thousands of articles have come out in the last few years on leadership. This points out how vital the subject is. Leadership really is the enabling art. The purpose of schools is educating kids, but if you have bad leadership, you have bad education. . . . We could give illustration after illustration to show that leadership is the highest of the arts, simply because it *enables* all of the other arts and professions to work." The gyroscope is the tool for viewing the enabling art. Within organizations and for leaders, the development of a written mission statement leads to setting a direction and can keep the organization on course when challenges and difficulties arise.

As leaders we have several tools available to assist us in our use of the gyroscopic view of leadership. A mission statement is one such tool. A mission statement is a concise statement that highlights why your organization is important. What is it that you hope to accomplish and what are the most important reasons why your organization exists?

Your organization's mission statement is a written proclamation of who you are and what you are about. Your organization's mission statement should provide an outsider the big picture of issues that are of importance to you and your members. Covey (1989) serves as an excellent resource for developing a written mission statement.

I believe that each leader should articulate a personal mission statement. Who am I, and what do I believe are the unique contributions that I can make? Covey (2004) encourages us to identify and create passions in life. He says, "The key to creating passion in your life is to find your unique talents and your specific role and purpose in the world" (p. 76). I believe that our individual mission statements ought to be written describing our passions for being engaged in English language teaching and learning. The mission statement gives us an opportunity for an in-depth view of what we believe we can contribute to the world. I have created my own mission statement and identified the key roles and identities that I have in my life. The role descriptions I have created for myself include individual, son-brother-husband-father-grandfather, professor, researcher, and ELT program administrator. In each of these roles, I have articulated for myself what I believe my reason for being is. My mission statement is a living document. I have a copy that I review regularly and update as my roles and responsibilities change. The mission statement then serves as a stabilizer and a guide for me as I lead.

Once you have written a mission statement, one useful way of letting it guide your work in your program is to have the elements of the statement be the organizing framework for meeting agendas. By using the elements in this way, your mission statement becomes a document that guides decisions you make and the work you do in your program.

A mission statement also serves as an assessment to help develop effective leaders. Recall once again Figure 1 and the role that assessment plays in developmental experiences. As we view leadership development from the view of a gyroscope, we must determine how a mission statement can be used in our educational contexts to help stabilize and guide decisions that we make.

## PREFIX #4: *KALEIDO*

Kaleidoscopes are instruments containing loose bits of colored material (glass or plastic) between two flat plates and two plane mirrors so placed that changes of position of the bits of material are reflected in an endless variety of patterns. I enjoy sitting with a kaleidoscope and watching the changing patterns that emerge as I turn the lens. One thing I have noticed is that many of the views last a very short time. The view from the kaleidoscope is dynamic and changing. The elements that go into making the view do not change but the conditions that the pieces are placed in change. I think that this provides instruction for leaders.

The kaleidoscopic view in educational leadership contexts will be influenced by what you see through the telescope and the microscope. It is here within the view of the kaleidoscope that everything gets blended together. I think the kaleidoscopic view allows leaders to plan for the long-range future of the organization. This is accomplished through strategic planning.

Strategic planning involves identifying the direction you desire to go as an individual or within an organization. Strategic planning is more than setting goals. It involves envisioning what influence you wish to have within your sphere of responsibility. Strategic planning involves making specific changes in what you as an individual or an organization do to accomplish your plan. Rowley and Sherman (2001, p. 202) define *strategic planning* as "a set of decisions that are designed to create a competitive advantage in order to achieve an organization's goals and objectives." As a leader in an educational context, you should want to create for yourself or your organization an advantage that will help you be the very best teacher, administrator, test developer, or curriculum designer and for your organization or program to be the best at what you offer your learners. Strategic planning is the process of identifying that competitive advantage.

The strategic planning process provides an opportunity to use what you have learned from conducting the historical sign-in and the SWOT analysis. You are now in a position as a leader to direct the writing of your vision of the future. Set some specific goals for the next year, the next two to three years, and the next five years. Record these goals in a place so that you can regularly refer to them and measure your accomplishments.

Just as the view from a kaleidoscope is dynamic, strategic planning should be dynamic. Do not think that a strategic plan will solve all your problems as a leader. The plan simply serves as a directional document for your organization. Use it to make adjustments in how you approach the future but also regularly review it to make sure that it is meeting your needs. A strategic plan incorporates both parts (a) and (b) from Figure 1 described earlier. The developmental experiences and the developmental processes are realized in the kaleidoscopic view of leadership.

A word of caution may be appropriate. Do not try to be all things to all people. In your organization, make sure you carefully identify who it is that you serve and do not try to meet everyone's needs. Acknowledge that there are other organizations you can work with to help accomplish goals and objectives.

This chapter has reviewed how four scopes can be used to assist individuals in the process of leadership development. Telescopes give leaders a big-picture view of the contexts in which they work. The tool of an historical sign-in can assist leaders in getting part of the big picture. Microscopes give leaders a detailed view of the context in which they lead. A SWOT analysis is an effective tool for obtaining that detailed view of an organization. Gyroscopes provide stability and direction just as a mission statement can for an educational organization. Finally, kaleidoscopes provide a blended view from the historical sign-in, the SWOT analysis, and the mission statement, which then leads to the development of a strategic plan.

I attended a Native American presentation at Tillicum Village in Blake Island State Park in Seattle, Washington. During the performance the script states, "The visions of our leaders are written in the hearts of our people." I believe that this statement summarizes effective leadership development. If those we lead have a vision written in their hearts, this signifies for me that everyone is working toward accomplishing the vision. Effective leaders use all available tools to improve themselves and the organizations in which they work. May we each strive to develop ourselves as effective leaders.

---

| Suggested Resources |
|---|

*Journal of Academic Leadership:* **www.academicleadership.org/**

> This online journal is particularly valuable because it addresses leadership in academia. The vast majority of material on leadership development focuses on the field of business. Because TESOL professionals are engaged in academic pursuits, I have found this site valuable in helping me to translate business principles into an academic context.

*The Center for Creative Leadership:* **www.ccl.org/**

> This website has a particularly useful link to new publications on leadership development. This, as well as many other websites, can alert us to new publications that may help us in our quest to develop as leaders. I recently

purchased the *Handbook of Leadership Development,* edited by McCauley and Van Velsor, from the Center for Creative Leadership.

### *The Greenleaf Center for Servant-Leadership:* **www.greenleaf.org/**

This website offers a free downloadable article on servant and teacher leadership, and it lists the Greenleaf Center's international offices in Japan, Korea, the Philippines, and Singapore. The fact that the Greenleaf Center has offices outside the United States shows that it is trying to reach beyond a leadership model based in a single country.

The contact information for four professional associations designed to help individuals develop as leaders follows. Check the websites for changes to contact information.

American Society for Training and Development
1640 King St., Box 1443
Alexandria, Virginia, 22313–2043 USA
Tel: 703-683-8100, Fax: 703-683-8103
www.astd.org/astd

Association for Supervision and Curriculum Development
1703 N. Beauregard St.
Alexandria, VA 22311–1714 USA
Tel: 703-578-9600, Fax: 1-703-575-5400
www.ascd.org/

National Center for Nonprofit Boards
2000 L St., NW, Suite 510
Washington, DC 20036–4907 USA
Tel: 202-452-6262, Fax: 202-452-6299
www.boardsource.org/

Teachers of English to Speakers of Other Languages
700 S. Washington St., Suite 200
Alexandria, Virginia 22314 USA
Tel: 703-836-0774, Fax: 703-836-7864
www.tesol.org/

*Discussion Questions*

1. Discuss Van Veslor and McCauley's model for Leader Development. What is your reaction to the model? What additional information do you need to better understand the model?
2. Prepare a timeline for a historical sign-in. Choose an educational program that you are familiar with. What dates would you include on the timeline? Why?
3. Conduct a personal SWOT analysis. What do you see as your strengths, weaknesses, opportunities, and threats as a leader or potential leader?
4. Review a written mission statement. (Possible sources could be the TESOL affiliate that you are a member of or the university or college where you are currently studying.) Do you think that the mission statement accurately articulates the mission of the organization? Why or why not?
5. How would you begin to develop a strategic plan for an ESL program? What resources would you need? Who would you involve in writing the strategic plan?

## REFERENCES

Covey, S. R. (1989). *The 7 habits of highly effective people.* New York: Simon & Schuster.

Covey, S. R. (2004). *The 8th habit: From effectiveness to greatness.* New York: Free Press.

Molecular Expressions. (n.d). Retrieved January 15, 2007, from http://micro.magnet.fsu.edu/primer/java/scienceopticsu/powersof10/)

Powell, C. L. (1995). *My American journey.* New York: Random House.

Rowley, D. J., & Sherman, H. (2001). *From strategy to change.* San Francisco: Jossey-Bass.

Van Veslor, E., & McCauley, C. D. (2004). Our view of leadership development. In C. D. McCauley & E. Van Velsor (Eds.), *Handbook of leadership development* (2nd ed.) (pp. 1–22). San Francisco: Jossey-Bass.

# Part 2

# Interpersonal and Communication Strategies

Leadership preparation must be carefully designed to broaden a teacher's knowledge of leadership theories and principles, as well as to develop interpersonal, communication, and organizational skills.

**Bailey** believes that the issue of encouragement is important to ELT teachers and leaders. In her chapter, she discusses the importance and impact of encouragement on the leadership potential and careers of ELT educators.

In their chapter, **Kamhi-Stein and de Oliveira** describe the mentoring relationship in which they (two NNES professionals with varying degrees of experience) have had and how this relationship has impacted their personal and professional growth.

**Coombe, England, and Schmidt** stress how important presentation and public speaking skills are to the professional development of English language educators. In their chapter, they point out that teaching and public speaking, although similar in many ways, require two different skill sets and provide recommendations for being better public speakers and presenters.

In her chapter, **McCloskey** reminds us that meetings are an essential element of leadership. She provides principles and recommendations for running effective meetings.

# Chapter 3

## Passing on the Light: Encouragement as a Leadership Skill

Kathleen M. Bailey

*"That light which has been given to me, I desire to pass undimmed to others."*
***(Campfire Girls Creed)***

In the autumn of 1976, I had just completed my master's degree in TESL at the University of California, Los Angeles (UCLA). I was working as the coordinator of the ESL Service Courses there, which entailed supervising about 20 teaching assistants (TAs) and making sure the curriculum was coherent, across sections of the same course, and across the courses at different levels. The work was challenging for me, since I had just graduated from the TA ranks myself.

My department chair, Russ Campbell, was contacted by some people who wished to organize a panel presentation at the next year's TESOL Convention, which would be held in Florida. The panel topic was supervising teaching assistants in university ESL programs. Russ told the panel organizers that he would participate in the panel if I could be his co-author, because I was the one who really knew what was going on with the teaching assistants in the service courses.

I was flabbergasted! I had only been to one TESOL Convention, and my job as a student volunteer had been to move chairs and make sure that speakers had water and sufficient numbers of handouts. Russ was suggesting that I should actually give a presentation—with him—on a panel of people whose work I had read all through graduate school. I didn't feel up to the task, but Russ encouraged me and together we produced a credible presentation. That was one of Russ Campbell's greatest talents: finding untapped abilities in his students and colleagues, and bringing them out into the open through encouragement and guidance. Like a water wizard with a divining rod, he could detect abilities in us (his students and colleagues) that we ourselves did not know we possessed.

Over the years I have come to believe that providing encouragement is one of the most important skills of leadership. It may well be the most important. In fact, encouragement has been described as a leadership skill in published writings (see, e.g., Dinkmeyer & Eckstein, 1996).

When we consider definitions of the verb *to encourage*, we can see its direct connection to leadership. *To encourage* is "to inspire with courage, spirit or confidence;…to stimulate by assistance, approval, etc.;…to promote, advance, or foster" (*Webster's*, 1996, p. 641). Synonyms for *encourage* are *embolden, hearten, reassure, urge, support, aid, help*, and *praise* (ibid.). As labels, these verbs all represent speech acts that have an important place in teaching or in any kind of leading.

## IMPORTANCE OF GIVING ENCOURAGEMENT AS A SKILL

The issue of encouragement is important to ELT teachers and leaders for several reasons. First, the ability to encourage is one of the fundamental skills of teaching. By scaffolding students' learning, providing feedback, bolstering confidence, and helping people move ahead as they grapple with difficult concepts or acquire new skills, teachers promote learning.

Second, unfortunately, teaching is a profession that sometimes leads to burn-out—a documented syndrome not uncommon among people involved in the helping professions (Maslach, 1982). *Burnout* is a type of job stress. It is defined as "a response to the chronic emotional strain of dealing extensively with other human beings, particularly when they are troubled or having problems" (p. 3). I believe that, coupled with appropriate action, encouragement from program administrators and colleagues can help teachers and other employees combat burnout. (I will return to the topic of burnout later in the chapter.)

Finally, the profession in general constantly needs renewing. As one generation ages, new leaders step up and move the profession forward. Encouraging young people to take on leadership roles is an important responsibility for present-day leaders in any profession, but perhaps especially in English language teaching. I say this because I see advocating as a necessary component of leadership, and our profession involves advocating for learners as well as providing language instruction and practice opportunities. For this reason, we continually need to develop teachers who are willing to be advocates and leaders.

## ENCOURAGING NEW LEADERS: SOME EXAMPLES

In this section I will look at some examples of encouragement, and how the smallest comment or suggestion can have important effects. We will begin with an illustrative anecdote, and then we consider encouragement and burnout before turning to a discussion of workplace fulfillment.

A few years ago, Andy Curtis and Mary Romney organized a colloquium for a TESOL Convention. The presenters all talked about their experiences of being TESOL professionals of color, and how issues of race and ethnicity had influenced them as youngsters and as adults. Repeatedly the speakers shared comments that a teacher or a classmate had once made to them—comments that had had powerful effects, whether positive or negative, on their self-image, their motivation, and their attitudes toward others. When the colloquium ended and the panelists were entertaining questions from the audience, I asked Mary and Andy what they planned to do next with this information, this momentum. They looked startled, because their efforts at planning and organizing the colloquium had led to a successful multi-ethnic, multi-national effort to discuss sensitive issues at a TESOL Convention. I am sure they thought they were done. (Andy didn't exactly say, "What do you mean, 'next', Bailey?" but that was what the look on his face said.) I encouraged them to collect the written versions of the presentations and produce a book, because I thought the ideas and experience I had heard about that day were important enough that they should be made available to TESOL professionals who had not been at the colloquium.

Later, Andy and Mary asked me to write the preface of the edited volume that came out of their colloquium: *Color, Race and English Language Teaching: Shades of Meaning.* This volume arose from a colloquium they had organized for a TESOL Convention. In the preface to the edited collection of these talks I wrote,

> What struck me most as I read the manuscript was how often an event that originally lasted only minutes (or even seconds) had so profoundly influenced a child, an adolescent, or an adult—how just a few words could make a lasting impact on the hearer, whether for good or for ill. Reading about these authors' experiences made me search my memory: As a classmate, as a teacher, had I ever said anything terribly hurtful, or particularly encouraging, to someone different from me—another student or one of my own pupils? (Bailey, 2005, preface)

In both listening to the speakers and reading their written words later, I was struck, again and again, at how small a thing encouragement is, and how little effort is needed to offer it. Likewise, I was struck by how profound an effect discouragement and disparagement can have on a person's life.

## BURNOUT AND ENCOURAGEMENT

I believe that encouragement, coupled with appropriate administrative action and self-help, can stave off burnout among language teachers (and people in the other helping professions as well). The role of a leader (whether that person is a supervisor, a principal, a department chair, a head teacher) in offering support and encouragement can be invaluable.

As noted, burnout consists of three factors. The first is *emotional exhaustion,* which occurs when a worker is overextended or over-involved emotionally (Maslach, 1982). As Maslach describes this response, "people feel drained and used up. They lack enough energy to face another day. Their emotional resources are depleted and there's no source of replenishment." (p. 3) Combating emotional exhaustion requires action—whether it be an administrative leave, diminishing one's workload, changing jobs, changing work habits, or taking a different job.

The second component of burnout is *depersonalization,* a psychological defense mechanism by which the people one serves (in our case, students or teachers-in-training) are depersonalized in the view of the service provider. Depersonalization involves seeing the people one deals with at work as cases or types, rather than as individual human beings—a stance Maslach describes as "viewing other people through rust-colored glasses" (ibid., p. 4). Depersonalization seems to occur when one has been in a particular service position too long, and the rewards of helping people begin to be outweighed by repetitious routine and the sense that what one does doesn't really matter.

The third factor, *reduced personal accomplishment,* occurs when service providers (including teachers and teacher educators) "have a growing sense of inadequacy about their ability to relate to recipients, and this may result in a self-imposed verdict of 'failure'" (ibid., 5). (See also Maslach and Jackson, 1986.) It is this component of burnout that can be directly (albeit partially) addressed by encouragement and appreciation.

Burnout "culminates in a build-up of negative feelings about students, colleagues, and administration" (Barduhn, 1989, pp. 2–3). If it is not addressed, burnout can lead to a downward spiral: "As motivation decreases and frustration increases, we lose the desire and energy to be creative, developing teachers" (ibid.). Eventually this pattern takes its toll, and "physical and emotional stress play on our self-esteem as we lose the sense of being in charge of our lives" (ibid.).

Possible burnout among ESL/EFL educators has been investigated by Pennington and Ho (1995). Using Maslach's research and definitions, they surveyed 95 teachers, most of whom were from the United States and Canada. Compared to the people in Maslach's original research (police, nurses, doctors, prison guards, social workers, etc.), the ESL/EFL teachers in Pennington and Ho's study experienced less emotional exhaustion, less depersonalization, and a greater sense of personal accomplishment.

The authors concluded that the ESL/EFL teachers they investigated were not experiencing burnout to the extent that some other people-oriented professionals do. It seems that in ESL/ EFL classes, at least some teachers experience substantial job satisfaction. This finding may seem surprising, given the poor conditions, low pay, and limited status of teachers in many ESL/EFL programs. However, it appears that the rewards and fulfillment of teaching can outweigh its problems.

## FULFILLMENT IN THE WORKPLACE

In fact, experienced language teachers may tell you that they have stayed in the profession—in spite of its poor conditions—because the work is enjoyable and satisfying. In other words, teaching people languages can be highly fulfilling.

Verity (2000) wrote about job satisfaction in our field. Intentionally setting aside factors such as compensation and status, she says that satisfaction means "leaving most classes, on most days, in most semesters, feeling good about a job well done" (p. 181). She continues, "From this perspective, a major reward of teaching well is the pleasure inherent in the activity itself; it serves as a creative enterprise" (ibid.).

As Verity notes, the satisfaction associated with teaching is largely internally motivated. However, in my experience, external appreciation and encouragement also play a role. It is worthwhile to recognize and acknowledge the talents and efforts of our colleagues, employees, and students. When a leader encourages someone to have confidence and go a step further (whether it may be in language learning, research, teaching, or writing), that person may be motivated to reach higher, to try harder, to take a risk they might not have taken without being encouraged.

The condition of feeling fulfilled in a teaching career has been discussed by Blumberg (1980). He notes that an individual feels fulfilled in his or her relationships with the employing organization (in our case, the school or program) when seven conditions are present (pp. 86–87 (italics and male pronouns in the original):

- He feels a communicative openness, when it is all right for him to share his concerns about himself with his supervisor, to disagree, to feed back to his supervisor any reactions he may have about their relationship, and so forth.
- He feels a sense of his own professional competence by way of helpful feedback from his supervisor and colleagues. This feedback, though it may be critical, is given in a supportive manner, inducing growth and confidence.
- He feels that his relationships with his supervisor and co-workers give him a *sense of colleagueship,* a collaborating share in the enterprise.
- He senses that his supervisor and his colleagues value his *worth as a person*; when he is not merely a cog, no matter how skillful or important, in a larger machine.
- He senses that the organization, primarily through the behavior of his supervisor, is concerned with his *personal and professional growth,* with providing the climate and opportunities for the individual to mature, to reach whatever potential his skills and pre-dispositions permit.
- He feels a sense of *personal independence and freedom,* when he can make decisions affecting his work on his own or with the help of his supervisor or colleagues. The decision to seek help is not seen as a confession of inadequacy.
- He feels a sense of *support for risk-taking* and a concomitant sense that the failure of a new venture is not taken as a sign of immaturity and incompetence.

Blumberg was writing specifically about teacher supervisors, but his comments can apply to other kinds of leaders as well. A concerned learner who communicates with and encourages co-workers and subordinates can have an effect on all seven of these conditions.

## ENCOURAGEMENT: PRINCIPLES AND RECOMMENDATIONS

Encouragement can take many forms. It may be informal, oral, and interpersonal, or it can be formal, written, and institutional. This section briefly discusses examples of each.

### Informal Encouragement

In 1989 I was privileged to return to UCLA to teach for a term at my alma mater. One of the courses I taught was a seminar on language classroom research, and one of the students who enrolled in that course was a woman named Amy Snyder Ohta. She was a doctoral candidate in applied linguistics, whose language of study was Japanese. In later years she went on to be a leading scholar in Japanese applied linguistics with important publications to her credit (see, e.g., Ohta, 2000). A few years ago, Dr. Ohta gave a plenary presentation at a conference hosted by my school, the Monterey Institute of International Studies. At a social event there, I told her how honored I was to have her visit the Monterey Institute as a guest speaker. She told me that in our class together all those years ago, I had been the first teacher ever to encourage her to publish a research paper she had written as a student. I was stunned, because (1) I did not remember that event at all, and (2) her work had been so good, I was surprised that no one else had encouraged her to publish it.

This anecdote illustrates a phenomenon I had been dimly aware of in the past, but Dr. Ohta's comment crystallized it for me. There have been many times that a former student has said to me, "I remember what you told me..." and then recounted a bit of advice or a funny story or a locker-room pep talk that had long since escaped my memory.

The point is, the smallest comment from a teacher or a leader can deeply influence another person. Like a tiny pebble in a pond, or the final snowflake that starts an avalanche, we sometimes have little awareness, and probably no foreknowledge, of the effects of our comments on others. The principle to be derived from these ideas is to offer encouragement to colleagues, students, and employees whenever it is appropriate to do so.

### Institutional Encouragement

Our profession provides many opportunities to encourage people officially, to nominate them for awards, and to express official appreciation for the work they do. One specific example of institutional encouragement that is especially important to me is the Leadership Mentoring Program of the international TESOL association.

The Leadership Mentoring Award represents induction into a program in TESOL. Its purpose is to prepare TESOL members for leadership positions within the association. Over the early years of TESOL, a dominant pattern emerged among board members and officers—i.e., most of them were Anglo-Americans working in university settings. This composition of the leadership did not necessarily represent the demographics of the members. For this reason, the Leadership Mentoring Program was begun to help prepare nonnative speakers of English, people who work in contexts other than universities, and members of underrepresented groups (e.g., ethnic minorities) to enter leadership roles in the association (see Bailey, 2000; see also Curtis, 2001).

A candidate for the Leadership Mentoring Award must be nominated by a TESOL member. The nomination process involves talking with the potential nominee to make sure he or she is interested and willing to take on the responsibility. There is a form to complete in which you must explain why you think your nominee has potential as a future leader in TESOL. Your nomination and the candidate's supporting materials are sent to TESOL's Central Office and reviewed by the Awards Committee.

Nominating someone takes a little work and forethought, but I believe it is worth the effort. My reason for thinking so is that I am pleased to have nominated about a dozen people for this award. The ten who have been selected have served on TESOL standing committees, on task forces, in the caucuses, or in interest sections. One has served on the Board of Directors and others have run for election to the Board or the Nominating Committee.

None of these people came to me and asked if I would nominate them for this program. In fact, some of them were quite surprised that I wanted to nominate them. Some even seemed to feel that they were not ready or not appropriate as nominees. For me, recognizing leadership potential in a young person is a rewarding endeavor and one I actively seek out. Each year when it is time to nominate someone for the Leadership Mentoring Award, I don't wonder whether I will nominate someone. I just think about who I will nominate. The principle arising from these comments is to make the time to provide encouragement by capitalizing on institutional opportunities.

Recently I had to articulate my teaching philosophy for a portfolio requirement at my work. I listed 12 principles that embody my philosophy. The tenth and eleventh, respectively, were "Challenge and critique students' work" and "Encourage, encourage, encourage."

When I think of the way significant changes in my life have come about through the encouragement of others, I am profoundly grateful for the time people have taken to help me move forward, to take risks, and to do new things I didn't know I could do. Receiving encouragement, whether it is a prestigious award or a simple comment, can profoundly influence a person's life. I believe that effective leaders use encouragement strategically and frequently to motivate others. It's like passing on the light of a candle or a torch. The original light is not diminished by being shared.

---

**SUGGESTED RESOURCE**

---

*The TESOL Leadership Mentoring Program:* go to the TESOL home page, www.tesol.org/, and search for Leadership Mentoring.

---

### Discussion Questions

1. Think of an effective leader you have known. Did he or she encourage you to extend yourself? Did you find that encouragement trustworthy? That is, if the leader expressed confidence in your ability to achieve a goal, did you feel confident in doing so? Why or why not?
2. Think of a time when *you* have been in a leadership role. Were you able to find ways to encourage the people you were working with (colleagues, students, employees, etc.)? If so, what was the result? If not, what was lacking?
3. When you are in a leadership role, what sense, skill, or talent enables you to find qualities in another person that are worth encouraging? In other words, when and how do you know to encourage someone?

---

### REFERENCES

Bailey, K. M. (2000). Leadership Mentoring Award nominations: Why bother? [Electronic Version]. *TESOL Matters, 10*(4), 4. Retrieved November 3, 2006, from http://www.tesol.org/s_document.asp?CID=195&DID=860

Bailey, K. M. (2005). Preface. In A. Curtis and M. Romney (Eds.), *Color, race and English language teaching: Shades of meaning* (pp. xi–xvi). Mahwah, NJ: Lawrence Erlbaum Associates.

Barduhn, S. 1989. When the cost of caring is too high. *IATEFL Teacher Development Newsletter, 11*, 1–3.

Blumberg, A. 1980. *Supervisors and teachers: A private cold war* (2nd ed.). Berkeley, CA: McCutchan Publishing.

Curtis, A. (2001). Learning about leadership from TESOL mentors [Electronic Version]. *TESOL Matters, 11*(3), 4. Retrieved November 3, 2006, from http://www.tesol.org/s_tesol/sec_document.asp?CID=194&DID=892

Dinkmeyer, D., & Eckstein, D. (1996). *Leadership by encouragement.* Boca Raton, FL: CRC Press.

Maslach, C., (1982). *Burnout: The cost of caring.* Englewood Cliffs, NJ: Prentice Hall.

Maslach, C., & Jackson, S. E. (1986). *Maslach burnout inventory manual* (2nd ed.). Palo Alto, CA: Consulting Psychologists Press.

Ohta, A. S. (2000). Rethinking interaction in SLA: Developmentally appropriate assistance in the zone of proximal development and the acquisition of L2 grammar. In J. P. Lantolf (Ed.), *Sociocultural theory and second language learning* (pp. 51–78). Oxford, UK: Oxford University Press, 51–78.

Pennington, M. C., & Ho, B. (1995). Do ESL educators suffer from burnout? *Prospect, A Journal of Australian TESOL, 10*(1), 4–53.

Verity, D. P. (2000). Side affects: The strategic development of professional satisfaction. In J. P. Lantolf (Ed.), *Sociocultural theory and second language learning* (pp. 179–197). Oxford, UK: Oxford University Press.

*Webster's encyclopedic unabridged dictionary of the English language.* (1996). New York: Random House.

# Chapter 4

## Mentoring as a Pathway to Leadership: A Focus on Nonnative English–Speaking Professionals

Lía D. Kamhi-Stein and Luciana C. de Oliveira

If U.S. academia is a "black box" for all professionals entering it, it's twice as black for those of us who come from the "outside" (that is, professionals who speak a language other than English as the home language, come from cultures that are not highly represented in academia, or have been educated in countries other than those in the Inner Circle) (Kamhi-Stein, 2004).

This statement, made at a presentation on TESOL teacher preparation and nonnative English–speaking (NNES) professionals at the 2004 TESOL Convention, reflects the way many of us who come from the "outside" feel when we enter U.S. academia. While it is true that many TESOL professionals who are "outsiders" become highly successful, it is also true that the path toward success is stressful and often times may come at the expense of a balanced life. In the case of NNES professionals, we believe that the "black box" can be made "less black" if they are initiated into the profession by mentors who help them deconstruct U.S. academia and give them career counseling and psychosocial support. In this chapter, we describe the mentoring relationship in which we, Luciana, a novice NNES professional from Brazil, and Lía, a more experienced NNES professional from Argentina, have had since 1998. We believe this is a topic that needs to be discussed since, to our knowledge, there are no publications focusing on issues of mentoring NNES professionals for leadership positions.

### INTRODUCTION: FIRST ENCOUNTERS

*Spring 1998:* We met at the first California TESOL (CATESOL) conference colloquium that addressed issues focusing on NNES professionals. Lía organized the colloquium, and Luciana was a member of the audience. As part of the lively discussion that followed the panel presentation, Luciana, who at that time was a graduate student in a TESOL M.A. program, made a strong statement about the need to create a group in CATESOL that would address issues related to NNES professionals in California. Lía was deeply impressed by Luciana's eloquence and passion about her ideas. Following the colloquium, in December 1999, a new interest group (IG), Nonnative Language Educators' Issues (NNLEI), was approved by the CATESOL Board of Directors.

*Spring 2000:* Lía was invited to give a featured talk focusing on issues related to NNES professionals at the 2000 CATESOL conference. Luciana attended the session and participated actively in it. Toward the end of the session, Lía mentioned that she was editing a special *CATESOL Journal* volume focusing on NNES professionals. Luciana offered to contribute an article to the volume. Once again, Lía was impressed by Luciana's determination and motivation. Therefore, after the session, we got together and discussed Luciana's ideas about the article. Luciana also suggested a variety of topics for future CATESOL colloquia and sessions and recommended directions for the future of the IG. Lía realized that Luciana was full of ideas, and she had a significant amount of experiences to contribute to, what at that time, was an emerging area of research and an emerging movement. She invited Luciana to write an article for the special volume of *CATESOL Journal.*

Over the next few months, Luciana (and her co-author, Sally Richardson) engaged in the process of writing the manuscript and Lía engaged in the process of reviewing it. Although Luciana lived in Northern California and Lía lived in Southern California, they managed to meet online through email and in person at regional and state conferences. Initially, the focus of our conversations was the manuscript, but our conversations moved on to topics such as our lives in the United States with a husband (in Lía's case) or a boyfriend (now Luciana's husband) as our sole support system, cultural differences between their countries of origin and the United States, our self-expectations as former successful EFL professionals. We also realized that Luciana was beginning a road that Lía had taken a few years back: that of Ph.D. student and future professional in the field of TESOL/applied linguistics. Therefore, we found ourselves spending more time talking about Luciana's professional future and her path toward leadership positions.

What had started as an author-editor relationship had slowly turned into a relationship of mentor and mentee, or "more experienced" and "less experienced" friend in a highly competitive field. However, central to our relationship was the fact that both of us demonstrated significant respect for each other and realized that we had a lot to gain from the relationship—though *what* exactly was unclear at the outset of our relationship. In the section that follows, we describe our evolving roles as mentor and mentee and show the importance of mentoring as a pathway to leadership for NNES professionals. We first review the literature on mentoring and relate it to our views about mentoring. We then describe our experiences working together and make recommendations for those professionals interested in entering into a mentoring relationship.

## VIEWS ABOUT MENTORING

Mentoring is traditionally defined as "a deliberate pairing of a more experienced person with a less experienced one, with the agreed-upon goal of having the less experienced person grow and develop specific competencies" (Murray, 1991, p. xiv). This definition emphasizes the distinct roles that both the more-experienced and the less-experienced person play: While the more-experienced professional "gives," the less-experienced professional "takes." In this view, it is the less-experienced professional who has opportunities to grow and develop. And the more-experienced professional imparts knowledge so that the mentee can grow within an organization or a profession.

We view this notion of mentoring as being rather limiting since it is parallel to a banking view of education (Freire, 1970), one in which the teacher "knows all" and students are expected to be filled with information. Such a view of mentoring assumes that mentors, much like teachers in the classroom, do not have anything to gain from the mentor-mentee relationship. Figure 1 presents a visual representation of this view of mentoring, which could be called Mentoring as a One-Way Directional Approach.

In contrast to this notion of mentoring, we propose the notion of "mentoring as transformational leadership." In this view of mentoring, there are three central characteristics: First, rather than looking at what mentors can provide mentees in a mentoring relationship, we view mentoring as a dyadic—two-way—relationship, one in which both mentee *and* mentor gain from the relationship. Both the mentor and the mentee create learning opportunities at different levels.

Second, in our view of mentoring, both the mentor and the mentee take and create learning opportunities to grow both professionally *and* personally (a point also proposed by Sosik, Godshalk, & Yammarino, 2004). Rather than solely focusing on career development (by providing support, protection, challenging assignments, exposure, visibility, career counseling, etc.), we believe that mentoring as transformational leadership should also emphasize the

---

**Figure 1:** Mentoring as a One-Way Directional Approach

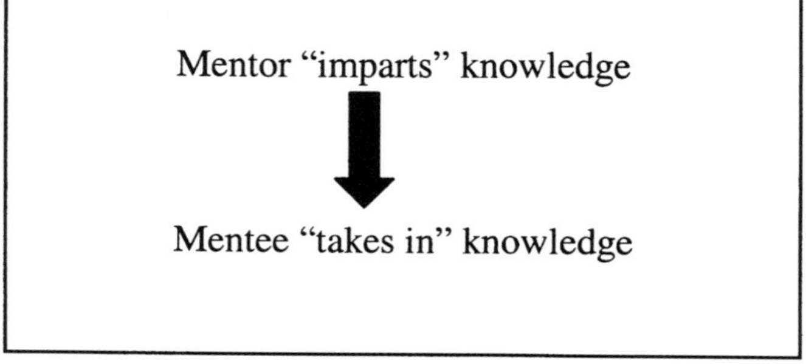

notion of psychosocial support—coaching, counseling, promoting self-confidence and acceptance, creating an awareness of the importance of a sense of personal and professional balance, sharing life lessons, and serving as a role model) (Godshalk & Sosik, 2003; Koberg, Boss, & Goodman, 1998; Scandura, 1992).

In looking at the lessons mentors share in transformational leadership, we found the work by Sosik, Godshalk, and Yammarino (2004) relevant to our relationship. They argue that mentors impart "values and standards of behaviors" (p. 245) and as a result of this, mentees view their mentors as "displaying various degrees of transformational leadership behavior" (p. 245) in the form of "idealized influence" (p. 245) (by showing personal achievement, serving as a role model of exemplary behavior, etc), "individualized consideration" (p. 245) (by coaching, counseling and giving personal attention), and "inspirational motivation" (p. 245) (by instilling positive self-perceptions and allowing the mentee to perceive himself/herself as a contributor and future contributor to the field).

The third characteristic in our notion of mentoring as transformational leadership is that as the mentor-mentee relationship evolves, there is a spiral process of meeting goals, setting new and higher goals accompanied by higher expectations (for both the mentor and the mentee), and creating conditions to meet such goals. It is through this spiral process that we see opportunities for leadership development. However, we should note that our definition of leadership is a broad one and does not necessarily require that the mentee be in a position of power (a point made by Boyatzis, Smith, & Baize, 2006) since leadership may take different forms for professionals working in different settings and at different stages in their leadership development process.

Figure 2 presents a visual representation of our view of mentoring.

---

*Figure 2:* Mentoring as a Two-Way Directional Approach toward Leadership Development

Mentor provides career and psychosocial support

Mentee acts and in turn affects the mentor

## Mentoring and Nonnative English–Speaking Professionals

Mentoring is often seen as an integral part of a novice teacher's development and is part of many induction programs that pair a novice teacher with a veteran teacher with the goal of supporting the novice teacher's development and providing support (Achinstein & Athanases, 2006). However, issues of mentoring and visible ethnic and language minority professionals have received limited attention in the field of TESOL. While professional associations like TESOL are making attempts to increase minority representation in leadership positions in the form of the Leadership Mentoring Program Award, to our knowledge, there are no publications that deal with the mentoring of NNES and minority professionals in the TESOL field. However, we believe that the literature on visible minority professionals is relevant to our discussion. Therefore, this section reviews the work, though limited, on minority teachers and mentoring.

While minority teachers bring to the teaching field valuable life experiences, they often report feeling isolated and incompetent in a new environment. When they are placed under the mentoring of a colleague, they tend to feel less intimidated as long as their colleague is not judgmental (Stallworth, 1994). Novice teacher support in the form of conferencing with mentors, being observed by mentors, etc., has been reported to be helpful. However, recent research by Ortiz-Walters and Gilson (2005) has shown that *who* mentors minority graduate students enrolled in Ph.D. programs makes a difference in the experiences of minority mentees. Ortiz-Walters and Gilson argue that professionals of color may benefit from having a relationship with a mentor of color because of the "comfort and interpersonal attraction that exists when individuals share similar racial/ethnic backgrounds" (p. 461) (an argument that could apply to NNES professionals). Therefore, they set out to investigate the extent to which a match in the race/ethnicity and/or in the values between mentors and mentees were associated with satisfaction and support. The results showed that graduate students perceived their mentors of color to provide them with a higher level of psychosocial and instrumental support, and reported a higher level of comfort and satisfaction, although sharing the same race/ethnic background was not an issue. In relation to values, the study showed that mentees who perceived their mentors to share their values were more satisfied, felt more interpersonal comfort, and received more support. At the same time, interpersonal comfort and commitment were found to mediate between race/ethnicity and values. As explained by Ortiz-Walters and Gilson (2005), this result suggests that it is important for mentors and mentees to have opportunities to get to know each other before collaborating and that while surface level characteristics like race/ethnicity do not influence the perceptions of mentors, they are still of consideration to mentees.

The notion that sharing similar backgrounds creates a feeling of comfort and facilitates the mentoring experience is also described in a recent article published in *The Chronicle of Higher Education*. In the article, Wilson (2006) describes the mentoring experiences of Hispanic female professors at Central Florida University. These women created an organization called "Mujeres Universitarias Asociadas" (Associated University Women) designed to mentor, network, and support female Hispanic professors, many of whom feel "like we're interlopers in academe" (p. B6) and are concerned that someone will say, "You don't really speak English, you don't really deserve this job, so get out" (B6). As explained in the article, the women attribute much of their survival and ultimate success on their campus to the support of the other women in the association.

The ideas reported by Wilson and Ortiz-Walters and Gilson have implications for the mentoring of NNES teachers and mentors in the TESOL field. It could be argued that sharing racial/ethnic backgrounds and/or the second language learning experience contributes to facilitating the mentor-mentee relationship and to increasing the degree of comfort needed to work in such a relationship. However, it could also be argued that coming from similar backgrounds is not the only factor that contributes to creating a high level of comfort. Factors such as shared values and beliefs also contribute to a feeling of satisfaction and comfort.

## MENTORING FOR TRANSFORMATIONAL LEADERSHIP: OUR EXPERIENCE

What did we learn from our experience working together? How did we succeed in having a mentoring relationship in which we both gained something, professionally and personally, and engaged in a spiral process of leadership development? We have been asked these questions several times, and we have always found ourselves providing quick answers. However, it was not until writing this chapter that we had an opportunity to look at the literature on the topic in detail, analyze our relationship, and become aware of the factors that have contributed to the success of our mentoring relationship as well as to the failure of other mentoring relationships that Lía had in the past. Therefore, to write this section, we looked back in time and reflected on conversations and emails that we have exchanged over the last few years. Following are some examples of how we engaged in a two-way directional approach toward career development and psychosocial support.

### Career Development as a Two-Way Directional Approach

Individual initiative is at the heart of a good leader, and Luciana learned early on that taking action is part of individual initiative that leads toward career development goals, particularly in the case of novice NNES professional leaders. Luciana realized that to be successful in a leadership position, one needs to take individual initiative very seriously. In turn, the mentor needs to encourage the mentees to participate in professional organizations and provide the kind of support needed to be successful. This encouragement can take several forms; what is fundamental is the mentee's initiation or beginning involvement. Being a leader in a professional organization means purposeful engagement attained by actively participating in several arenas, such as attending business meetings to get to know the organization's workings, conducting presentations, and reading proposals for regional and state meetings. Lía always encouraged Luciana to participate actively, and in some occasions suggested ways in which Luciana could participate. Lía encouraged Luciana to become active in the CATESOL IG by presenting on the topic of NNES professionals. To this end, Lía invited Luciana to co-present with her, which made Luciana very comfortable because she knew she could count on Lía for feedback and guidance.

In 2001, Luciana was nominated and elected coordinator-elect of the NNLEI IG in CATESOL and started becoming more involved in the CATESOL association. Luciana was IG coordinator from 2002 until 2004. Once Luciana was involved in the IG, Lía then suggested that Luciana run for a Level Chair position on the CATESOL Board of Directors, a position elected by the CATESOL membership. Luciana, at the time going through qualifying exams in the Ph.D. program, was not sure about her nomination because of the work involved. Lía explained to Luciana what the work would entail and how important it would be for the organization to have another minority professional on the Board. In 2004, Luciana was elected Assistant College/University Level Chair and became Chair in 2005. Lía's career development support helped Luciana to become more *visible* (Sosik, Godshalk, & Yammarino, 2004) as a presenter and leader in the association. Throughout Luciana's terms in leadership positions, she and Lía engaged in conversations about the association and Luciana's roles. These meaningful conversations led to the development of new levels of trust and respect for one another.

Another career development function includes the provision of specific feedback, guidance, and advice, described by Sosik, Godshalk, and Yammarino as important career development functions. In the early stages of leadership, new leaders may feel they may not be dealing with some issues appropriately. Advice and guidance can help new leaders become more confident in their own decisions. However, mentees must take the feedback and advice from mentors seriously and, rather than following the mentor's advice without critically reflecting about specific choices and decisions, the mentor and mentee share and bounce ideas off of each other to reach a particular decision together. For instance, on one occasion, Luciana and Lía discussed what should be done to increase leadership in CATESOL's IG. They talked about specific strategies, such as involving more graduate students in presentations and conducting meetings at regional conferences where potential leaders could be recruited. Luciana identified several potential IG leaders and encouraged them to become involved in the IG. As the women in Wilson's article attributed their success on their campus to the support of their minority mentors, Luciana attributes her accomplishments in several leadership positions to Lía's continuing support and guidance. However, Lía always reminds Luciana that her accomplishments can't be attributed to Lía. Had Luciana not been motivated to grow into leadership positions, Lía's encouragement would not have mattered.

While the mentor-mentee relationship provided Luciana several benefits, it also contributed to Lía's career development. For example, Lía helped Luciana with her job search process. In this process, Lía was forced to reflect upon her own job search strategies. This process of reflection allowed her to develop explicit awareness about the strategies she had used to obtain her current position at California State University, Los Angeles. She went back in time and recalled how a colleague, an ethnic minority professional himself, had made her aware of the importance of matching her skill sets to the job call. So in some way, Lía was passing on to Luciana what she had learned from someone else. Moreover, by working with Luciana on her job search, Lía gained an understanding of the current market expectations for a new Ph.D., a fact that is important for any faculty member in a TESOL Program that may be running a search for a new position in the near future.

A second career development benefit that working with Luciana provided Lía was in the area of writing. One of the challenges Lía experienced as an author was related to her difficulty in "showing her voice" as a writer. Giving feedback to Luciana on her (and Richardson's) co-authored chapter for a volume Lía was editing allowed her to develop increased awareness about some of the challenges she herself faced as a writer. Both of our home languages are Romance languages, and we perceive our languages to allow written discourse that is less direct than that of English (when writing for academic purposes). Therefore, sometimes, Lía could see Luciana's writing reflecting the same pattern of indirectness that Lía's writing exhibited. So by providing Luciana with feedback on her writing, Lía was able to develop increased awareness of how to adapt her writing to meet the expectations of different audiences.

A third career development benefit for Lía was when Luciana invited Lía to serve on her Ph.D. Qualifying Examination Committee. Lía took this invitation as a great honor since she knew it would allow her to have access to Luciana's ground-breaking research that investigated the writing for academic purposes of middle school and high school history students using a functional linguistics approach. In addition, by serving on Luciana's Qualifying Examination Committee, Lía had an opportunity to meet colleagues from disciplines other than TESOL/applied linguistics.

## Psychosocial Support as a Two-Way Directional Approach

Another important function in a mentor-mentee relationship is psychosocial support for purposes of transformational leadership behavior. Included in this function is role modeling. Role modeling may be the most important mentoring function for NNES professionals since it provides mentees with examples of "idealized influence" (Sosik, Godshalk, & Yammarino, 2004, p. 245). Mentors of NNES professionals who are leaders serve as role models for new leaders in a variety of ways. Role modeling from the part of the mentor may not be a conscious effort but is undoubtedly a very important part of the mentoring relationship for the novice NNES professional leader. Mentees look up to the mentors' actions and observe how they act and react in situations that deserve particular attention. This is especially important for novice leaders learning to deal with difficult situations. Part of the mentee's role is to observe and reflect on the mentor's actions in certain situations and consider what the situation prompted the mentor to do. This is leading by example. Lía, having been in several leadership positions, is a role model of personal achievement. Lía inspires Luciana in several ways at a personal and professional level.

First, because of Lía's background, a Latina and nonnative English speaker in academia, she serves as a role model at a personal level. At a professional level, Lía is a role model of professionalism and professional competence. For NNES mentees, the act of receiving positive affect from the mentor encourages greater development, which in turn may lead to more involvement, as the NNES mentees feel supported and confident in continuing their contributions and improving as leaders. This was the case with Lía and Luciana. In addition to her involvement in CATESOL—which with approximately 3,900 members is the largest TESOL affiliate in the United States—Luciana started getting more involved in the TESOL association after she participated in TESOL's Leadership Mentoring Program, which is designed to help underrepresented groups get more involved in the organization. Lía nominated Luciana for this program, and Luciana was selected as one of the 2005–2006 program participants. Lía was her mentor, and together they organized a New Leaders Forum, a workshop for novice professionals that provided participants with practical tools and strategies to help them to understand how to get more involved in leadership.

Several features can be highlighted in Lía and Luciana's mentoring relationship. First, the collaborative work that Lía and Luciana engaged in at the TESOL convention in Tampa shows Lía's continuing belief in Luciana's leadership and involvement. To Luciana, this means that Lía believes she is able to take on tasks and be successful, which leads her to believe in herself as a leader even more. This is an important source of psychosocial support for Luciana. In addition, Luciana's continuous involvement shows a level of commitment on which Lía can count.

While Luciana perceives Lía to be a role model for her, Lía also perceives Luciana to be a role model for her and for other NNES professionals. In what ways was the notion of Luciana as a role model realized? First, when Luciana and Lía met at the CATESOL Colloquium on NNES professionals, Luciana, though sitting in the back of the meeting room, did not hesitate to express her ideas in a vocal and assertive manner. Lía immediately admired Luciana's determination to overcome her fear to participate in front of a large audience since it had taken several years to overcome her silence and to develop the confidence needed to express her ideas. Once we established a relationship, Luciana's work as an emerging leader in CATESOL and TESOL became a topic of conversation with Lía's graduate students. Lía used Luciana's experiences to motivate her students to become involved in professional organizations.

Another source of psychosocial support from Luciana toward Lía was in their work in the CATESOL association. Luciana and Lía served on the Board. In Luciana's first year as coordinator of the NNLEI IG (2002), Lía was serving as CATESOL President and the subsequent year, she was the Past President. Lía was CATESOL's first NNES professional to become President. Therefore, besides the responsibility that comes with serving as the President of TESOL's largest U.S. affiliate, Lía felt responsible for representing NNES professionals in the best possible way. During Lía's presidency, Luciana was a sounding board for Lía. Luciana represented the professionals that CATESOL wanted to reach: novice professionals, with the added bonus that Luciana's status as a triple minority (female, Latina, and nonnative speaker) provided her with a perspective that did not reflect that of the mainstream in CATESOL.

## RECOMMENDATIONS

This section includes recommendations for specific leadership guidance for novice professionals.

- **Introduce yourself to experienced professionals and leaders when you attend professional conferences.** As you meet these people, reflect on whether or not there is some level of comfort with them. Think of what you have in common with these people, whether it is values, ethnicity, background experiences, country or city of origin, etc. Knowledge about or expertise in the field of study should not be the sole factor in a mentoring relationship. To be in a mentoring relationship, it is important that both the mentor and the mentee feel some level of interpersonal comfort and that as mentor and mentee work together, the level of comfort grows.
- **Make your voice heard.** Do not be afraid to speak up during a session or to offer to submit a chapter or an article. Individual initiative is an extremely important feature of new leaders.
- **Initiate your contributions early in your career**. This will allow you to meet professionals who will become interested in your work. This in turn may result in a collaborative relationship with successful leaders.
- **Always think of the mentoring relationship as two-way support.** This means that you will not only be receiving support but providing it, too. When you contact a leader in the field, think of ways in which the relationship can be two-way support. If you describe the potential benefits that mentors can gain from working with you, potential mentors will be more open to the idea of working with you.
- **Find a mentor who can give you continuous feedback.** Continuing encouragement is important for novice NNES professionals.
- **Have realistic expectations.** Mentoring relationships, like all relationships, evolve. Start by working on small projects; as the relationship grows, so will the nature of the projects in which you and your mentor become involved.

As we wrote this chapter and reflected on our collaborative experiences, we were concerned about depicting a picture that was too rosy. However, we were not able to find anything that did not work in our mentor-mentee relationship. Our explanation for this is that a combination of factors, which we have described in the chapter, contributed to the growth of our relationship. These factors are: our values and beliefs, our experiences as former international students with very limited support systems in the United States, our background as South American women, our status as NNES professionals, and our willingness and openness to learn from each other.

Early in our relationship, we realized that the mentor-mentee relationship provided both of us with opportunities for personal and professional growth that might otherwise have been missed. Central to these opportunities was the fact that each of us valued and respected the other personally and professionally and that we were, and still are, willing and open to learn from each other. A good example of this openness and mutual respect was the writing of this chapter, which allowed us to reflect on and learn from our past experiences as a way to build toward the future.

## Suggested Resources

### The TESOL Leadership Mentoring Program

This program is designed to help underrepresented groups become more involved in the TESOL association. To be considered for the award, a TESOL member must be nominated by another TESOL member. For more information on this program, go to www.tesol.org/.

For further information on the topic of mentoring and leadership, we recommend consulting the following journals:

- *The Leadership Quarterly*, published by Elsevier, in affiliation with the International Leadership Association (www.ila-net.org/)
- *Journal of Vocational Behavior*, published by Elsevier
- *Group & Organization Management*, published by Sage.

### Discussion Questions

1. According to the authors, what are the most important features of mentoring NNES professionals in leadership development? What other kinds of support do you think are essential for new NNES leaders?
2. Reflect about mentoring relationships in which you have been involved. Have they been similar to or different from what the authors described? What were the most important features of the mentoring?

3. To what extent, if any, should mentors and mentees share common characteristics for the relationship to work? Why or why not?
4. This chapter described mentoring functions that were particularly important for the authors. In what ways can mentoring functions strengthen the leadership skills of new NNES leaders?

## REFERENCES

Achinstein, B., & Athanases, S. Z. (2006). Introduction: New visions for mentoring new teachers. In B. Achinstein & S. Z. Athanases (Eds.), *Mentors in the making: Developing new leaders for new teachers* (pp. 1–20). New York: Teachers College Press.

Boyatzis, R. E., Smith, M. L., & Baize, N. (2006). Developing sustainable leaders through coaching and compassion. *Academy of Management & Learning, 5*(1), 8–24.

Freire, P. (1970). *Pedagogy of the oppressed* (M. B. Ramos, Trans.). New York: Seabury Press.

Godshalk, V. M., & Sosik, J. J. (2003). Aiming for career success: The role of learning goal orientation in mentoring relationships. *Journal of Vocational Behavior, 63*(3), 417–437.

Kamhi-Stein, L. D. (2004, March/April). Addressing nonnative English-speaking teachers and teacher educators needs. Paper presented at the Academic Session, Teacher Education Interest Section, held at the annual convention of Teachers of English to Speakers of Other Languages, Long Beach, CA.

Koberg, C. S., Boss, R. W., & Goodman, E. (1998). Factors and outcomes associated with mentoring among health-care professionals. *Journal of Vocational Behavior, 53*(1), 58–72.

Murray, M. (1991). *Beyond the myths and magic of mentoring*. San Francisco: Jossey-Bass.

Ortiz-Walters, R., & Gilson, L. L. (2005). Mentoring in academia: An examination of the experiences of protégés of color. *Journal of Vocational Behavior, 67*(3), 459–475.

Scandura, T. (1992). Mentorship and career mobility: An empirical investigation. *Journal of Organizational Behavior, 13*(2),169–174.

Sosik, J. J., Godshalk, V. M., & Yammarino, F. J. (2004). Transformational leadership, learning goal orientation, and expectations for career success in mentor-protégé relationships: A multiple levels of analysis perspective. *The Leadership Quarterly, 15*(2), 241–261.

Stallworth, B. J. (1994). *New minority teachers' perceptions of teaching.* (ERIC Document Reproduction Service No. ED 383 660).

Wilson, R. (2006, September 29). At Central Florida, Hispanic women give each other advice and a sympathetic ear. *The Chronicle of Higher Education,* B6–8.

# Chapter 5

## Public Speaking and Presentation Skills for ELT Educators

Christine Coombe, Liz England, and John Schmidt

As ELT professionals move into leadership roles, effective public speaking and presentation skills are essential to their success. An educator in a leadership position speaks to inform, persuade, inspire, or entertain, or any combination of these four purposes of public speaking.

An educator speaks informatively in public to teach, lecture, or demonstrate. In a leadership role, an educator moves outside the classroom or lecture hall to chair meetings, discussions, and presentations. Educational leaders also give reports and technical speeches. Most educators' use of persuasion follows their informative course lectures when they promote their theories or ideas in class and when they encourage their students to excel by delving into the instructional material, doing homework, preparing reports or assignments, and studying for tests. Leaders in education take their skills of persuasive public speaking beyond the classroom to convince others, both inside and outside the educational system. Successful educators inspire their students, and a few have even achieved fame through their portrayal in books and movies. Educational leaders also speak to inspire others outside the classroom. They inspire a range of audiences large and small in administrative offices, boardrooms, committee chambers, and meeting halls when they coach, announce, honor, toast, and commemorate. Both inside and outside the classroom, educators are very successful as communicators when they can entertain while speaking. When we laugh, we relax. When we relax, we are most receptive to listening, accepting others and their ideas, and to learning. Thus, educators who can incorporate subtle elements of entertainment with finesse and good taste into their public speaking tend to effectively influence their audiences. Finally, many educators communicate across cultures, a dimension that adds richness and complexity to the act of communication. This requires them to be conscious of the actual linguistic and non-linguistic characteristics of oral interaction, and to work to confirm that their message has been accurately understood.

Many classroom teachers take on the dual roles of teacher and leader, often moving back and forth between these roles on a given day, week, or semester. Having spent countless hours before a room full of students, teachers develop an ease of communication and adaptation before an audience. While there is overlap between teaching and public speaking, the considerable learning curve for an educational leader to become a highly competent public speaker often goes unaddressed when the teacher assumes the role of leader without attentive and systematic focus on the development of the skills set of an effective public speaker. For most educators, this development requires a depth of awareness, study, and practice through a structured and ongoing training program.

Attaining a consistent level of competence and excellence as a public speaker in diverse modes of communication on the part of an educational leader involves extensive work over time. The knowledge base encompassing the principles and recommendations in this chapter is designed to foster an awareness and understanding of the breadth of factors that an educational leader should develop in order to become an accomplished public speaker and thus a highly effective leader. A critical eye and ear, along with keen sensitivity toward the range of factors that educational leaders must systematically work on and take into account with each opportunity to speak publicly, initiates them on the journey toward becoming consummate leaders equipped to excel as communicators in a range of contexts with varying purposes and a diversity of audiences.

There is a myth that teachers have an advantage over most other public speakers, as teachers spend so much time in front of an audience. While educators have clocked significant amounts of time up front in a classroom, teaching is very different from public speaking. Teaching and public speaking require substantially different strengths, strategies, and techniques. Excellent teachers know how to effectively communicate and explain course content to students. Accomplished public speakers are able to eloquently connect with diverse audiences and inform, persuade, inspire, or entertain.

A summary of differences between teaching and public speaking follows.

1. Teachers know their students well. Public speaking often requires speaking to diverse and unfamiliar audiences.
2. Teaching allows for a second chance. A teacher can say, "I don't know. I'll find out and tell you in the next class." Public speakers have one chance to present the information and often only a short question-and-answer period to respond to issues and inconsistencies and to make clarifications.
3. Teaching usually occurs either in a familiar classroom or online on a standardized schedule. Public speaking venues can vary widely, and the acoustics, seating, timeframe, and other critical factors may be outside the speaker's control.

4. Teachers regularly use spontaneity and informality with students. Therefore, teachers can take advantage of verbal and nonverbal communication skills to get their message across. Public speakers, on the other hand, must use spontaneity and informality very carefully to maintain the professional edge and the unambiguous approach expected by nonstudent audiences.
5. Teachers can rely on others—colleagues, parents, and supervisors—to support the instructional goals for their students. Conversely, a public speaker is "The Lone Ranger," and must present information and check for understanding within the time constraints of the given session.

Teaching and public speaking are similar as they both require thorough and systematic study, practice, and preparation. They also require good organization and clear communication to effectively convey the message and engage the listener.

As a language teacher, your communicative skills are already exceptional. You have a broader vocabulary than most people; your grammar is better than the average person; and your ability to make a concept clear is well established. Take advantage of these language skills in your speeches.

## BACKGROUND LITERATURE

Research shows that public speaking and presentation skills are in much demand in today's world: In a survey conducted by the National Association of Colleges and Employers (NACE), 11 fundamental skills that recruiters seek in job candidates were identified. The most important of these skills was oral communication. We believe that like job candidates, leaders in education also want to be marketable and competitive in their profession. In a similar study conducted by the Center for Public Resources, 250 companies rated speaking and listening among the most critical areas in need of improvement for people entering the work force. Similarly, in a report published by the American Council on Education, experts advised that "good oral and written skills can be your most prized possession" in getting and holding a top position (Osborn & Osborn, 2004, p. 5). Giving effective presentations involves the mastery of a broad range of skills, which are essential in public speaking and important to personal, professional, and leadership growth.

People have been speaking in public since humans first developed the ability to talk. The first known textbook detailing the how to's of public speaking was written more than 2,400 years ago. Most of our rules and techniques, particularly when it comes to the art of persuasive speaking, come from guidelines written by Aristotle, a Greek philosopher in the 3rd century BCE. These basic principles have undergone modification as societies and cultures have changed; despite this, they have remained surprisingly uniform. Aristotle saw great potential in rhetoric (one person addressing many). He believed it was an art that should be studied and that good rhetoric was not only persuasive but ethical as well. Aristotle identified *ethos*, *pathos*, and *logos* as three methods a speaker uses to persuade, and he believed that all public presentations are some balance of these three rhetorical proofs. *Ethos* refers to a speaker's credibility and character as revealed through communication, *pathos* refers to the emotions felt by the audience during the rhetoric, and *logos* to the speaker's actual words.

Greco-Latin tradition suggests five principles for successful public speaking: *inventio, dispositio, elocutio, memoria*, and *pronunciatio* (O'Meara, 1993, p. 43). In today's jargon they mean:

- Decide what you want to say *(inventio).*
- Decide how to structure your message *(dispositio).*
- Choose the best medium for your message *(elocutio).*
- Learn it by heart *(memoria).*
- Use whatever it takes—voice, gestures, body language—to get your message across *(pronunciatio).*

Effective public speakers such as Ghandi and John F. Kennedy have incorporated Aristotle's teachings into their presentations.

A more in-depth review of the literature on public speaking and presentation skills is not possible, given chapter space constraints and the amount of work published on the topic. Some of the literature on this topic that we feel English language educators need to know is presented in context in the sections that follow and is listed in the resources section at the end of the chapter.

## PRINCIPLES AND RECOMMENDATIONS

There is a myth that great speakers are born and not made. It is commonly believed that somehow certain people have an innate ability to calmly stand in front of an audience with no anxiety and deliver a well-developed, organized, and dynamic speech. To do anything well takes practice and knowledge of the basic skills and abilities involved. Public speaking is no exception. The principles and recommendations included here should help most educators become better speakers.

### Have the Requisite Knowledge

Knowledge is essential for giving good presentations. First **know yourself** as an educator, a leader, and a speaker. Critically evaluate your strengths and weaknesses from a personal and a professional standpoint. Knowledge of what you do well and what you need to work on will help your growth as a public speaker.

Many people resist public speaking because they fear embarrassment or failure. It is perfectly normal to be nervous before delivering a speech, no matter how many times you have spoken before. The single best way to control and harness nerves is to rehearse until you are very well prepared and **know your speech.** No one attends a presentation hoping that the speaker will fail. The audience wants you to succeed. If you are prepared and exhibit confidence, your mistakes may go unnoticed.

**Knowledge of your topic** is crucial. Do not attempt to speak on a topic about which you are not knowledgeable. Care about the topic and have a strong desire to impart your knowledge. Audiences can tell if you lack knowledge, interest, or passion.

It is important to **know about your audience**. Make your presentation relevant to your listeners. As you prepare your speech, find out the following:

- audience demographics (age, gender, religion, ethnicity, educational background)
- audience values, attitudes, and beliefs
- appropriate language level, avoiding or incorporating certain words or phrases, jargon or topic-specific vocabulary, and keeping in mind nonnative speakers
- wants or needs of the audience and tailor your tone and content accordingly
- audience perspective of you, the speaker—as an expert, a leader, a facilitator, or a peer

Logistical **knowledge about the venue** is essential. Advance considerations include room set-up and equipment. Arrive early to check arrangements, test equipment, and determine your position and mobility. Then allow advance time to mingle with incoming attendees, thus establishing rapport and giving you an opportunity to confirm what you anticipate to be the audience wants and needs.

Additional considerations as you prepare your presentation include the following:

- Lectern, staging, and seating arrangements.
- Time of your presentation and its fit in the program (as an opener or a closer or before or after a meal. One word of advice—do not try to compete with food—you will not win!)
- Time allotted for your speech. Plan the amount of content accordingly. Allow ample time for questions and answers, and avoid running overtime.
- Technical equipment in working condition and someone to set it up or operate it, if necessary.
- Additional equipment needs—power source, extension cord, extra overhead projector bulb, equipment stand at appropriate height.
- Back-up plans, equipment, and supplies, in the event of a technology problem.

## DEVELOPING YOUR SPEECH

Knowledge is essential for a successful speaker, and research is one of the keys to a good speech. The audience will look up to someone who is well prepared and has done his or her research. To research speech topics, you can use a variety of sources like print media (newspapers and magazines), broadcast media, libraries, reference books, the Internet, and informants or experts in the field you're speaking on.

Provide additional support for your topic by using personal experiences. You can infuse your own relevant stories, anecdotes, interesting facts, and statistics into your speeches. These tools can enhance your speech, but carefully select only useful ones and try not to use too many. Citing authoritative sources can also bolster your credibility. Famous quotations can support the theme. Humor can also be an effective tool. Once you have written your speech, double-check your facts and make sure you have cited sources properly.

## Speech Support Dos and Don'ts

| Support | Dos | Don'ts |
|---------|-----|--------|
| Stories and anecdotes | • Tell stories or anecdotes with a purpose.<br>• Tell stories about people.<br>• Try out your stories first.<br>• Collect stories or anecdotes for future use.<br>• Use a variety of different types of stories (success, personal, human interest, fables, etc.). | • Tell stories you don't know well. |
| Statistics and numerical data | • Round off numbers.<br>• Get statistics from a credible source.<br>• Repeat key numbers.<br>• Put statistics into familiar terms.<br>• Use shocking statistics.<br>• Limit your examples (one good one is better than two so-so examples). | • Spew numbers.<br>• Use numbers to impress people. |
| Quotations | • Relate quotation to a point in your speech.<br>• Use quotations from unpredictable sources for maximum effect.<br>• Keep them brief<br>• Be careful about citing—if you're unsure, say "I believe it was Mr. Famous person who once said….." | • Drop names.<br>• Say "quote" and "unquote." |
| Humor | • Keep it simple.<br>• Limit self-deprecating humor.<br>• Make sure joke is related to the topic. | • Tell off-color, racist, sexist, or prejudicial jokes.<br>• Make fun of your audience. |

## Start Out and Finish with Style

Since your opening sets the stage for the rest of your speech, you want it to be great. Research shows that people form opinions about others within several seconds of meeting them. Even if the rest of your talk is extemporaneous, memorize your opening. A good speech opening always **grabs the audience's attention.** Some good ways to do this include a startling fact or statistic, a rhetorical question, a challenge to the audience, a good quotation, a story, or a funny anecdote. The purpose of your introduction is to give the audience a reason to listen to you. You can do this through a **significance statement.** This statement will tell them why your speech topic is important to them. The introduction is also an opportunity to **establish your credentials** as a speaker. Research shows that people listen more intently if they perceive the speaker to be an expert in the field (Markham, 1988), so make sure you give the audience reasons why you're qualified to be giving a speech on this topic. Once you've gotten the audience's attention, given them a reason to listen, and established yourself as a speaker, you will want to make a brief **statement about the topic and purpose of your speech.** You can then follow up with a brief **review of the main points** you will cover in your presentation.

Sometimes what you do not say in your introduction is as important as what you do say. Here are some common pitfalls to avoid in presentation openings: Don't......

- open your speech with an apology.
- get names wrong.
- admit you're not prepared.
- admit you've given the same presentation several times.
- ask about the time.
- begin with endless greetings and acknowledgements.

If your introduction is your first chance to make an impression, your conclusion is your last. The conclusion plays a key role in determining how your audience will remember you and your message. Your closing is a way of ending your talk, reinforcing ideas that you have talked about, and letting your audience know what you expect of them. Your closing should be memorized as well and should effectively tie up your speech. It should indicate to the audience that the speech is ending.

Very often, a closing will relate to the opening. Your closing should also give audience members an opportunity to ask questions. You may want to close by summarizing your points, demonstrating what you talked about, or by appealing to the audience for action. Whatever closing strategy you use, your final statement should be powerful and direct as its purpose is to leave an impact on your audience.

Kushner (2004) recommends a simple formula for setting up your closing: Just say, "I have one final thought that I want to leave you with. . . ." or "If you remember just one thing I've said today, remember this. . . ." Then give them one very strongly worded, relevant thought. Since your conclusion should only constitute 5 percent to 10 percent of your speech, make sure you sum up and then sit down.

### Have Structure, but Be Spontaneous

Before you can organize your presentation, you must choose the material you want to use. Probably the most difficult task you will face is deciding what not to use. No matter what you're speaking on, you can always find more material than you need. Your job is to find a lot more than you need so that you can select the best content to use and the best content to keep in reserve.

Once you have decided on a speech purpose, it is necessary to pick an organizational pattern for your speech. A few of the most common patterns you can use to shape your presentation are problem/solution, cause/effect, and chronological.

The next step to structured speaking is to create an outline. This can help you see what points you want to make, how your examples relate to your main points, and whether your points are arranged in the correct order. Another important decision you will make is choosing the right number of points to make. The most important recommendation here is **do not try to include too much information.** Most presenters make the mistake of packing too much information into a single presentation. Only include the number of points that are essential to your message.

Since your opening and closing should be memorized, the body of the speech gives you the opportunity to adapt and ad-lib. Personalizing your talk by asking questions or by talking directly to an individual can help build good rapport with the audience.

### PRESENTING THE SPEECH

### Oral Delivery Skills

Dynamic speakers use variety in volume, rate, pitch, and rhythm. They also use pauses and emphases on key words to make important concepts stand out and to convey meaning. If you want to become an exciting speaker, learn to use vocal variety to add vitality and excitement to your speeches. Perhaps the single best thing you can do to improve your delivery is to vary the pace, pitch, volume, pausing, and tone of your voice to fit the words you are saying.

During presentations, speak clearly and concisely, placing emphasis when you want to make a point. Use your voice to exaggerate your emotions, but be careful not to constantly talk at an excited level. As far as volume is concerned, on a scale from 1 to 10, aim for a 6 to 7. In many conference presentations, you might have to use a microphone. Keep in mind that the type of microphone you use (i.e., built-in podium, hand-held, lapel microphones) will affect other aspects of your presentation like your ability to move around and gesture.

It is common to speak too quickly when you are inexperienced or under prepared. A good pace is between 125–160 words per minute. You may want to practice your speech in front of a friend or record yourself to see if you should make any changes.

### Physical Delivery Skills

Physical delivery skills and nonverbal communication can have a great impact on your presentation.

- **Appearance.** The first thing to consider when giving a presentation is your appearance since it can affect your credibility. Obviously, you should convey a professional appearance when giving a formal presentation. However, you will need to dress differently for different occasions (i.e., school assembly, conference presentation, retreat, meeting, etc.). A good rule of thumb concerning appearance is to dress just a little more formally than members of your audience.
- **Body Language.** Body language refers to the messages you send through facial expression, posture, and gestures. Effective body language is important every time you step in front of an audience. The single most important facial expression is the smile. Although some formal speeches or presentations call for subdued movements, you should not be afraid to let your body speak. Body movements should be deliberate and precise but look natural and spontaneous. Your movements should always enhance what you are saying. Common body language includes showing physical characteristics (size, shape, direction, location), displaying importance or urgency (running, arm-waving, fist-pounding), and comparing or contrasting (moving hands together or in opposition).
- **Posture.** Sloppy posture is generally viewed negatively. Experts recommend that you stand up straight with your feet slightly apart and ready to gesture and that you lean slightly toward the audience. Leaning forward gives audience members the impression that you're actively involved with them. Good posture is said to improve your breathing, voice projection, and appearance.
- **Eye Contact.** Eye contact is essential for a successful presentation. For small audiences, strive to make eye contact with every individual in the room at least once during your talk. If your audience is large or if you are speaking under bright lights, try your best to look around the room.

## OTHER PRESENTATION SKILLS

### Time Management

A major challenge for both novice and experienced speakers is managing time during a presentation. This essential task begins as one develops the speech, whether it is a new presentation or a variation on a previously delivered, familiar topic.

When preparing the presentation, the speaker needs to know how many minutes to plan for, not counting the introduction and a question-and-answer period. Good time management is obvious to the audience. Speakers who fall short of their allotted time frame tend to fumble to stretch the presentation with a rambling conclusion and an extended question-and-answer session—or simply adjourn early.

More common are speakers who have too much material to cover in the allotted time, often including too many PowerPoint slides to cover or too many sections on their handouts to address. When these speakers realize they are out of time, they have five minutes left and a considerable amount of uncovered material, as well as a summary and a conclusion. Thus, the end of their speeches tends to be a race through an extensive amount of content, leaving the audience dazed. The speaker does not have an opportunity to end with a strong, eloquent, and memorable conclusion. Time management, starting with the speech preparation, beginning with the new or revisited material for the speaker, and continuing through the closing sentence, is of great importance to all types of presentations—half-day workshops, hour-long speeches, and ten-minute panel presentations. In addition, when participating in question-and-answer sessions, limit responses to a crisp two or three minutes.

### Use Media Effectively

Christison and McCloskey (2006) recommend that you keep AV equipment to a minimum to achieve your presentation goals. Remember that your overhead projector bulb could blow out at any moment or your laptop might not be compatible with the projector, but you will have to proceed with your nonmedia plan B (p. 2).

Whichever option you choose, remember that your participants will not be able to see any text in a font that is smaller than 24 point.

> # This is how big a 24 point font looks in Arial.

Consider the 7-7 rule for each overhead transparency (OHT) or PowerPoint slide—no more than seven lines of text with about seven words for each line. And do not hesitate to include illustrations, photos, diagrams/charts, and sounds, which take advantage of the potential of multimedia. When presenting, do not read your slides; use them as an outline or to provide examples of points you are making.

## Have Strategies to Cope with Problems

As with anything, circumstances can occur that have the potential to weaken or even ruin your presentation. Even plenary presentations given by well-known TESOL leaders can be significantly diminished due to a simple technology glitch, an unawareness of how to most effectively use PowerPoint, or a problem participant. Because teachers regularly present content in front of an audience—their students—they already have some back-up plans or troubleshooting strategies at their disposal. The most important thing to remember is to be prepared. Presenters who are prepared have a back-up plan or two in case of technology problems (i.e., PowerPoint slides put on OHTs in case of computer/projector malfunction). Teachers who are prepared also have the confidence to remain calm when things start to go wrong. Remaining calm and being able to think on your feet are skills that only come with practice and preparation.

As you attend meetings, conference presentations, and lectures, pay attention to what kinds of problems speakers generally have. Then think about ways you would address these problems should they occur in your presentations.

## Become a Student of Public Speaking

After you speak, take the time to reflect on your presentation, noting what you did well and what you want to improve. You may also want to ask a trustworthy friend or colleague to evaluate part or all of your speech.

A professional pianist or athlete keeps training and practicing constantly. They, like leaders, shouldn't stop being a student when they retire! There is no better place to acquire and hone effective public speaking and presentation skills than in a Toastmasters Club. These clubs, found in virtually every country in the world, provide members with different types of public speaking opportunities.

Public speaking and presentation skills are essential for professionally engaged teachers. Do not be fooled into thinking that these skills are an innate ability—they are a learned skill. Behind every successful presentation are hours of careful preparation.

---

| **SUGGESTED RESOURCES** |
| --- |

The leading university textbook, Stephen E. Lucas's *The Art of Public Speaking*, 9th ed., (2007), McGraw Hill, is accompanied by ancillary materials for students and instructors and a website, www.mhhe.com/lucas8 with numerous resources—summaries, puzzles, flash cards, study questions, and a Learning Center with PowerPoint tutorials and the 100 most important American speeches. (ISBN 007321650X)

Allyn & Bacon, a division of Pearson Education, publishes comprehensive university textbooks, as well as the *Essence of Public Speaking* series for both aspiring and professional speakers. Endorsed by both Toastmasters International and the National Speakers Association, partial titles include *Choosing Powerful Words, Delivering Dynamic Presentations, Motivating Your Audience,* and *Writing Great Speeches.*

A volume in the bestselling Dummies series, *Presentations for Dummies* (2004), Wiley, is an invaluable resource in the public speaking literature. Written by professional speaker and humor consultant, Malcolm Kushner, this publication is chock-a-bloc full of traditional and non-traditional information.

Natalie Rogers' *The New Talk Power: The Mind-Body Way to Speak without Fear,* (2000), Capital Books, Inc., is a thorough resource with charts, self-talk monologues, and speech templates.

A handy pocket guide relevant in its focus on leaders in professions and in the community is *The Elements of Great Public Speaking* by J. Lyman MacInnis (2006), Ten Speed Press.

Toastmasters International publishes useful and affordable materials, including reference books, speech project manuals, and club materials in seven languages, available online www.toastmasters.org.

---

### *Discussion Questions*

1. What is the overlap and what is the gap in the public speaking roles and demands of a teacher and of an educational leader?
2. Why and how should aspiring educational leaders enhance their public speaking skills?
3. Educators provide students with a wealth of information and considerable amounts of homework. They regularly and systematically evaluate students' knowledge and performance. How and why should educational leaders apply this classic academic model to their own study of public speaking?
4. There are four fundamental objectives of public speaking. Provide examples of each type based on the activities of educational leaders whom you know.
5. Reflect on an educational leader you know. Describe one who stands out for his or her public speaking skills. What are the strongest attributes of this leader's abilities as a communicator?

## REFERENCES

Christison, M., & McCloskey, M. L. (2006). What makes an excellent TESOL session? Tips for presenters [Electronic Version]. Retrieved from http://www.mlmcc.com/File/PUBLICATIONS/2006TipsforPresenters.pdf

Kushner, M. (2004). *Presentations for dummies.* Indianapolis, IN: Wiley.

Markham, P. (1988). Gender differences and the perceived expertness of the speaker as factors in ESL listening recall, *TESOL Quarterly*, 22, 397–406.

O'Meara, F. (1993). Presentation tips from old dead Greeks. *Training, 30*(1), 43.

Osborn, M., & Osborn, S. (2004). *Public speaking* (5th ed.). Boston: Houghton Mifflin.

# Chapter 6

## Behind Door #3: Effective Meetings for the ELT Profession

Mary Lou McCloskey

Effective meetings are an essential element of leadership no matter what philosophy or approach is taken. Yet many professionals are not satisfied with meeting experiences and do not find them a valuable use of their time. Principles and recommendations are provided for deciding when meetings are needed, preparing for meetings, carrying out leadership roles during meetings, and following up on meetings. The goal is to provide meetings in which members are actively involved, listen carefully and respectfully to one another, and see the effect of their work on moving the organization forward toward its goals.

Most institutional meeting scenarios take one of the following three forms.

- *Behind Door #1:* A meeting is scheduled without a clear agenda. Several groups of attendees have their own ideas about what should happen, and much of the meeting is spent arguing about what will be discussed and then arguing opposite sides of motions made on the spot. Cell phones ring many times during the meeting, and members step aside to respond. Little is accomplished, and the arguments continue beyond the meeting into the greater organization.
- *Behind Door #2:* A meeting is scheduled to inform participants about organization goals, policies, and activities. During most of the meeting, participants listen to several speakers summarize written materials that are provided to members. Many participants are bored and restless as they have no stake in meeting outcomes. They make excuses for missing future meetings.
- *Behind Door #3:* A meeting is scheduled with an agenda that is negotiated among participants beforehand and with links to the long-range strategic plan of the organization. Participants have prepared by reading advance materials. Several participants take leadership roles in presenting important matters relevant to the goals of the organization, which are to be decided.

Participants are engaged, feel that they are listened to, see that their contributions prove useful to the work of the group, and feel that their time is well spent. They complete the tasks taken on at the meeting and come back to future meetings, eager to contribute.

Many studies have reported widespread dissatisfaction with both the process and outcomes of group meetings. Planning and managing meetings are important elements of your leadership in an ELT organization. How you manage meetings reflects the effectiveness of your leadership, the willingness and effectiveness with which fellow leaders complete their responsibilities, and how an organization achieves short- and long-term goals. An effective meeting leader facilitates good planning and decision-making by the group and helps to make things happen. What's more, how you manage meetings not only affects the decisions you make at those meetings but it affects the leadership development of all of the meeting members in the months and years ahead. Your management of professional meetings can lead to the future use and development of the leadership skills of all your participants. When meeting members are actively involved, when they listen carefully and respectfully to one another, and when they see the effect of their work on moving the organization forward, their contributions will continue and expand.

## BACKGROUND LITERATURE

A number of prominent theories of leadership and of educational leadership have been influential in guiding leaders in the ELT profession.

*Transformational leadership* and *transactional leadership* are concepts associated with the work of James Burns (1978), and revisited by Bennis (2003), considered by many the founder of modern leadership theory. Transactional leadership involves exchanging one thing for another, while transformational leadership focuses on change.

*Total Quality Management,* a concept developed by Edward Deming (1986), provides the framework for the restoration of manufacturing in post–World War II Japan. Though developed for business, it has been highly influential in education, and it focuses the actions of an effective leader as change agency, teamwork, continuous improvement, trust building, and eradication of short-term goals.

*Servant Leadership* (Greenleaf, 1977) is based on the belief that leadership emerges from the desire to help others. A servant leader is a person within an organization who nurtures the development of those in the organization through understanding their needs, healing wounds, stewarding resources, developing others' skills, and being an effective listener.

*Situational Leadership* (Blanchard & Hersey, 1996) involves the leader adapting behavior to the "maturity" of followers. So, when followers are new to a task, the leader provides direction and guidance in a "participating" style. When followers are unable and unwilling to perform the task, the leader must be directive in a "telling" style. When followers are able but not willing to perform the task, the role of the leader is persuasive in the "selling" style. When followers are able and willing to perform tasks, the leader's role is in letting followers accomplish the task on their own in the "delegating" style.

*Instructional Leadership* (Smith & Andrews, 1989) is a theme in educational leadership that has been related to transformational leadership. It involves four dimensions or roles of instructional leaders: resource provider, instructional resource, communicator, and visible presence.

*Principle-Centered Leadership* (Covey, 1992), focuses on the needs of effective leaders to have a strong sense of purpose in their own lives and principles that guide their actions. He offers seven directives: (a) be proactive, (b) begin with the end in mind, (c) put first things first, (d) think win-win, (e) seek first to understand and then to be understood, (f) synergize (cooperate and collaborate), and (g) sharpen the saw (develop skills and learn from mistakes).

*Change-focused leadership* (Fullan, 2001), specifically applied to education, addresses the dilemma that educational systems continually seek change but are inherently averse to change. Fullan offers five characteristics of effective leadership for change: (a) having a clear moral purpose, (b) understanding the change process, (c) developing strong relationships, (d) knowledge sharing, and (e) coherence, or making connections between existing knowledge and new knowledge.

Regardless of the approach taken to leadership, meetings are one of the necessary tools to accomplish leadership goals. Yet many—perhaps most—professionals are dissatisfied with both the process and outcomes of group meetings, and this is well documented in the research (e.g., Mosvick & Nelson, 1987). The goal of this chapter is to provide you principles and recommendations for effective meetings that will support your leadership, whichever approach it takes, and support those who work with you as well toward the kind of productive meeting you might find behind Door #3.

## PRINCIPLES AND RECOMMENDATIONS FOR EFFECTIVE MEETING PLANNING

This chapter offers principles and recommendations that will help you make your professional meetings successful, effective, satisfying, and enjoyable.

### Before the Meeting

Your efforts before your meeting will prepare the way to a productive outcome.

1. *Clarify the purpose.* Meetings need to be purposeful—to serve the goals of the organization. Clearly define the purpose of the meeting. A meeting may be held for many reasons: to design a strategic plan, to inform members about the

organization and their leadership roles, to share knowledge, to brainstorm ideas or solutions, or to make important decisions. Meetings are expensive in terms of time and travel and should be held only when they are necessary—when the knowledge and experience needed are distributed among participants and goals can be met more effectively through their meeting together. If goals can easily be accomplished through written communication, they should be done that way. If a meeting is needed, determine who needs to be there and what needs to be addressed.

2. *Develop an agenda in collaboration with key participants.* Send out a request for items for the agenda and/or a draft agenda inviting comment. The final agenda should include only items that demand a face-to-face discussion. Use other means to distribute information that does not need discussion. Whenever appropriate to increase investment and participation, spread the workload, and incorporate needed expertise, delegate agenda items to individual participants or specially invited guests. Discuss with the person in charge of each agenda item how the item will be addressed. The sample agenda for a Board of Directors (BD) in Figure 1 shows the distribution of meeting responsibilities among BD members. A further advantage of this distribution is that it gives the meeting leader opportunities to let someone else be in front of the group so that he or she can focus on what is being said. Delegating leadership responsibilities both frees you for other activities and provides means to develop others' leadership qualities, itself one of the responsibilities of leadership. Note in Figure 1 that members of this BD, at its first meeting, have already established their own ground rules for operation, and these are included on each agenda that is distributed.

3. *Distribute the agenda,* background material, and any lengthy documents or articles prior to the meeting and make it clear that members are expected to come well prepared for the discussion. Figure 1 shows a sample agenda for a TESOL Affiliate Organization. Also note that the agenda items are aligned with the strategic goals of the organization and have been given time allotments that make it possible to complete these items during the meeting. Having and holding to time limits can increase the likelihood that the agenda will be covered as well as increase the efficiency of the meeting. If an item must exceed the time allotted, members can decide to extend the meeting, postpone an item to a future date, or delegate the item to a subgroup.

4. *Choose an appropriate and convenient meeting time and place.* Schedule only the time needed to accomplish the goals—participants will be more willing to contribute if their time is well spent. Choose a convenient location suitable to your group's size. A small room with too many people is likely to get stuffy and create tension. A larger room is more comfortable when available. Vary meeting places if possible to accommodate different members. Be sure everyone knows where and when the meeting will be held and how to get there.

*Figure 1:*   Sample Board of Directors Meeting Agenda

**Meeting of the TESOL Affiliate Board of Directors (BD)**
March 20, 2007

**Meeting ground rules.** *We will:*

1. Be prepared for meetings
2. Be attentive listeners
3. Be active contributors
4. Promote safe and professional communication

5. Be open to compromise and negotiation
6. Be respectful of others' passions; express our own passions with control
7. Be mindful that our decisions are to be in the best interest of the Affiliate

1:30–1:40   Welcome and Opening Remarks from the President (A.Z.)

1:40–1:45   Consent Agenda:
Action Item #1: Revised Awards Committee Charge

1:45–2:15   Committee 3-minute Reports
*Membership, Professional Development, Chapters, Sociopolitical Concerns, Finance Committee, Awards Committee*

2:35–2:55   Selection of 2007–2008 Nominating Committee Chair (M.P.)
(Strategic Goal #2: Leadership)
*Action Item #2: Chair of the 2007–2008 Nominating Committee*

2:55–3:15   Strategic Plan Update (V.M.)
(Strategic Goal #2: Leadership, #3: Organizational Soundness)
*Action Item #3: Approval of 2008 Update of the Strategic Plan*

4:05–4:30   Finance Report (Q.E.)
(Strategic Goal #3: Organizational Soundness)
*Action Item #4: Approval of Affiliate Proposed FY 2008 Budget*
Outcome: to be knowledgeable on the financial status of the association and to make informed financial decisions

4:30–4:45   Preview of Next Year's Convention (B.B.)

5:05–5:30   Professional Position Statement on Teaching English to Young Learners (J.L.)
(Strategic Goal #1: Public Policy and Understanding)
*Action Item #5: Position Statement on the Teaching English to Young Learners*
Outcome: to take position on issues pertaining to the profession

5:30–5:50   Unfinished Business

5:50–6:00   Wrap-Up (A.Z.)
Board Meeting Evaluation

*5. Make arrangements for the meeting room.* If at all possible, have the room arranged so that members face one another. Use a table that is circular or semi-circular whenever appropriate and practical. For larger groups, try a U-shaped arrangement. Arrange seats so that everyone can see, hear, and participate. Provide comfortable chairs. Provide for, and encourage the use of, visual aids for interest (e.g., posters, diagrams, slides, etc.). Post a large agenda up front to which members can refer, or provide individual copies. Make arrangements for light refreshments: They are good icebreakers and make your members feel welcome and comfortable. Refreshments are essential if the meeting is held over a mealtime or after a long workday. Note: in any group, but particularly in a multicultural group, there are likely to be food restrictions or preferences. Some may refrain from sugar or caffeine. Others may be vegetarians, or have allergies, or have religious fast days. When distributing the agenda, ask participants to let you know about their preferences and restrictions, and make sure that appropriate food and drink are available for all.

## During the Meeting

1. *Your role as meeting chair.* During the meeting, the chair must focus on the decisions required of the meeting, ensure that all participants are accorded adequate time, decide when to end debate on each topic, use appropriate questions to elucidate information or redirect discussion, listen carefully to all contributions, and clearly summarize proceedings with an emphasis on decisions taken and future plans. An effective chair demonstrates qualities of *impartiality* and *assertiveness*, while performing functions of *keeping the meeting on course* and *summarizing* discussions and decisions.

An *impartial* chair ensures that all participants have opportunities to express their points of view. As chair, you withhold the expression of your own views in lieu of making sure that others are heard. If there is an item on which you feel it is important to speak, turn your gavel over to another member for the discussion of that item. To ensure that everyone gets a hearing, you will sometimes need to show *assertiveness.* This does not imply being rude or dogmatic but being clear and firm in using such phrases as, "Let's wait to hear from you again until others have spoken," or "I think it's time we hear from someone on the finance committee on this topic," and then ensuring that the new speaker is not interrupted. Feel free to ask for only constructive and nonrepetitive comments. Tactfully end discussions when they are getting nowhere or becoming destructive or unproductive. You must also act to *keep the meeting on course,* and on agenda, addressing the importance of each topic and closing the discussion when the allotted time for that topic is up. If one issue begins to dominate, you must take control and suggest a future meeting to discuss the issue, or that a concerned sub-group could continue the discussion at the end of the meeting. Sometimes it will be necessary to call for a decision and then move on to the next topic. You need alertness and judgment to ensure that an issue is given an adequate and impartial hearing within the time allotted.

Finally, summarize a meeting discussion to end a topic, to end a discussion, and make sure that at the end of the meeting all participants have a clear overview of what took place or what action is now required. Summarizing requires active listening. You have to state concisely what was said in an impartial way and end with a clear statement about what is expected to happen next, by when, and who is responsible. It takes careful, active listening and practice to summarize well, but it is a skill well worth developing.

2. *Keeping track of decisions and assignments.* A RAP (Responsibility Action Plan) Sheet (Figure 2) (adapted from Schlessman, 1998) is a tool to assist with this summarizing and record-keeping role. The term Rap Sheet is slang for a form for listing accusations of crimes by law enforcement officers. The word derives from the use of the word rap to mean giving a punishment. The meeting RAP sheet, however, has a more positive purpose: to help meeting participants to remember decisions and responsibilities determined at the meeting and to follow them to completion. During the meeting, someone takes notes on action decisions made using a RAP Sheet as summarized by the chair. This person

**Figure 2:** RAP Sheet (Responsibility Action Plan)

| RAP Sheet<br>Responsibility Action Plan | | | |
|---|---|---|---|
| | | | *Last Updated: March 28* |
| Action | Who is responsible | Target date | Status/ Completion Date |
| Thank-you letter to committee chairs | A.C. | April 1 | |
| Contact and orient selected nominations chair | M.D. & C.L. | April 5 | |
| Final revisions to strategic plan update | A.C. | April 15 | |
| Call new editor re: negotiations. | T.J. | April 3 | |
| Timeline & process for policies manual | EXC<br>R.Z. | May 1 | |
| Standing Rules follow-up<br>  To BD<br>  BD feedback<br>  Staff edit to EXC<br>  EXC review<br>  To committee chairs: Plan for presentations<br>    to committee chairs at convention | <br>A.C.<br>BD<br>Staff<br>EXC<br>A.C. | <br>April 2<br>April 15<br>May 1<br>May 7<br>By June 1 | |
| Contact potential lobbyist re: representation of affiliate & report to BD | R.R. | By May 1 | |
| Board of Directors: BD<br>Executive Committee: EXC<br>M.C., C.L., A.C., T.J., R.Z.: Initials of responsible individuals | | | |

writes down the planned action, who is responsible for completing the action, and the target date for completion (See Figure 2).

The RAP sheet is sent out to all participants after the meeting. At each meeting, the current RAP sheet is reviewed to monitor progress made on the tasks. Each time the RAP sheet is used, completed tasks are dropped and new ones added. An updated RAP sheet is sent out after each meeting. A blank RAP sheet for your use is included in Appendix A.

3. *Getting the meeting started.* Arrive early so that you can greet members and make them feel welcome. (Greet late members, too, when appropriate.) Start and end on time. Do not repeat information for latecomers; rather ask them to get it from a colleague during the break. You may choose to begin with a brief icebreaker or get-acquainted activity that can serve to build a team atmosphere and to generate enthusiasm. The icebreaker helps participants get to know one another and creates group cohesion based on trust and understanding. Timing is important, but it will depend on the size of the group, the overall length of the event, and the purpose of the event. An all-day retreat might warrant a half-hour ice breaker, but a one-hour meeting may merit only a minute or two. Appendix B includes suggested icebreaker activities for both getting acquainted and focusing participants on meeting goals.

As the formal meeting begins, remind everyone of and agree on the major items to be accomplished. Review and approve the agenda. Use the "unfinished business" slot for items that members wish to add to the agenda, or schedule these items for a future meeting. Establish and/or review agreed upon ground rules for the meeting. (See the example in Figure 1.)

4. *Modeling effective communication and participation.* As leader and role model, how you treat those at the meeting will affect how they treat one another. Show interest, appreciation, and confidence in others. Demonstrate your professionalism in demeanor and your fairness and impartiality toward everyone present. Be aware of your body language and use effective body language to communicate your interest in and openness to the ideas of others. Generally, show interest by leaning forward, looking at the speaker, and use posture and gestures that welcome contributions. In the English language teaching profession, however, your meeting participants are likely to come from a variety of cultural and linguistic backgrounds, and body language may be interpreted in different ways. Actions and their meanings as well as meeting expectations and language use may vary according to culture. In one culture, moving very close to someone to speak might be the norm, whereas in another it may be a signal of aggression. In some cultures, but not in others, it may be customary to defer to the chair or to senior members of the group. You will need to observe carefully and to ask cultural informants how actions and language are interpreted by individuals from different cultures. It is also important to encourage everyone

to ask questions when they don't understand someone else's motives, and not to jump to conclusions quickly when something sounds strange or potentially offensive.

5. *Encouraging group discussion.* You will have better quality decisions as well as highly motivated members if everyone is engaged, if you get all points of view and ideas, and if members thus feel that attending meetings is worth their while. When one or two members seem to be doing all the talking, make it clear that everyone will have an opportunity to address an issue before anyone gets a second turn. If the time limit is up for an item, offer the group choices: Move to another item, extend the meeting, delegate the decision to a subgroup, or postpone the discussion until the next meeting. Encourage everyone to contribute feedback. Ideas, activities, and commitment to the organization improve when members see their impact on the decision-making process.

6. *Ending the meeting positively.* End on time, noting meeting accomplishments and summarizing future commitments. While everyone is still together, set a date, time, and place for the next meeting. Acknowledge that even a good meeting can be improved upon, and set aside five minutes at the end of every meeting to evaluate how you did. Ask: What did we do in this meeting that really worked well? What happened that we never want to repeat? Are there bad habits that we seem to keep falling into? Take notes on responses and implement needed improvements in future meetings.

**After the Meeting**

Take a few steps after your meeting to ensure that your accomplishments are implemented. First, *write up and distribute minutes* within three or four days. Quick action will reinforce the importance of the meeting and reduce errors of memory. Second, *follow-up on decisions and delegated responsibilities.* Good leadership empowers everyone—you have distributed responsibilities, now see that all members understand their jobs, have what they need to accomplish the jobs, and then carry out their responsibilities. Third, *recognize success.* Give recognition and appreciation to excellent and timely progress. Fourth, *start on the next agenda.* Put unfinished business on the agenda for the next meeting, check with long-term planning documents, and start planning for next time.

Managing meetings is one of the primary ways you implement your leadership in your profession. It is your responsibility for taking the needed steps before the meeting to help participants understand its goals and come prepared, during the meeting to promote positive and productive interactions, and after the meeting to follow through on decisions taken and continue progress toward goals. These steps will make your organization's meetings purposeful, efficient, effective, and worthwhile.

SUGGESTED RESOURCES

Hindle, T. (1998). *Managing meetings*. New York: DK Publishing.

Marzano, R. J., Waters, T., & McNulty, B. A. (2005). *School leadership that works: From research to results.* Alexandria, VA: Association for Supervision and Curriculum Development.

McNamara, C. (1999). *Managing meetings.* The Management Assistance Program for Nonprofits. Available from http://www.mapnp.org/library/grp_skll/meetings/meetings.htm

Miller, R. F., & Pincus, M. (2003). *Running a Meeting that Works.* Hauppauge, NY: Barron's Educational Series.

Streibel, B. J. (2003). *The manager's guide to effective meetings.* New York: McGraw-Hill.

Zimmerman, D. P. (1997) *Robert's Rules in plain English.* New York: HarperCollins.

### *Discussion Questions*

1. What is your leadership philosophy/approach? Transformational Leadership (Burns, 1978; Bennis, 2003)? Total Quality Management (Deming, 1986)? Servant Leadership (Greenleaf, 1977)? Situational Leadership (Blanchard & Hersey, 1996)? Instructional Leadership: (Smith & Andrews 1989)? Principle-Centered Leadership (Covey, 1992)? Leaders as Change Agents (Fullan, 2001)? Draw connections between your philosophy/approach to leadership with principles of how meetings should be run.

2. How might you adjust the management of meetings for different purposes, e.g., an information-sharing meeting, a strategic planning meeting, or a problem-solving meeting?

3. Discuss how you might apply the principles outlined in this chapter in dealing with difficult participants at your meetings. For example, what might you do about:
   • Someone who doesn't participate—who perhaps leaves to take phone calls or sends email during the meeting
   • Someone who dominates the discussion
   • Someone who doesn't come prepared or doesn't follow through on tasks

4. How can your meetings achieve a balance between providing structure to make them efficient and effective and providing opportunities to take advantage of the face-to-face interaction for free exchange of information to encourage innovation?

## REFERENCES

Bennis, W. (2003). *On becoming a leader.* New York: Basic Books.

Blanchard, K. H., & Hersey, P. (1996). Great ideas revisited. *Training and Development, 5*(1), 42–47.

Burns, J. M. (1978). *Leadership.* New York: Harper & Row.

Covey, S. R. (1992). *Principle-centered leadership.* New York: Simon & Schuster.

Deming, W. E. (1986). *Out of crisis.* Cambridge: MIT Center for Advanced Engineering.

Fullan, M. (2001). *Leading in a culture of change.* San Francisco: Jossey-Bass.

Greenleaf, R. (1977). *Servant leadership: A journey into the nature of legitimate power and greatness.* New York: Paulist Press.

Mosvick, R. K., & Nelson R. B. (1987). *We've got to start meeting like this: A Guide to successful business meeting management.* Upper Saddle River, NJ: Scott, Foresman.

Schlessman, A. (1998). *Organizational design: Policy and planning, development and coordination, supervision and implementation.* Tucson, AZ: Evaluation, Instruction & Design.

Smith, W. F., & Andrews, R. L. (1989). *Instructional leadership: How principals make a difference.* Alexandria, VA: Association for Supervision and Curriculum Development.

## APPENDIX A:  BLANK RAP SHEET

| Action | Person Responsible | Target Date | Completion Date |
|---|---|---|---|
| **RAP Sheet** | | | Last Updated: |
| | | | |
| | | | |
| | | | |
| | | | |
| | | | |
| | | | |
| | | | |
| | | | |

## APPENDIX B:  ICEBREAKERS

| Meeting Icebreakers |
| --- |
| *To get acquainted:* <br> • **Partner Interview/Introductions.** Have participants briefly interview partners, then introduce their partners to the group. <br> • **Favorite things.** Have participants choose two items from their wallets/purses and explain them to a partner or the group. <br> • **Get-Acquainted Bingo.** Give each person a 5 x 5 grid with characteristics that they must find in common with the people around them. They can write the name of the person with that characteristic in its box. Sample items could be: "Find someone that…was born in the same month…lives in your state…drives the same model of car…read a book you read recently…has visited three continents. <br> • **Uncommon commonalities.** Have small groups of about four try to come up with three things they have in common that no other group has in common. <br> • **To Tell the Truth.** Have participants share three facts about themselves—two true and one fiction. Group members guess which item is not true. |
| *To focus the meeting:* <br> • **Burning Questions.** Ask participants to state one or two burning questions they hope will be answered in this session. <br> • **Resource sharing.** Have participants describe one strategy/resource they have used successfully (that is relevant to the topic of the meeting/training). <br> • **Definitions.** Have participants state their personal definitions of the topic being addressed. <br> • **Koosh Toss Ground Rules.** Have participants throw around a beanbag or koosh ball. It must be thrown to every participant, and when the participant receives the item, he or she suggests a ground rule for the meeting, e.g., "Cell phones off." "Let everyone finish." |

# PART 3

# Personal Organizational
# Skills and Strategies

In addition to knowledge about the theory of educational leadership, English language educators need to have personal organizational skills and strategies to function effectively. In this section, skills like time management, managing the tenure process, and event planning are described.

In their chapter, **Murphey and Brogan** discuss the importance of time management on the leadership potential of ELT professionals. They propose nine strategies that they feel will assist educators in being more effective time managers.

**Taylor, Sobel, and Al-Hamly** share a collection of structures and strategies identified in the literature and in their own successful tenure journeys that they feel will facilitate the process for ELT educators.

**Algren, Dwyer, Eggington, and Witt** feel that one skill teacher leaders need to have is event and conference planning. The authors, four former TESOL convention chairs, present skills and strategies associated with organizing professional development events both large and small.

# Chapter 7

## The Active Professional's Balancing Act: Time and Self-Management

Tim Murphey and Jim Brogan

*Time is that quality of nature which keeps events from happening all at once.*
*Lately it doesn't seem to be working.*
*(Anonymous)*

### THE IMPORTANCE OF TIME MANAGEMENT FOR TEACHERS

When you want to be more relaxed and happy, accomplish more, and feel better organized (at least most of the time), then good time management (TM) is important for you. You probably know already that you can continually improve the balance between productivity and enjoying the quality of your life. Many high-performers find this balance by regularly looking for ways to be more efficient and productive and, at times, completely relaxed. We think that the Nine . . . Ates framework that we describe can be a valuable tool to help teachers continually look for this balance and adjust to their particular situations.

We think that you most likely already have some good TM strategies and that you realize how they allow you to contribute more to the world and to help others be more productive. Yet still you want to know how you can cultivate even more of these peak productive moments, as well as having calm and relaxing times when things are running smoothly, when you can slow down and just enjoy life. Of course, what you are managing at these times is not time, but your behavior, choices, decisions, and thinking.

> Time management is really a misnomer, because we all have exactly the same amount of time. . . .Self-management is a better term, because it implies that we manage ourselves in the time allotted us. (Covey, 1990, p. 138)

As an active professional, you may enjoy intensive multi-tasking much of the time but you probably also dread those overwhelming moments when you realize you have too much to do. Finding a balance that includes just enough facilitative stress and healthy relaxation is most people's preferred setting. We suggest that the appropriate balance continually changes throughout our lives and is individually and situationally specific. No matter how good we are at the balancing act, however, we sometimes find that things pile up too high and we feel overwhelmed. We need to be aware of the signs that tell us we have too much going on. "Less" and "slow" can often improve the quality of our work. We recommend that you fine-tune the suggestions we offer below to your own context.

Let us confess up front that we are also writing this for ourselves as much as we are for anyone else. We sometimes find ourselves knee-deep in half-finished manuscripts, projects, association and departmental obligations, while trying to teach effectively.

We also want to address the idea that one's TM balancing act affects, and is affected by, everyone else's, and that being aware of others' values and time schedules can help us avoid a lot of time-consuming conflict. For example, full-time staff and adjunct faculty work under greatly different conditions. Thus, while many teachers may be full time (e.g., Tim), they often must deal with a great number of staff members who are part-time and may see TM priorities very differently (e.g., Jim).

## BACKGROUND LITERATURE

Most professionals learn quickly to thin-slice their work (Gladwell, 2005), that is, they decide the quality of something by examining a few crucial characteristics, as a thin slice of food would inform the palate of a gourmet. For active teachers and students, the first degree of thin-slicing most often begins with choosing which publications to read. For example, unless you are writing an article on the topic yourself, you probably don't read the literature reviews in most articles; you will actually thin slice them when you skim the references. However, some reviews actually contain a lot of useful information, as we hope this one does for you.

In our short human history, time management research and theorizing has taken up volumes. We got 28 million hits from a simple Google® search on September 16, 2006, for "time management"! "Developing time management skills" got a reasonable 970, that and "education" got 644, and that and "teachers" got 624.

Since people have been conscious of time, they have been worried about how we might misuse it. Even Marcus Aurelius Antoninus (121 CE–180 CE) recommended saving time by not being overly concerned with what others think: How much time he saves who does not look to see what his neighbor says or does or thinks.

The true beginning of modern time management as we know it dates from Taylorism and the 19$^{th}$ century industrial revolution. Frederick Taylor researched and measured the time it took to carry out different tasks in factories. He then calculated what could be accomplished in certain amounts of time. While Taylor and his research have been highly praised by industrialists and demonized by humanists, close readers report that, "A careful reading of Taylor's work will reveal that he placed the worker's interest as high as the employer's in his studies, and recognized the importance of the suggestion box, for example, in a machine shop" (Ockerbloom, n.d.). He also advised regular breaks from work to increase productivity (which, however, many industrialists decided were unnecessary). These are two things that seem to have a lasting ring in the literature of TM: we need periodic breaks in our daily, monthly, and yearly work schedule to be most productive, healthy, and happy—(and, yes, according to Koch (1998, p. 153), these three do usually come together). Second, it is a good idea to learn from others about how we can be more efficient through their feedback, a suggestion box of sorts.

## Steven Covey

Steven Covey did the most popular recent reconception of time allotment when he divided our time into quadrants. With urgent and nonurgent columns crosslinked with important and nonimportant ones, he suggested to readers to fill in the quadrants with relevant activities from their lives and reflect on how they were spending their time. Examples, for educators, for the four general spaces could be: a crying student (important and urgent), professional development (important but not urgent), some telephone calls (not important but urgent), and much of the television we watch (not important and not urgent).

*Table 6.1: Covey's Time Management Matrix (Adapted)*

|  | Urgent | Not Urgent |
|---|---|---|
|  | (SPACE 1) | (SPACE 2) |
| **Important** | • Crises | • Study/Prof. Development (crises prevention) |
|  | • Pressing problems | • Relationship-building |
|  | • Deadline-driven projects | • Recognizing new opportunities |
|  |  | • Planning, recreation |
|  | (SPACE 3) | (SPACE 4) |
| **Not Important** | • Interruptions, some calls | • Administrivia |
|  | • Some mail, some reports | • Busy work |
|  | • Some meetings | • Some mail, some phone calls |
|  |  | • Time wasters |

*Source:* Dornyei and Murphey, *Group Dynamics in the Language Classroom,* Cambridge University Press, 2003.

As explained by Dornyei and Murphey (2003, p. 10),

> Covey argues that any one of the four quadrants can become bigger and bite into the time of the others. When the *'Important/Urgent'* quadrant (Space 1) is dominant, we seem to continually be putting out fires and can burn out. On the other hand, if we spend a great deal of time on *'Important/Not Urgent'* (Space 2) activities, this tends to reduce the number and severity of the fires that occur in the first place. Those who concentrate on *'Not Important/Urgent'* (Space 3) activities are not understanding goals and plans and have a short-term focus. And finally those whose activities are mostly in the *'Not Important/Not Urgent'* space (Space 4) are irresponsible, depend on others a lot, and may often get fired.

Important continual teacher development (Space 2) is where we go to get our thin-slicing tune-up so that we can react more intelligently. A more simplistic and yet practical way of looking at your day is the simple "to do" list prioritized by the urgency of the task. For example, tasks or telephone calls can be prioritized by whether or not they must be completed today or completed time permitting.

## PRINCIPLES AND RECOMMENDATIONS: THE NINE ...ATES

We propose considering TM by use of a new framework we call "the nine . . .ates": Abbreviate and Automate, Celebrate, Collaborate and Cooperate, Differentiate, Delegate, Decelerate, and Propagate. Note that we conceptualize these as overlapping and interconnected concepts, nonlinear and noncircular. In the text of this chapter, we have listed them alphabetically for convenience but this does not represent their potential order of importance with respect to an individual's life and dynamically changing circumstances and needs.

### Abbreviate and Automate

Abbreviating routines and chunking processes into more simple and comprehensible pieces usually leads to better learning and performance. The acronym KISS typically stands for "Keep It Short and Simple." Good teachers know this works well for classroom organization and instruction. Managers higher up also understand that the more complex the organizational system, the less controllable it is. Meetings especially can benefit from a good dose of KISS (see Chapter 6).

*Automate* refers to making some things—things that really do not need your constant attention—automatic. For example, downloading sound files for a listening class can now be automated by Rich Site Summary (RSS) feeds that collect all the recent sound files from your preselected locations. For those writing many articles, citation management software like EndNote® can save a lot of time. Rather than accumulating stacks of paper, there is now software for assisting grading and keeping e-records online, for example, with WebCT or

Blackboard. Get administration to send you e-copies of all class lists, pictures of students, and email addresses. Communicating with students through e-lists saves time, and email work gets rid of illegible hand writing. Remember to have back-up files. Software tool use is extremely important for professionals in any field and, as we suggest later, collaborating with colleagues and observing how they work can teach us new ways to automate our own everyday tasks, freeing up time for more quality reflection. In our experience, it is more often part-time teachers rather than full-time teachers, who learn to streamline classroom activities with similar structures and routines. In Japan where full-timers may only be teaching five classes a week, part-timers may teach more than 20 classes at several institutions. In such cases, automizing routines, as much as possible, becomes crucial to one's sanity. Productive full-timers have also learned to be more efficient in order to increase the depth and breadth of their academic contributions. Many teachers, however, conservatively persist in working in the ways we always have. Challenging ourselves to try something new and different can open up new opportunities. We strongly suggest inviting computer-literate students into your office to watch you work and have them suggest alternative ways to work more efficiently.

Another aspect of abbreviate is limiting the time you are "available" in your office and for taking phone calls and responding to emails. In the *Decelerate* section that follows, we will talk more about relaxing and going slowly and occasionally "turning off." Many of us feel pressure to be available 24/7, but being "on" all the time can add to our stress. What we suggest is having set office hours and reasonable times when we can be reached.

## Celebrate

Take time to celebrate your successes; relax after having worked hard. Pat your-self and your team on the back and take a break. Tom Peters also advises us to "Celebrate what you want to see more of." This is aligned with the 20-year-old business management field of "appreciative inquiry" (Cooperrider & Whitney, 2005) that tells us that when we spend time asking people what is working well and celebrating these successes, rather than focusing on what is not working well, productivity increases and many problems simply disappear. The old adage, "Energy goes where attention flows," explains this. When we concentrate too much on problems, they only seem to get bigger and people often burnout. Celebrate what is going well, and you give everybody more energy. The point is that, as busy professionals, sometimes we jump from one problem to the next without pausing to realize that we are doing a good job. At the end of the day, we risk thinking it is all about problems, when really it is about solving them—we just do not take the time to appreciate what we accomplish. This is where appre-ciative inquiry steps up to ask us (and our colleagues and students) about these successful moments that we experience. So, celebrate what you want to see more of. It will instill a more can-do attitude in the minds of those you work with.

One can also celebrate being asked to do tasks and to join teams without necessarily saying yes. When someone asks you to join a new research or writing team and you are not so inclined, it is a good idea to first thank them for considering you. Compliment them on a good project idea or plan. You might say, "Wow, this sounds like a fascinating project and I would love to join it. Unfortunately, I am just overbooked at the moment. Give me your email, and I will send you a few names of people who might be suitable for the job." The point is to confirm the generosity of the offer and thank them for the offer. Then *Collaborate* with them to try to find another suitable candidate. This skill of knowing how to say no while still being helpful and encouraging to the asker is good professional courtesy.

## Collaborate and Cooperate

Folk wisdom tells us "Many hands make short work" and "Two heads are better than one." The research on cooperative learning (CL) also leads us to the same conclusion: Working with others is usually more efficient, faster, and fun (Kagan, 1994; Slavin, 1995). We also learn more and produce a better product! However, often in academia, teachers can feel isolated and compelled to work alone. For example, in many Japanese universities, coauthored articles are, unfortunately, frowned upon when teachers are being considered for promotion. Collaborative research and publication, we feel, should in fact be encouraged as preferable to solitary work.

Many effective leaders realize that collaborating with staff on managerial decisions provides everyone with a fuller understanding of organizational objectives. When time management issues are discussed, open reasoning and consensus through collaboration allow everyone to sing off the same hymn sheet.

Deutsch (1949), expanded upon by Johnson and Johnson (1998) and further by Jacobs, Power, & Inn (2002), identified three windows through which students and teachers can see their peers: individual, competitive, and cooperative. The individual window makes them feel unconnected to others; the competitive one makes them feel that what helps their peers hurts them; and the cooperative one makes them feel that what helps others helps them, and what hurts others hurts them. Jacobs et al. go on to explain:

> CL encourages students to see peers through the cooperative window, as resources, as people to share with, as fellow adventures in the search for knowledge. Clearly, individual work and competition still have their place, particularly when preparing students for the real world outside school. With CL, [however] we attempt to tilt the balance in favor of cooperation, not to eliminate the other two perspectives. (2002, p. x)

One easy way to increase collaboration among your staff is to ask them to do one of the activities or discuss some of the questions at the end of this chapter.

By asking people how they work efficiently, you show that you want to learn from them and you have opportunities, through their ideas, to develop your TM toolbox. Don't forget to also collaborate with your students by asking them more open questions: "How could these materials/tasks/activities be more interesting for you?"

## Delegate

"Delegate" is an often-repeated recommendation to those who are overly busy. Teachers need to heed this advice in and out of the classroom. In the classroom, teachers can include students in classroom management tasks such as distributing and collecting papers, setting up equipment, and writing things on the board. Sharing responsibilities with learners creates a collaborative environment that can build student ownership and is good pedagogy. Activities and tools that build both student responsibility and increase learning can free teachers of some unneeded work. A few examples are student action logging (Murphey, 1993), peer-corrected essays, self-assessment schemes, and student-made tests (Murphey, 1989; 1995).

Out of class, teachers can also develop their skills at delegating work in their departments and associations. In administrative positions, it helps to become aware of tasks you do not need to do personally and to think about who might learn from, and enjoy doing, these things (see the section on differentiating that follows). Doing things, collaboratively at first, will help you learn what your colleagues are capable of and what can be delegated. Asking for small things initially, which will not cause you too much trouble to redo if they are not done well, lets you find out if colleagues can be relied on and what kind of workers they are.

When delegating it is important to keep in mind how positive delegation can give a person more of a feeling of involvement and allow him or her to learn something. Negative delegation just shifts your workload onto them and can cause resentment. So, before delegating, spend a little of your precious time to think of ways of pointing out how that person will benefit from the task. When you are delegated tasks, paraphrase what you have been asked to do, making sure you both agree on definitions and goals. In a profession of unclear boundaries and inexact goals, we need to set realistic achievable targets.

## Differentiate

With experience, we acquire the ability to do what Gladwell (2005) refers to as thin-slicing which is to size up a project, person, or idea and quickly assess whether or not we wish to invest our time and energy. We thin-slice all the time, whether we are judging a book, boss, colleague, or student. We simply do not have the time to thoroughly look at each decision in detail. Of course, we make mistakes when thin-slicing, but that goes with the territory of trying to be more efficient. As Kaufman & Wetmore (1994, p. 31) contend, "All decisions have an element of risk. The most successful people have made the most mistakes and view setbacks as a challenge."

It is important to know *what* you want to invest your time in, choosing opportunities that can be reasonably handled with your expertise, and, at the same time, develop your competence. When you make such selections and decisions, you find that your projects tend to complement one another rather than distract from one another. For example, researching and writing articles about whatever you are doing administratively or pedagogically is much easier and more focused than writing about something that you are not doing every day. Researching and writing articles about topics that you think will make you more efficient "feeds many birds with one scone." Differentiating the TM concerns of different stakeholders can also make us more efficient in the long-run. Good TM isn't just making good decisions for ourselves. We should also take into account the time constraints of our students and colleagues in planning our work. For example, teachers might ask their students to tell them of upcoming events that may prevent the accomplishment of certain tasks or influence their ability to study for a test (e.g., Please let me know if you have more than one test on the same day!). When planning a meeting, it is a good idea to send a few choices around to the people involved so they can tell you what times are easiest for them. Also remember that others, especially part-time staff members, may have different time concerns than you do. Consulting them when making decisions can save you "problem" management time in the future.

### Decelerate

Honeré (2004, p. 104) says *In Praise of Slow* that, "In the war against the cult of speed, the front line is inside our heads. Acceleration will remain our default setting until attitudes change." His book was greatly inspired by the slow food movement (cooking at home with fresh, organic, local foods) that originated in Italy and has now become internationally popular. There are a growing number of "slow" aspects of our lives that Honeré covers in his chapters: slow cities, slow exercise, slow sex, slow work, slow leisure, and even slow schooling. He further cites a wide range of people who have eschewed the rat-race and learned to slow down to improve the quality of their lives and work. He also talks of some slow thinkers:

> The greatest thinkers in history certainly knew the value of shifting the mind into low gear. Charles Darwin described himself as a "slow thinker." Albert Einstein was famous for spending ages staring into space in his office at Princeton University (p. 106) . . . Benjamin Franklin was among the first to envision a world devoted to rest and relaxation. Inspired by the technological breakthroughs of the latter 1700s, he predicted that man would soon work no more than four hours a week. (p. 162)

When trying to slow down, it is useful to remind ourselves that we do not have to do everything at once, and that trying to do so can be overwhelming. Multi-tasking may be thrilling for a while but exhausting if done without a break. Doing some things later or more slowly may be better, especially if the optimum choice is not yet clear. Rather than sticking rigidly to a preset lesson plan or work plan, slow down and let student production or the flow of work guide you where it is most useful to go. Find out what you don't need and do need to teach. Just-in-Time Teaching (Edwards, Mehring, & Murphey, 2006), like the Just-in-Time factory production model, provides the teaching that is actually needed, rather than that forecast by the syllabus.

## Propagate

By propagate we mean to "prodigiously produce good work concerned with your own area of focus and expertise." For example, we both know colleagues who seem to be able to use a newspaper article in a class in 15 different ways while still keeping their students interested and motivated. And then they can write about it in a teacher's publication and do a presentation about it at a conference to contribute to their's and our professional development.

Most educators repeat activities that work well for them, refining them over the years. These same activities could be sources for articles in publications and presentations at conferences. In addition, by working with like-minded colleagues, your output and learning can greatly increase in a fraction of the time you would spend working alone.

The Nine . . . Ates can work together and overlap to provide an efficient and healthy work and living environment. After organizing our list of Nine. . . Ates alphabetically, we realize that probably the most important one is Collaborate. By collaborating with colleagues and students on TM strategies, you can develop your toolbox for improving all the other ". . . Ates": abbreviating and automating our everyday activities, celebrating success, differentiating tasks and responsibilities, delegating behavior, propagating production, and knowing how to decelerate for a healthier lifestyle.

Educators who have been socialized into the profession as independent solitary workers may at first find collaboration unnecessary and too time consuming. They may, however, be missing out on one of the best parts of getting things done: the mental and affective growth that occurs when interacting with other minds. Margaret Mead said, "Never doubt that a small group of thoughtful, committed citizens can change the world. Indeed, it is only thing that ever has." Feeling such camaraderie in successful teams, making the world a bit better, has been one of the greatest rewards of our professional lives.

All of the . . .Ates can save time in the long run, but more importantly they change our behavior and make much more pleasant and satisfying use of our time. They allow us to (to paraphrase Koch, 1998, p. 152), "Do the things we like to do, make them our job, and make our job doing them well."

| SUGGESTED RESOURCES |
| --- |

Gladwell, M. (2005). *Blink: The power of thinking without thinking.* New York: Little, Brown, & Co.

Hindle, T. (1998). *Manage your time.* London: Dorling Kindersley.

Honoré, C. (2004). *In praise of slow: How a worldwide movement is challenging the cult of speed.* London: Orion.

Kaufman, P., & Wetmore, C. (1994). *Brass tacks manager.* New York: Doubleday.

### *Discussion Questions*

1. As a teacher, what things do you do to save time and be more efficient?
2. As a teacher, how do you use time that seems to be wasted time for others productively?
3. What do you do to re-energize yourself when you are tired? What things work for you? What are your methods of relaxation?
4. What time-saving tips would you give to beginning teachers?
5. Henry David Thoreau (1817–1862) said, "*A man is rich in proportion to the number of things he can afford to let alone.*" What things do you "let alone," time-wise, that already simplify your life? What others things might you forgo in the future?

## REFERENCES

Antoninus, M. A. The quotations page. Retrieved November 26, 2006, from http://www.quotationspage.com/quote/9044.html

Cooperrider, D., & Whitney, D. (2005). *Appreciative inquiry: A positive revolution in change.* San Francisco: Berrett-Koehler.

Covey, S. (1990). *The 7 habits of highly effective people.* New York: Fireside Books.

Deutsch, M. (1949). A theory of cooperation and competition. *Human Relations, 2,* 129–152.

Dornyei, Z., & Murphey, T. (2003) *Group dynamics in the classroom.* Cambridge, UK: Cambridge University Press.

Edwards, J., Mehring, J., & Murphey, T. (2006). Exploring JiTT: Just-in-Time-Teaching. *The Language Teacher, 30*(12), 9–13.

Gladwell, M. (2005). *Blink: The power of thinking without thinking.* New York: Little, Brown & Co.

Honoré, C. (2004). *In praise of slow: How a worldwide movement is challenging the cult of speed.* London: Orion.

Jacobs, G., Power, M., & Inn, L. (2002) *The teacher's sourcebook for cooperative learning.* Thousand Oaks, CA: Corwin Press.

Johnson, D., & Johnson, R. (1998) *Learning together and alone* (5th ed.). Boston: Allyn & Bacon.

Kagan, S. (1994). *Cooperative learning.* San Clemente, CA: Kagan Publications.

Koch, R. (1998). *The 80/20 principle.* New York: Doubleday.

Mead, M. Retrieved December 3, 2006, from http://www.quotationspage. com/search.php3?Search=Never+doubt&startsearch=Search&Auth or=Margaret+Mead+&C=mgm&C=motivate&C=classic&C=coles& C=poorc&C=lindsly

Murphey, T. (1989/1990). Student-made tests. *Modern English Teacher, 17*(1 & 2), 28–29.

———. (1993). Why don't teachers learn what learners learn? Taking the guesswork out with Action Logging. *English Language Teaching Forum,* Washington DC USIS. pp. 6-10. http://exchanges.state.gov/forum/vols/ vol13/no1/p6.htm

———. (1995).Tests: Learning through negotiated interaction. *TESOL Journal, 4*(2), 12–16.

Murphey, T., & Sato, K. (2005). *Communities of supportive professionals.* (PDLE series, Vol. IV pp.) Alexandria, VA: TESOL.

Ockerbloom, J. (Web ed.) (1993–2004). (onlinebooks@pobox.upenn.edu) Frederick Taylor. Retrieved November 26, 2006, from www.ibiblio.org/ eldritch/fwt/taylor.html

Peters, T. Retrieved September 28, 2006, from http://www.brainyquote.com/ quotes/quotes/t/tompeters166169.html

Slavin, R. E. (1995). *Cooperative learning: Theory, research, and practice* (2nd ed.). Englewood Cliffs, NJ: Prentice Hall.

Thoreau, H. D. Retrieved December 3, 2006, from http://www.quotationspage. com/search.php3?Search=&startsearch=Search&Author=Henry+D avid+Thoreau&C=mgm&C=motivate&C=classic&C=coles&C=poor c&C=lindsly

# Chapter 8

## The Tenure Journey: Shining the Spotlight on Structures and Strategies for Success

Sheryl V. Taylor, Donna M. Sobel, and Mashael Al-Hamly

> *"Tenure is a topic better illuminated by multiple spotlights than a single floodlight. . . ."*
> *(Chait, 2002, p. 2)*

The system of tenure in institutions of higher education has been clearly defined for more than half a century. Viewed as indispensable to the success of an institution of higher education in meeting its obligations to students and society, tenure is directly linked to the faculty's pursuit of truth in their research and teaching ("1940 Statement," 1940). Assuming that "institutions of higher education are conducted for the common good and not to further the interest of either the individual teacher or the institution as a whole ("1940 Statement," 1940, p. 1), the faculty's work is crucial to the advancement of these outcomes. If tenure is directly linked to the success of an institution, what factors contribute to a faculty member's successful journey toward tenure?

How do highly qualified faculty members successfully maneuver the rigorous process of tenure? Successful scholars understand the twofold foundational purpose of tenure: to firmly ground academic freedom related to teaching and research activities and to provide a core of outstanding faculty. According to a study conducted by Tschannen-Moran and Nestor-Baker (2004), productive scholars learn to manage an array of competing demands while managing the pressures of academic life. That said, how do faculty successfully balance and excel at the conflicting demands of teaching, research, and service? How do faculty members focusing on the education and diverse needs of English language learners find success in academia?

In the field of English language education, leaders often find themselves in the context of higher education. Of the 47,000 total members in International

TESOL (Teaching English to Speakers of Other Languages), results of a recent membership survey indicate that slightly more than one-fourth of the members (26.3 percent) work in higher education (TESOL, 2006). While the International TESOL membership provides only a partial indicator of the English language professionals involved in higher education, it is fair to assume that for many, success in academia involves attaining tenure.

In the present chapter, we illuminate a path for excelling at tenure. First, we provide a brief review of the tenure literature. Next, we share a collection of structures and strategies identified in the literature and our own successful journeys.

## BACKGROUND LITERATURE

Most would agree that universities are complex organizations with a strong foundation in academic freedom and traditions of learning. The principle of academic freedom grew from the need to protect the university from political interference, both in international and U.S. contexts (Mas-Colell, 2003). In 1940, the American Association of University Professors (AAUP) and the Association of American Colleges jointly approved the "Statement of Principles on Academic Freedom and Tenure," thereby updating an original statement (1925). The purpose of the statement is to "promote public understanding and support academic freedom and tenure and agreement upon procedures to ensure them in colleges and universities ("1940 Statement," 1940, p. 1)." In the 1940 statement, a tenure system is articulated to include at minimum: (1) a probationary period of fixed duration; (2) a high-stakes evaluation at the conclusion of the probationary period, and (3) an indefinite appointment for those whose evaluation is successful, grounded in principles of dismissal for cause with due process for the individual and peer review.

Tenure is prevalent in university and college systems in the United States and internationally. In particular, tenure at public research institutions in the United States is highly predominant. According to a report on characteristics of the new professoriate from the American Council on Education in which Anderson (2002) clarifies data from the National Center for Education Statistics (NCES), only .6 percent of all faculty at public research institutions are at institutions without tenure. Despite questions about the economic feasibility of the tenure system, about half of the American professoriate is now tenured (Finkelstein, 2003). In Europe, the tenure ratios tend to be lower than in the United States. The range in Europe varies from a high of 90 percent of the faculty tenured in Italy, 80 percent in France, slightly below 50 percent in Germany, and 40 percent in Portugal (Enders, 2001).

A recent trend in U.S. institutions involves the hiring of faculty into nontraditional, nontenure track, alternative appointments (Bland, Center, Finstad, Risbey, & Staples, 2006). Given that nearly half of the U.S. higher-education faculty anticipate retiring by the year 2015, this shift in hiring practices has potential for long-term impact. Such nontenure, contract positions tend to be less costly and can be advantageous because they are easily terminated if revenues decrease or programs change. As a result, the number of nontenure-track, full-time faculty appointments in U.S. higher education institutions increased 88 percent while probationary tenure-track appointments decreased 9 percent between 1975 and 1993 ("1940 Statement," 1940). By 1998, almost half of the appointments in institutions of higher education were nontenured positions (53 percent) as compared to 47 percent full-time tenure-track faculty (Bland et al., 2006). No doubt, an attractive feature of these hiring changes is their tendency to offset increasing costs and decreasing state funding.

Despite the changes in appointment types, tenure has proven to be durable (Finkelstein, 2003). In a National Study of Postsecondary Faculty, results indicated research institutions of higher education tend to hire full-time tenure-track faculty more often, both in the public and private sector (U.S. Department of Education, 2002). Additionally, in a recent study by Bland et al. (2006), findings indicate that faculty on tenure appointments are significantly more productive in research and education, work about four hours more per week, and are more committed to their positions than their nontenure track colleagues.

Finkelstein's critical review of three major works about academic tenure in the United States (2003), highlights important questions:

- Can a university still provide serious, scholarly higher education without tenure?
- With the declining rate of tenured faculty, how far can the tenure ratio decrease before it negatively affects organizational stability and educational quality?
- What is the role of tenure in attracting the best faculty to available positions?

Finkelstein concludes that much of the variation in the system created for faculty appraisal and to promote the university mission is dependent on the context of the institution. "What is functional in one setting may be dysfunctional in another (p. 508)."

What constitutes a tenure system? The AAUP 1940 Statement on Academic Freedom and Tenure asserts that: (1) terms and conditions of an appointment be stated in writing and include a probationary period of fixed duration; (2) an evaluation at the conclusion of the probationary period be provided; and, (3) an indefinite appointment be offered for those whose evaluation is successful and this appointment be grounded in principles of dismissal for cause with due process for individual and peer review. Common practice consists of a tenure review to occur in about the seventh year of a faculty appointment preceded by a mid-point appraisal in year three or four. Generally, the tenure evaluation takes into account the faculty member's teaching ability (instruction, curriculum, program work), research work (publications, refereed journal outlets, grant writing activity), and professional/public service activities (university, local, state, national, international). It is not uncommon for these performance areas to be weighted, with teaching and research each carrying more weight (e.g., 40 percent) and service less (e.g., 20 percent).

What prompts some faculty to generate the effort, ideas, and productivity needed to be successful in attaining tenure? An investigation by researchers Tshannen-Moran and Nestor-Baker (2004) shed light on this topic. The researchers categorized interview data, identified behavioral themes among successful scholars, and revealed 12 categories contributing toward their success.

Tschannen-Moran and Nestor-Baker found that prolific scholars were driven by a clear set of values resulting in making research their priority. Keeping focused on research was crucial as the faculty continually faced competing demands. Moreover, their research focus helped them maintain direction through tedious aspects of research. These prolific scholars articulated how they managed time and emotions when coping with the pressures of academic life, the criticism involved in peer review, and the politics of organizational life. They formed collaborative networks for both emotional support and intellectual challenge.

## STRATEGIES, STRUCTURES, AND RECOMMENDATIONS

Building on the literature review and the study by Tschannen-Moran and Nestor-Baker (2004, p. 1493), we used the identified categories as a framework to ground our structures for success.

| | |
|---|---|
| • Navigating institutional context | • Knowing yourself and your interests |
| • Setting a research agenda | • Maintaining standards of rigor |
| • Connecting research to practice | • Perseverance through obstacles |
| • Collaboration and social support | • Writing skills |
| • Coping with competing demands | • Coping with publishing and peer review |
| • Setting and maintaining goals | • Political skills to gain resources (p. 1493). |

Working within these categories, we spotlighted structures and strategies that led to our own successful tenure journey.

### Spotlight on the Big Picture: Navigating Institutional Contexts

Becoming informed of the institutional regulations is essential behavior for successful faculty. Each university generally publishes an institutional manual addressing tenure. These typically provide faculty with regulations, review procedures, preparation guidance, and mentoring opportunities as faculty: (1) develop teaching and research skills; (2) advance their research agenda; (3) participate in service activities; and, (4) prepare for reappointment and tenure. For example, the *Strategies for Success* manual (Office of the Provost, 2005) offers University of Colorado at Denver faculty suggestions for excelling in teaching, research, and service. Following these guidelines aids faculty in avoiding disappointments along the tenure journey.

Navigating the institutional context also involves taking note of the "actual facts of the situation as one discovers them" (Neisser, 1976, p. 137). Applied regulations, accepted practices, and behavioral norms can evolve into something quite different from the stated principles. Moreover, regulations or established norms can be counter to one's development as a productive scholar. For example, teaching loads, program work, and service demands placed on new faculty can easily derail their research and writing schedule. Highly productive scholars were identified as being "astute observers of their contexts" and able to adapt to the norms of an academic environment (Tschannen-Moran & Nestor-Baker, p. 1487).

In our contexts, we quickly learned to pay attention to explicit and subtle recommendations particular to the institution and our disciplines. For example, we noticed contradictions related to scholarship, authorship, and publication outlets. While collaboration is a core value of the School of Education and Human Development (University of Colorado context), independent scholarship and single authorship are critical to tenure success. Hence, we continued to collaborate, but we each nurtured an independent line of published work. Moreover, we pursued clarification about institutional and school values regarding refereed outlets, published books, refereed or invited book chapters that allowed us to make informed, strategic decisions related to our goals, time management, and publication outlets. Last, we learned to use indexed guides such as *Cabell's Directory of Publishing Opportunities* (2002) to confirm a journal's readership, intended audience, circulation, and acceptance rates.

In the case of ELTs, those in university contexts often find themselves at language centers. Hiring practices in language centers range from part-time or full-time alternative appointments to full-time tenure-track faculty positions. Some language centers hire ELTs with a master's degree for nontraditional, nontenure track appointments. In this case, their primary responsibility is language instructor. In other contexts, ELT professionals with a Ph.D. are found in departments of English Language where they are hired into tenure-track positions to teach linguistics and language, pursue a research agenda, and become a published researcher. In some contexts, ELT professionals hired into alternative positions coexist with tenure-track colleagues. Both quickly learn to negotiate distinct behavioral norms for their success. Clearly, navigating the institutional context is (1) dependent on one's ability to adapt to environmental norms, and, (2) crucial to one's success.

## Spotlight on the Research Agenda

Personal motivation must lie at the core of every tenure-track faculty member's research agenda. In fact, the prolific scholars articulated a desire to make a contribution through their research and writing. Moreover, they began by shaping a research agenda with an anticipated duration of up to a decade or more. What steps does a pretenure faculty member need to take prior to initiating his or her research agenda?

The developmental phase of one's research agenda is the ideal time to seek support in the institution of higher education. Most pretenured faculty can benefit from the insights of experienced scholars despite risk of intimidation. Moreover, articulating one's research goals and agenda to a mentor forces junior faculty to become clear about their questions and methodology. Last, pretenured faculty need to take advantage of campus research facilities, grant management offices, and campus library.

In the urban university context of Denver, we (Taylor & Sobel) were able to fuel our research through insights gained from our teaching and supervision of preservice and inservice teachers in local schools. Driven by our desire to make a difference through our teaching, research, _and_ writing, we have found the integration of these three to be an ideal "fit" for our work in a school of education focused on innovation, leadership, and applied problems of practice. Without a doubt, our research continues to inform our teaching, and our teaching informs our research (Sobel & Taylor, 2005; Taylor & Sobel, 2001). And, while it has taken a concerted effort and numerous planning sessions to maintain a balanced interplay of research, writing, and teaching, we whole-heartedly agree that this has been worthwhile and contributed toward our tenure success.

## Setting and Maintaining Goals

Regardless of one's passion for research or one's drive to make a difference, faculty need to manage a multitude of demands associated with implementing their research. Prolific scholars tracked their research and productivity, committed time for their research, and followed up on details related to research, writing, and publishing. Last, they took advantage of cycles of conference proposal deadlines to design and finalize writing projects.

"The devil is the details" is a phrase that must have been created for junior faculty negotiating the tenure process. Pretenure faculty must plan for a research agenda in ways that genuinely match one's learning and life style. In the early planning stages of our first decade-long longitudinal study begun at the University of Colorado, we pushed ourselves to participate in backward planning, working backward from our anticipated outcomes. We began with refining our research questions. Next, using a template we created (see Table 1), we recorded detailed thinking around methodology, anticipated data sets, potential manuscripts, audiences, authorship, timelines, and conference presentations.

Our detailed planning provided a clear path for our needs and timelines— needs such as securing human subject approval, locating subjects, making arrangements for data collection, and analysis. Moreover, we compiled a list of potential journal outlets directed at the designated audiences for particular manuscripts. We previewed journal calls for themed issues as a strategy for

*Table 8.1:* Research Agenda Logistics

| Research Questions | Data Sets | Authorship | Manuscript Focus | Possible Outlet | Timeline | Conference Alignment |
|---|---|---|---|---|---|---|
| How can we best prepare teachers for organizing and managing the inclusive, culturally and linguistically diverse classrooms they will encounter? | Pre- and post-surveys from current cohort of teacher candidates | | • IHEs and programmatic issues (How do you prepare? How do we know if they are getting it?) <br> • Ideas for new certificate programs <br> • Recommend customized aspects for professional development in school districts. | | Survey: Sept. & May <br><br> Data analysis: June <br><br> Writing: July–Aug. <br><br> Submission due date: Sept. 15 | |

disseminating our work. We planned manuscripts to coincide with refereed conference programs to ensure that our efforts were directly linked to manuscripts. Last, we used conference materials for forthcoming manuscripts that facilitated swift conversion of conference presentations to manuscripts.

While we were tempted to adhere to the cliché, "out of sight, out of mind" after submitting a manuscript for refereed review, we quickly learned that monitoring the review process required mindful focus. We suspect that every author can cite horror stories about lengthy review processes, late feedback, or lost materials. In response to delayed reviews, we devised a tracking system to follow manuscripts from submission through revisions to ultimate publication (see Table 2). Ultimately, our tracking template helped minimize the "sting" of negative reviews and served as a tool to focus our attention on feedback, revision, and resubmission.

### Collaboration and Social Support

All the prolific scholars interviewed by Tschannen-Moran & Nestor-Baker (2004) discussed the value of collaboration. Successful scholars collaborated with partners and mentors regarding complementary strengths, access to new opportunities, and professional networks. As researchers and writers, we have found the synergy of the collaborative process to be a powerful and cherished gift. In our case, we come from two different disciplines that directly influence our research interests, perspectives, and ideas for outlets. Consistent and clear communication has contributed to our long-term collaboration. We concur that working together with someone you trust and respect is a benefit like no other.

*Table 8.2:  Tracking Research and Writing Logistics (Taylor & Sobel, 2002)*

| Manuscript title | Journal outlet | Submission date | Review time period | Editor name & contact info. | Reviewers' feedback received (Y/N date) | Revised & resubmitted (date) |
|---|---|---|---|---|---|---|
|  |  |  |  |  |  |  |
|  |  |  |  |  |  |  |
|  |  |  |  |  |  |  |
|  |  |  |  |  |  |  |

Faculty members who are considering a collaborative research and writing project need to be clear, realistic, and honest in articulating goals and needs with their partner. Likewise, partners need to be aware that successful collaboration includes: voluntary involvement; shared decision-making and agreed-upon structures for decision-making; and shared responsibilities, resources, and accountability for the outcomes (Friend & Cook, 1996). Once faculty members decide to collaborate, we assert that the issue of authorship is one that warrants honest conversation at the onset of every project. Without a candid conversation, faculty risk misunderstandings, hurt feelings, and irreparable damages to a rich partnership. Once a project is launched, partners need to regularly check in with each other. Such conversations should address author sequencing; writing responsibilities; tracking review processes; and coordinating revisions, resubmissions, timelines, and outcomes.

## A Spotlight on Maintaining Relevance while Coping with Job Demands

Prolific scholars identified constructive strategies to cope with competing demands of the professoriate. Demands like teaching load, student advising, committee assignments, and service commitments must be met while faculty members simultaneously make progress on their research. Managing a barrage of diverse activities necessitates one's thoughtful prioritization. We learned to find a "symbiotic relationship" between scholarship and teaching similar to the other successful scholars (Tschannen-Moran & Nestor-Baker, 2004, p. 1497).

The integration of our research, teaching, and service has been crucial to our successful tenure journey. We have maintained a deep commitment to research that informs our teaching and makes a contribution to improving fair, equitable practices for all students (Sobel & Taylor, 2005; Taylor & Sobel, 2001). This integration of research and teaching has occurred within graduate-level teacher education situated in multilingual, multicultural, and inclusive school settings in urban and suburban Denver. Similar to the prolific scholars, we found two consistent factors for this successful integration. First, we aspired to meet both the standards of rigor and relevance required by the university; and, second, we consciously maintained research grounded in the work of schools because we did not want to disconnect from practitioners and learners.

Besides integrating our research and teaching, we have found that research and writing must become regularly scheduled commitments just like courses and standing committees. We suggest that faculty schedule research and writing time as "nonnegotiables." Also, we have become selective about the opportunities we accept; in fact, we have even learned to say no to some tempting initiatives for the sake of not derailing our research. Last, we recommend that faculty be strategic in conference presentations so that attendance at one conference results in the delivery of multiple papers, thereby minimizing travel time and expenditures.

Tenure—despite recent controversies and changes in hiring practices—continues to be a durable system situated within higher education in the United States and international contexts. If tenure is directly linked to the success of universities, then what factors contribute to success of the faculty? The answer to this question is of paramount interest to tenure-track faculty and administrators in higher education.

The literature supports a range of recommendations for tenure success. A passion for one's research is only one element that comes into play. Certainly, maintaining a focus on rigorous and relevant research situated within one's research agenda is a crucial component to success. But, a promising research agenda may be doomed for failure if the faculty member cannot concurrently manage competing demands of teaching, research, writing, and service. These compelling demands can become the downfall of junior faculty.

We recommend the categories articulated by prolific scholars (Tschannen-Moran & Nestor-Baker, 2004) and the structures we have spotlighted. We suggest faculty members find success in the tenure journey using clarity, direction, durability, and rigor relevant to their research agenda. Concurrently, it is necessary to effectively manage one's time and emotions in the pursuit of advancing one's research and writing. Once these components are in place, faculty can pursue collaborative and supportive relationships while attending to contextual politics. Certainly, the most rewarding elements of the tenure journey are the professional partnerships and collaborative networks formed for emotional support and intellectual challenge.

---

**SUGGESTED RESOURCES**

www.aaup.org (American Association of University Professors). The AAUP mission is to advance academic freedom and shared governance and ensure higher education's contribution to the common good. This organization assists faculty members with advice and assistance about their questions when due process rights have been violated. The AAUP also works with Congress and state legislators to promote effective higher-education legislation and promotes the profession and purpose of higher education in the public eye.

http://chronicle.com/ (The Chronicle of Higher Education). The *Chronicle* offers a regular overview and update of current and highly pertinent topics affecting higher education with a focus on the United States and occasional international coverage.

www.tesol.org/ (Teachers of English to Speakers of Other Languages). In particular, the higher-education interest section offers a variety of resources, relevant topics, and networking opportunities for ELT professionals involved in higher education. You can access this at http://www.tesol.org/s_tesol/seccss.asp?CID=29&DID=34.

---

### *Discussion Questions*

1. Consider your research goals and agenda: What contribution do you hope to make through your research, writing, and teaching?
2. How would you describe your 5- to 10-year research agenda?
3. Which audiences do you hope to address through your writing (e.g., researchers, practitioners, classroom learners, administrators, etc.)?
4. Which refereed journals might serve as appropriate outlets for your research?
5. What are the organizational structure and format for articles published in journal outlets in your discipline?
6. Locate an associate professor who was recently awarded tenure:
   - What is the faculty member's research agenda and goals?
   - How does the faculty member make time for an active and productive research agenda?
   - What strategies does the faculty member use to track his or her research activities? To capitalize on cycles of conference proposal deadlines related to his or her writing projects or research studies?
   - What collaborative structures or professional relationships does the faculty member have? In what ways do these provide support for his or her research and writing?
   - How does the faculty member cope with competing demands of the professoriate (e.g., teaching load, student advising, committee assignments, and service commitments) and still make progress on his or her research agenda?
7. Identify an institution of higher education as the focus for the following questions:
   - What are the terms, conditions, and evaluation policies and practices of tenure-track positions at the institutions?
   - What are the characteristics of hiring patterns and personnel policies at the institution of higher education?

## REFERENCES

AAUP. (1940). 1940 Statement of principles on academic freedom and tenure. Retrieved August 2, 2006, from the American Association of University Professors website, http://aaup.org/AAUP/pubsresearch/policydocs/ 1940statement.htm?PF=1

Anderson, E. L. (2002). *The new professoriate: Characteristics, contributions, and compensation.* Washington, DC: American Council on Education, Center for Policy Analysis.

Bland, C. J., Center, B. A., Finstad, D. A., Risbey, K. R., & Staples, J. (2006). The impact of appointment type on the productivity and commitment of full-time faculty in research and doctoral institutions. *The Journal of Higher Education, 77*(1), 89–123.

Cabell, D. W. E., & English, D. L. (2002). *Cabell's directory of publishing opportunities in educational curriculum and methods.* Beaumont, TX: Cabell.

Chait, R. (Ed.). (2002). *The questions of tenure.* Cambridge, MA: Harvard University Press.

Enders, J. (2001). *Academic staff in Europe: Changing contexts and conditions.* Westport, CT: Greenwood Press.

Finkelstein, M. J. (2003). Floodlights, spotlights, and flashlights: Tenure meets the glare of empirical social science. *The Review of Higher Education, 26*(4), 503–513.

Friend, M., & Cook, L. (1996). *Interactions: Collaboration skills for school professionals.* White Plains, NY: Longman.

Mas-Colell, A. (2003, November/December). The European space of higher education: Incentive and governance issues. *Rivista di Politica Economica 93,* 9–28.

Neisser, U. (1976). *Cognition and reality: Principles and implications of cognitive psychology.* San Francisco: Freeman.

Office of the Provost and Office of the Associate Vice Chancellor for Faculty Affairs. (2005). *Strategies for success: A mentoring manual for tenure track faculty.* University of Colorado at Denver and Health Sciences Center.

Sobel, D. M., & Taylor, S. V. (2005). Diversity preparedness in teacher education. *Kappa Delta Pi Record, 41*(2), 83–86.

Taylor, S. V., & Sobel, D. M. (2002). Making sense of our journey: Lessons learned by novice researchers implementing a four-year research agenda. Paper presented at the 20th annual conference of the Northern Rocky Mountain Educational Research Association, Estes Park, CO.

Taylor, S. V., & Sobel, D. M. (2001). Addressing the discontinuity of students' and teachers' diversity: A preliminary study of preservice teachers= beliefs and perceived skills. *Teaching and Teacher Education, 17*(5), 487–503.

Tschannen-Moran, M., & Nestor-Baker, N. (2004). The tacit knowledge of productive scholars in education. *Teachers College Record, 106*(7), 1484–1511.

Teachers of English to Speakers of Other Languages (2006). *Membership statistics report.* Retrieved August 15, 2006, from http://www.tesol.org

U.S. Department of Education & National Center for Education Statistics (2002a). *Tenure status of postsecondary instructional faculty and staff: 1992–1998,* (NCES 2002–210), by Basmat Parsad and Denise Glover. Project Officer: Linda J. Zimbler. Washington, DC: U.S. Department of Education.

# Chapter 9

## So, You've Agreed to Chair a Conference!

Mark Algren, Eric Dwyer, Bill Eggington, and Beth Witt

> *Only fools and newcomers predict weather.*
> **Anonymous**

We four former conference chairs welcome you in joining this elite group of masochists, believing that fools not only predict weather, they also chair professional organization conferences. We hope to convince you that (1) conferences are worth organizing, (2) they are unpredictable, and (3) you are not required to attend to every conference detail all by yourself. We'll also describe how conferences are designed and, finally, offer suggestions on how to organize a small, local conference. In light of tightened budgets, an additional goal of this chapter is to assist teachers in their ability to defend their attendance at conferences.

A common element in the many definitions and descriptions regarding the notion of an academic or professional conference is the "humanity" of a conference. Thompson (1995) notes that the word *conference* comes from Medieval Latin *conferentia* meaning "to bring together." Barton (2005) emphasizes that academic conferences should yield what periodicals cannot. Thus, while conference attendance can foster knowledge-based professional development, it can also provide unparalleled opportunities for professional networking. Given this interpersonal value of conferences, conference chairs have at least two principal responsibilities: (1) getting the job done, and (2) promoting the interpersonal nature of the conference through networking.

### THE "GETTING-THE-JOB-DONE" REFRAIN

Having listed the two principal responsibilities of conference chairs, you may assume that we will now discuss the one we listed first. You are mistaken. Instead, we offer the following paragraph as a "getting-the-job-done" refrain or chorus that we will invite you to revisit at strategic places throughout the remainder of this paper. We do so because this refrain is simply so important.

### *The Refrain:*

With respect to the nitty-gritty of conference organization, you may feel tempted to assume responsibility for every single detail. Doing so entails madness, to say nothing of miring yourself in a micromanagement morass. Recruit colleagues who take pride in their work, help them to define their tasks clearly, establish feedback and reporting mechanisms, and then step back and trust them to do their jobs. You may want to view your role as the chief cheerleader and the "big picture" organizer. Incorporate fun elements into your planning meetings, get silly, praise extravagantly, and don't forget the chocolate. (The authors are strongly convinced that any meeting—even at breakfast—runs better when good chocolate is available.) It's definitely possible to have fun <u>and</u> to do good work. In fact, we see it as preferable, and the results are more creative.

We will return to the nitty-gritty of conference organization, but first we want to spend some time discussing the human value of conferences by discussing the networking structure and potential of conferences.

## The Importance of Conferences

*Networking:* Conferences bring people together to share expertise and wisdom. In doing so, we enter a structure, i.e., a network, from which we operate. A newsletter for a Pacific Regional YWCA conference (1990) explains that a network is

> a group of people who have a common interest and link together to share information, skills, ideas, and resources. A "Network" can be large or small. It can link individuals to each other, individuals to small groups, small groups to large groups, and so on. No matter what the size, all networks have one common theme—SHARING! (p. 4)

Riles (2000) describes a network as: (1) an information center from which more global and substantial information might flow, and (2) peripheral areas where issues pertinent only to factions of the region may be discussed.[1] From Riles's description, we derived the following visual model of a conference network.[2]

---

[1]  Riles (2000, pages 23–24) describes a direct outgrowth of the Pacific Regional YWCA model: PAWORNET—the Pacific Women's Information/Communication Network.

[2]  For further examination of such frameworks, please see Riles's (2000) schematic of the Asia and Pacific NGO Working Group from the 1995 Beijing NGO Forum, page 49.

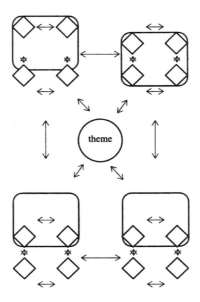

Here we show a relationship with the conference chair's nexus, represented by the circle

beginning with the conference theme, and the relationship with information flow, represented by all the arrows. The theme is transmitted in all directions to pods,[3] represented by

The pods represent groups of related interest sections or groups. Riles might refer to these pods as "kinship" (p. 93), which at their best promote social relevance by their inclusion, or at their worst create marginalization by their exclusion. Professional academic organizations call these pods by different names, often special interest groups (SIGs) or interest sections (ISs). Pods can also include exhibit areas where publishing companies and other business interests spotlight their products. The pods then include presentation sites, represented by

often held in session rooms, hotel ballrooms or breakout rooms.

---

[3]   We implemented the term *pods* for such use during scheduling.

Finally, ⟵⟶ represents communication and information. Facilitating information exchange is a principal consideration for conference site selection; we purposefully provide areas where natural and unstructured communication occurs outside of workshops, presentations, colloquia, meetings, poster sessions, or exhibits. Furthermore, organizers and attendees may depend as much on the space between presentation venues for their dialoguing as they do upon the actual meetings attended.

## ADMINISTERING CONFERENCES

Now we return to discussing how to get the job done. Please go back and read *The Refrain.*

When people think of conferences, the format that usually comes to mind is a one- to four-day event with presentations of papers and workshops. Organizing the facilities and program can indeed be daunting; however, when broken down into small tasks distributed among a core of dedicated volunteers, any conference can be manageable and successful. There's no way to sugarcoat the amount of work that goes into planning and running a conference, but providing professional opportunities to one's colleagues is perhaps one of the most rewarding of leadership endeavors. Please think of *The Refrain* again.

### Reasons Educators Attend Conferences

An early step in conference organization is to ask why people attend conferences. New and experienced teachers overwhelmingly report that they want more training and appreciate any dynamic professional development experiences (Darling-Hammond, 1997, p. 34). Feedback from our own conference evaluations have indicated that educators attended for a variety of reasons, including:

1. Participants want information of professional value that they can *use* immediately. This suggests that conference organizers need to remember that adults want immediate value in new information. You can do much to ensure that presentations include useful, applicable content.
2. Networking opportunities are essential. Conference organizers should set up opportunities for collegial sharing, such as a long lunch break, or informal small group discussions around a "hot topic." Provide lists of area restaurants and bars. Be sure that the event venue has lots of chairs and tables for "accidental" discussions.
3. Educators want access to the latest materials and publications. Consequently, program time should be dedicated to the exhibits.
4. Other factors include amassing professional development "hours" for recertification, individual professional growth plans, and school district requirements. Organizers should be prepared to issue certificates of attendance

that will satisfy such local requirements. Assign volunteers from area school districts to research acceptable formats so your event attendance certificates will be useful.

### Reasons Why Organizations Hold Conferences

It is important to define clearly why the organization is even holding a conference. A conference presents significant financial risk to an organization and is not to be undertaken lightly. Be sure that your group is clear about its conference goals. You may consider the following questions:

- Who is the intended audience, and how many attendees can you expect?
- Who is your competition? Are there other conferences or professional development opportunities where your intended audience might consider spending their funds?
- Even with no notable competition, will the program attract an audience?

### Scheduling Your Conference

Once you have determined that there is an audience and that the conference will meet professional development needs, then the actual planning begins. Please read *The Refrain* one more time.

Start by setting dates. Talk to many people from your intended audience to make sure you avoid major conflicts. Contact the host city Convention and Visitors Bureau (CVB) to avoid damaging conflicts with other events. Be sure to account for holidays or observances. Prioritize potential conference dates, and then go shopping for a venue.

### Selecting a Location

Ask your colleagues to suggest conference locations. If your date doesn't interfere with classes, schools and colleges often have suitable facilities and can be inexpensive or free. Someone with personal or professional connections can help negotiate a favorable deal.

Although highly suitable, hotels and city convention centers can be expensive. If you choose to hold the conference at a hotel, be very aware that you're entering a contract with a corporate salesperson. While it may be possible to arrange for some complimentary sleeping rooms or meeting space (usually based on the number of room nights booked by your attendees), be certain that you know your financial obligations if the anticipated number of sleeping rooms is not booked. Get every detail of your agreement in writing. Know the cost of last-minute, on-site changes or requests for equipment or services; they can be very expensive.

Questions you may want to consider for potential venues include:

- Are there sufficient meeting rooms of appropriate size?
- Can you bring your own audio/visual equipment? If not, how much does the venue charge for these items?
- What computer/Internet services are available for attendees' personal use and in presentation rooms, and what is that cost? (Brace yourself for sticker shock.)
- What are the food and beverage costs? (Catering contracts usually prohibit your bringing in any snacks or drinks.)
- How much does parking cost?

We don't intend to discourage you from using professional conference facilities, but we do want you to be an informed consumer. The bill for hotel services is presented after your event, and you don't want to discover that your organization is responsible for significantly higher expenses than you had anticipated.

While you think about costs to your association, also think about costs to attendees such as registration, accommodation, meals, airfares etc. For international attendees, what will a visa cost, and how easy is it to procure one? If a conference venue is too expensive or difficult to get to, you may find that you have a willing audience, many of whom cannot attend.

## DESIGNING AND IMPLEMENTING A CONFERENCE

Now that the date is set and there is a place to meet, the conference needs to start taking shape. And here we ask you to revisit *The Refrain*. Having done so, please read on.

Divide the work into manageable parts, assembling a team to take on management and oversight responsibilities. You can first divide a conference into large areas—e.g., speakers, publicity, concurrent sessions, special sessions, special events, and so on. Once the teams are determined, recruit volunteers to lead them. In some cases, a leader may also be the do-er, but just as often it is this person's job is to provide leadership to a team of volunteers who do the required work. Together, you as chair and each team leader should develop a timeline.

Another early step is to develop a theme. The theme will give your program development committee a framework upon which they can base their selection of sessions. The theme can reflect the values of the organization, areas of current concern, or reflect an aspect of the venue.

### Concurrent Sessions

Concurrent sessions form the core of educational conferences; these usually run from 45 to 90 minutes and are presented by attendees. Depending on the size and complexity of the organization, there may be only one or multiple presentations in a given time slot. Concurrent sessions may include but are not limited to:

- individuals or groups presenting their own work or research
- workshops with active participation by attendees
- panel discussions
- moderated discussions

One could plan for alternative formats, such as round tables, poster sessions, half-sessions, or combined sessions grouped by topic. Amid planning for time slots and concurrent sessions, also consider the following:

- How long will time slots be?
- What time do you think attendees are ready to start working?
- How many time slots will you schedule during a day, and can you allocate more than one time slot to a single presentation?
- When will invited speakers talk? Do you schedule other sessions against them?
- How long should break times be so attendees have time to move from one event to the next?
- Will there be breaks for beverages or meals?
- How much time will venue staff need to rearrange rooms if furniture set-ups need to be changed between events? (There will be a charge for this.)
- What time of day will sessions finish?

Conferences are not composed of presentations only. Many other events are often attached, such as meetings of groups or subgroups of the association, social events, field trips, and tours. Association business is often conducted during early morning, late afternoon, and early evening hours, or over lunch.

## Conference Session Content

With the framework in place, content is needed. You will need to develop a calendar for soliciting and selecting proposals. Write guidelines for proposal submission (we have seen these run from the very informal submission of a title and descriptive paragraph to carefully vetted, highly detailed submissions requiring recommendations regarding the presenters' presentation skills). Set up a committee to review proposals and develop the program. Time to read *The Refrain* again. (Are you getting the message?)

The conference proposals committee develops the *call for proposals*. Include all the information needed: name, address, email address, session title, session description and how long it can be, and a longer, more complete description of the content and activity of the session. (See the annual TESOL call for proposals for a thorough, professional example.) The call should include a rubric so that proposers can know what elements in their proposals will be used for evaluating them. Some possible criteria include a title that clearly describes the session, a topic that is highly relevant, and a description of the presentation that is clear and complete.

We strongly recommend a blind peer-review process undertaken by a proposal selection committee. This group uses the published rubric to evaluate proposals.

## Invited Speakers

Invited speakers can be a major draw for attendees; many attendees make their decision to attend based on their desire to hear a particular speaker. Strive for speakers and speaker topics that either have broad appeal or particular interest to various segments of a diverse audience. We advise issuing speaker invitations early, even a year or more in advance, and offering sufficient financial incentives to invited speakers (i.e., hotel, per diem, registration, air fare, honorarium, complimentary tickets to conference meals and social events).

If you are located in an area of interest to travelers, offer your speakers a guided tour. Use the uniqueness of your locale to appeal to prospective speakers. Many conference organizers have successfully (and cheaply) lured otherwise expensive speakers by providing them with a unique cultural experience in lieu of an honorarium.

The conference theme is important information to any invited speaker. They will also need background information on your organization, the purpose of the conference, and a description of the audience they will address (size, gender make-up, work settings, professional interests, etc.). Plan invited speaker presentation times carefully to maximize attendance. Remember that the "luminaries" talk to each other; your hospitality and good care of an invited speaker can help ensure that others will want to come in the future.

## Conference Publicity

Be sure your prospective attendees have enough time to plan to attend. If the event is costly and involves attendees' institutional support, plan at least one year in advance so that institutions can build costs into their budget cycle. International attendees will have to budget time and funds to obtain a visa and get their passports in order.

Publicity clearly deserves its own team. Team members should work hard designing and sending flyers to association members, nonmembers, and, if possible, administrators who have budgetary authority to approve expenditures. Publicity should also extend to local school district teachers and principals, civic organizations like the Chamber of Commerce, and local media.

## Conference Exhibits

An important group at any conference is the educational materials exhibitors. They want to participate because they can sell products, make sales contacts, and turn a profit. But more importantly for you, exhibits draw attendees. Be sure to include time in the conference dedicated to the exhibits. You could arrange for light refreshments to be served in the exhibit hall during conference breaks. Hold any raffle or prize drawings there as well. Exhibitors can also make strong contributions to the conference program. Their sessions are often popular with attendees, so allocate some concurrent presentation time to them. Ask exhibitors about their needs. The sale of exhibit tables can bring significant revenue to your organization. Build a reputation for treating your exhibitors well, and they'll support your organization by attending your meetings annually. Many will be inclined to make sponsorship donations if asked.

## Something Will Go Wrong

We can guarantee that something will go wrong with the conference. Don't worry, you and your conference will survive. Our philosophy: It's not a problem; it's an opportunity to excel! What if a major/plenary speaker cancels at the last minute? You, the brilliant planner that you are, have a back-up standing by. What about "no-show" session presenters? Communication is the key here. Be sure that your team has had positive confirmation from each session leader. Use whatever means necessary to get in touch; it's worth the time and effort.

Mistakes in the conference program book are inevitable, no matter how many times it is proofread. Enlist several people to read the semi-final draft so your printed program is as accurate as it can be. Have some readers focus on the content, and have others concentrate on logistical information, such as session times and locations. Then have a plan for communicating last-minute changes to conference attendees such as announcements from the podium, signs on session doors, posters in high-traffic areas, flyers in the conference packet, or all of the above.

Some audio/visual (AV) equipment will fail. If your venue has an AV company on site, be sure that your planning team knows the protocol for contacting technicians. If you're handling AV equipment yourselves, have tech-savvy volunteers standing by with spare projectors, extension cords, and replacement bulbs. Be sure that a "techie" is available to assist plenary speakers to set up and test their presentation gear.

Unpreventables happen, such as power outages, building evacuations, severe weather, or faulty sprinkler systems. Brainstorm with your team leaders to have some strategies in mind should you find yourself coping with such an event. You should NOT be the only person with knowledge and information for problem-solving. Share this responsibility with your planning team, and solicit their input for potential solutions. Remember *The Refrain*!

## Appreciation

All volunteers need to know their efforts are recognized. Be sure your planning team volunteers are aware of your appreciation. Small gifts are nice, but your regular praise and thanks for a job well done are even more valued. Conferees will be very kind and compliment you. Let folks know a team of volunteers is responsible for the conference and share kudos with your team.

## Conference Evaluations

The most useful evaluation form is one that can be used from year to year, guiding future planners as they tailor the conference to meet attendees' needs. Focus on aspects of the conference over which you have control. The return rate on evaluation forms is usually very low, unless there's an incentive, such as a free prize raffle ticket, or a chance for complementary conference registration at your next event. Delay evaluation reading until your post-conference team's debriefing meeting, a week or two after the event. Bolstered by chocolate and a few good nights' sleep, everyone can be more sanguine about negative comments, using them to improve future conference experiences. But what about the attendee who is unhappy and vents distress in person at the conference? Advise your team to listen respectfully to complaints and to take them seriously. Apologizing and acknowledging how your upset attendee feels goes a long way.

## Post-Conference Products

Administrators who pay the conferees' bills often want to see something tangible when their teachers return home. Many conferences, as a result, offer newsletters, press releases, special interim meetings, reports, or proceedings as part of their conference packages. Particularly expensive conferences may even offer audio/video recordings, and/or electronic versions of presenters' handouts. Much of this material could be made available through online resources attached to the association's webpage. In order to maintain professional integrity, we recommend that online material be made available only after it has undergone extensive quality control mechanisms such as peer review.

## ORGANIZING A SMALLER CONFERENCE

We have tried to provide a breadth of information that includes suggestions for organizing conferences ranging in size and scope from international to regional to local. We are aware, however, that most of you will be organizing smaller conferences. The following is a list of additional considerations specific to organizing local or regional conferences. For this context, *The Refrain* at the beginning of this paper is absolutely vital. Please read it again. We have noted that too many professionals "burn-out" after organizing one or two local conferences because they have tried to, or been forced to, do it all. So in addition to all of the preceding, please consider the following.

Local conference chairs should always verify that what they have been told has been done has actually been done. Communication procedures are essential. Publicity for the conference needs to come out early and be constant. Be creative in getting the word out. Bring in good outside speakers as a draw; link up with local sister associations; involve local college and university personnel (faculty and students); use door prizes and raffles as attendance enticements; and make the program intense and very rewarding. It's sometimes more difficult justifying giving up a Saturday to go to a conference within a few hours' drive than attending one that's across the country, so creating a sense of value for attending the conference is paramount.

Planning a conference is a complex job, but there's help available. Many organizations have documented their own planning and implementation processes in detail, and you will find a list of print and electronic resources at the end of this article. We wish you well and ask you to visit *The Refrain* one more time and then have a piece of your favorite chocolate.

---

**SUGGESTED RESOURCES**

---

Mundry, S., Britton, E., Raizen, S., & Loucks-Horsley, S. (2000). *Designing successful professional meetings and conferences in education: Planning, implementation, and evaluation.* Thousand Oaks, CA: Corwin Press.

Migliore, P. E. Conference planning guide. Columbus, OH: Office for Victims of Crime, U.S. Department of Justice. http://www.ojp.usdoj.gov/ovc/publications/infores/res/confguid/welcome.html

*International Association of School Librarianship. Conference planning and management: A handbook.* http://www.iasl-slo.org/confmanprog.html

*National Academic Advising Association. Regional conference chair handbook.* http://www.nacada.ksu.edu/RConf/index.htm

National Association for Developmental Education. *Conference planning: Chapter and national.* http://72.14.203.104/search?q=cache:gStlh9cBW0kJ:www.nade.net/documents/CONFBOOK.doc+conference+planning&hl=en&gl=us&ct=clnk&cd=57

National Council of Teachers of English. Conference and meeting planning checklists and worksheets. Documents prepared by Jacqui Joseph-Biddle, NCTE Convention Director. http://www.ncte.org/groups/affiliates/mtgs/124410.htm

*Discussion Questions*

1. How valid are the sentiments contained in "The Refrain"? Why do you think the authors ask their readers to constantly revisit it?
2. Why do you think people attend conferences? What do they hope to go back to their work with?
3. What teams do you need to develop in order to lead a successful conference?
4. With a partner or small group, brainstorm some no- or low-cost ways to provide substantive follow-up for conference attendees.
5. What ideas do you bring to conference organizing that are not described in this chapter?

## REFERENCES

Barton, K. (2005, December). Advancing the conversation: The roles of discussants, session chairs, and audience members at AERA's Annual Meeting. *Educational Researcher,* 24–28.

Darling-Hammond, L. (1997). *Doing what matters most: Investing in quality teaching.* New York: National Commission on Teaching & America's Future.

National Council for Accreditation of Teacher Education (2006). *Professional standards for the accreditation of schools, colleges, and departments of education.* Washington, DC: NCATE.

Pacific Women's Information/Communication Network (PAWORNET) (1990, June). *Tok Blong Ol Meri, 2.* Suva: PAWORNET.

Riles, A. (2000). *The network inside out.* Ann Arbor: University of Michigan Press.

Thompson, D. (1995). *The concise Oxford dictionary of current English* (9th ed.). Oxford, UK: Clarendon Press.

# PART 4

# Program Organizational
# Skills and Strategies

In order to be effective, ELT leaders need skills in the functions of planning, organizing, leading, and coordinating activities and supporting individual and collective learning. This section contains articles that are critical in the area of program organizational skills and strategies.

**Curtis's** chapter presents seven practical principles to keep in mind when creating a professional development program. **Christison and Murray's** chapter defines strategic planning, describes the role of strategic planning in business and English language programs, and presents a flexible process of strategic planning. **Siskin and Reynolds** remind us that a leader sets the tone for technology use among teachers, and they provide useful information on what technological skills and abilities they feel ELT educators need to have and where and how to acquire these skills. **Brady's** chapter discusses fundraising, a vital leadership strategy that contributes to our personal development as teachers and researchers. He defines fundraising and why ELT professionals need to engage in this important activity. **Currie and Gilroy's** chapter helps guide leaders as they build their skills and knowledge to become more effective recruiters of quality language teachers and future teacher leaders. **Panferov's** chapter on program promotion introduces some current methods of promotion and suggests steps for establishing a promotional plan for a typical intensive university ESL program. **Quirke and Allison's** model of DREAM management is presented in their chapter as a way of defining best ELT leadership practices employed at their institution.

# Chapter 10

## The Seven Principles of Professional Development: From A to G

Andy Curtis

### THE IMPORTANCE OF PROFESSIONAL DEVELOPMENT

"The most complex society ever assembled in a single place" is how Vivian Paley (1997, p. 122) described the classroom. Such a high degree of complexity gives classrooms—perhaps especially multilingual, multicultural English language classrooms—an organic quality, where growth must constantly be occurring to avoid stagnation and death. Not, of course, the death of the individual, but perhaps the death of the kind of passion that first attracted us to this field. This, then, is one of the key reasons for the importance of professional development: to enable a language teaching organization to maintain a state of positive, productive growth and change. This is in itself reason enough, though there are many more reasons (see Curtis, 2006, for a discussion of these reasons).

Professional development can be an effective form of community-building (Curtis, 2005) when used to overcome what Dan Lortie (1975) refers to as the isolation of "the egg carton profession" (p. 223), which is what he calls teaching because of the ways in which teachers work in a classroom, usually separated from other teachers. As Bailey, Curtis and Nunan (2001) point out: "once we close the doors to our classrooms, we are relatively isolated from our peers" (p. 10). Professional development can be carried out in isolation (see the literature review that follows), but it may be most effective when carried out collaboratively and cooperatively, which helps prevent isolation and creates communities.

Another compelling reason for engaging in professional development is burnout prevention. Christina Maslach, who developed the Maslach Burnout Inventory (Maslach & Jackson, 1986), defined burnout as "a syndrome of emotional exhaustion, depersonalized, and reduced personal accomplishment that can occur among individuals who do 'people work' of some kind. It is a response to the chronic emotional strain of dealing exclusively with other human beings, particularly when they are troubled or having problems." (Maslach, 1982,

p. 3). Maslach goes on to explain that "what is unique about burnout is that the stress arises from the *social* interaction between helper and recipient" (1982, p. 3). It is possible that the relationship between an English language educator (ELE) and students struggling to understand and make themselves understood in a foreign language and culture is precisely the kind of exhausting, people-intensive relationship described by Maslach. Professional development is one way of preventing this kind of burnout (Bailey, Curtis, & Nunan, 2001) and helping teachers avoid what Diane Larsen-Freeman (1998) has called "excessive routinization" and the "deskilling of teaching" (p. 220).

## BACKGROUND LITERATURE ON PROFESSIONAL DEVELOPMENT AND REFLECTIVE PRACTICE

In a chapter such as this, a review of the literature on professional development is neither possible, because of space limitations, nor necessary, given the practical orientation of this book. Also, some of the literature on professional development that ELEs need to be familiar with is presented in context in the section that follows. However, where the literature can help is in developing a firm understanding of the meaning of *professional development* and *reflective practice*. Focusing on so fundamental a starting point as defining terms may seem obvious, but it is commonly overlooked. For example, in the recent state-of-the-art, encyclopedic article on professional development in English language teaching "in the new century," Michael Breen (2007) explains that, in his chapter, "the terms *teacher development* and *professional development* are treated as synonymous" (p. 1). However, he does not offer a definition of either term beyond explaining that both terms "refer to any in-service program or course for experienced English language teachers, be they planned or provided by teacher educators or others or generated locally by and for teachers themselves in planned or spontaneous ways" (p. 1). An example of the sometimes limited usefulness of scholarly definition is provided by Michael Knapp (2004), whose exhaustive 50-page paper on *Professional Development as a Policy Pathway*, includes the following: "Professional development can be understood productively as a 'channel' or 'pathway' connecting…learning process and outcomes with policy events" (p. 116). Knapp continues: "In essence, the pathway comprises of a stream of activities spanning levels in the educational system that are, in some intentional sense, related to support for professional learning" (p. 116).

A more accessible and practical definition of professional development was provided some years earlier by Dale Lange (1990): "Teacher development is a term used in the literature to describe a process of continual intellectual, experiential, and attitudinal growth of teachers" (p. 250). Lange (p. 250) also referred to the need for "continued growth both before and throughout a career" and added that teachers should "continue to evolve in the use, adaptation, and application of their art and craft." Although this definition is now nearly 20 years old, it is useful and accessible as it captures a complex set of relationships simply and clearly. The first tripartite set of relationships refers to three distinct types of knowledge—intellectual, experiential, and attitudinal—which is connected to and balanced with another set of three more skills-based aspects, i.e., use, adaptation, and application. The ongoing nature of professional development is also referred to three times in Lange's definition (1990).

Taking Lange's definition, professional development can be carried out in isolation. Similarly, Richards and Lockhart's definition (1994) also suggests that reflective practice can be carried out individually: "teachers and student teachers collect data about teaching, examine their attitudes, beliefs, assumptions, and teaching practices, and use the information obtained as a basis for critical reflection about teaching" (p. 1). However, Julian Edge (1992) has developed a collaborative approach that he calls *Cooperative Development*. Edge states that "I need someone to work with, but I don't need someone who wants to change me and make me more like the way they think I ought to be. I need someone who will help me see myself clearly" (p. 4).

One of the best-known and most accessible works on reflective teaching is Ken Zeichner and Dan Liston's (1996) introduction, which at only 80 pages can be read by even the busiest of ELEs. In their chapter on the Historical Roots of Reflective Teaching, Zeichner and Liston acknowledge the influence of John Dewey's *How We Think* (1933), which continues to influence the reflective practitioner more than 70 years after it was first published. Zeichner and Liston paraphrase Dewey's definition of reflection as "active, persistent and careful consideration of any belief or practice in light of the reasons that support it and the further consequences to which it leads" (1996, p. 9). Another key thinker in this area was Donald Schön (1983, 1987), who distinguished between two different timelines in relation to reflection. Reflecting on teaching before and/or after the teaching event he called *reflection-on-action*. Reflection on teaching during the teaching event he called *reflection-in-action*.

In terms of broader definitions that can also apply to ELEs in administrative and managerial roles, the action researcher Stephen Kemmis (1986) pointed out that "Reflection is not just an individual, psychological process. It is an action oriented, historically-embedded, social and political frame, to locate oneself in the history of a situation, to participate in a social activity, and to take sides on issues" (p. 5). This kind of more politically inclined definition is likely to be of use to ELEs negotiating the politics of professional development seen in many areas of education, including English language teaching organizations.

## PRINCIPLES AND RECOMMENDATIONS

Fifty years ago, George Miller published his famous paper entitled The Magical Number Seven, Plus or Minus Two: Some Limits on Our Capacity for Processing Information (1956). This paper is still being cited today, for example by Robert Glassman (2000), who stated that: "The capacity of working memory [short-term memory] for about seven plus or minus two serially organized simple verbal items may represent a fundamental constant of cognition" (p. 163). Add to this fact the difficulty of remembering all the useful advice contained in books like this one during difficult or challenging times, when such advice might be most needed, and the question becomes: How to present practical principles in ways that make such information most accessible when it is most needed? My solution to this conundrum was to present seven principles in alphabetical order, from A to G, using alliteration where possible to assist with recall. This arrangement will, hopefully, help the reader access this information effectively when it is most needed. Although the seven principles, which are designed to overlap and complement each other, are supported by some references to the literature, they are primarily derived from my years as the executive director of an EAP/IEP school of English, referred to below as "the School" at a Canadian university from 2002 to 2006.

## 1. Articulate Your Awareness

It is possible that all development starts with awareness—an awareness of what might be thought of simply as a gap in one's knowledge, skills, or understanding. This is an over-simplification, but this definition does help highlight the fact that before anyone can attempt to fill such a gap they must first be aware that a gap exists. This is not as obvious as it might at first seem. For example, some ELEs live and work in contexts and cultures in which a teacher who publicly admits that he or she does not know something runs the risk of damaging, if not ruining, his or her credibility. If the prevailing assumptions and cultural norms within a particular context are based on the transmission model of education in which the job of the teacher is to transmit knowledge from themselves to their students, acknowledging such gaps—even privately—may be difficult.

According to Bailey et al., "Self-awareness and self-observation are the cornerstones of professional development" (p. 22), but if we accept that articulating awareness is an important and logical first step in professional development, this then raises the question, What is awareness? Leo van Lier (1998, p. 131) described four levels of consciousness, one of which is *Awareness,* which he describes as "transitive" consciousness, i.e., "consciousness *of* something, which involves 'perceptual activity of objects and events in the environment, including attention, focusing, and vigilance'" (Bailey, Curtis, & Nunan, 2001, p. 25).

But awareness of what? In this case, the awareness is focused on possible gaps that may be addressed through some form of professional development. It is, though, important to note that this is not the kind of gap-filling or cloze activity that many EFL and ESL students are asked to complete. A more appropriate analogy for the gap in professional development would be the Big Bang Theory of inflationary cosmology in which the Universe is thought to be constantly expanding. The point is not to fill the gap, but to feed it.

## 2. Be an Example

Although the importance of leading by example has been stressed to the point of being a tired leadership literature cliché, it is not at all uncommon, in my experience, to find university administrators who constantly advocate the benefits of professional development, but who engage in little if any themselves—a typical case of "do as I say, not as I do." As the executive director of the School, one of my main goals was to promote professional development in an environment that was suffering severely from stagnation. All staff members hired after my arrival were required to make a commitment to engage in ongoing professional development, funded and supported by the school. This funding was both direct, for example, reimbursing the costs of attending a full-day workshop on conflict transformation, and indirect, for example, granting release time to attend an undergraduate course on intercultural communication offered by the university. For full-time clerical staff, the time commitment was the equivalent of one working day per semester, i.e., seven to eight hours. For full-time teaching staff, the commitment was the equivalent of one week per semester of paid professional development time. Although some staff resisted this arrangement, claiming that they did not have enough time for professional development, it became increasingly difficult for them to make this claim when they saw that I was willing and able to make the commitment and sustain my own professional development over the years.

## 3. Count the Cost

Cost is a constant concern in English language education these days, especially in zero-funded, cost-recovery, income-generating units within universities, which is the category into which our School fell. Therefore, the costs and benefits of professional development must be considered. However, for most ELEs—whether teachers, administrators, or managers—the notion of cost-benefit analysis is an entirely unknown area. What then is a cost-benefit analysis?

According to Watkins (n.d.), Cost-Benefit Analysis (CBA) "estimates and totals up the equivalent money value of the benefits and costs to the community of projects to establish whether they are worthwhile. These projects may be dams and highways or can be *training programs* and health care systems" (emphasis added). Some key distinctions between training and development are discussed in the point that follows, but the reference to "training programs" makes that definition relevant to this discussion. Another definition of CBA is given by the American National Institutes of Health (1999), which uses the term *Benefit-Cost Analysis,* which it defines as: "A systematic quantitative method of assessing the desirability of Government projects or policies when it is important to take a long view of future effects and a broad view of possible side-effects." Although attempts to assess the relative costs and benefits of professional development are currently extremely rare, such calculations are likely to become more common as demands for "financial accountability" increase. Therefore, ELEs lobbying for professional funding for themselves and their staff, if they are also fulfilling managerial roles, would be well advised to start posing and responding to questions such as: What are the costs of ELE professional development in this school? What are the benefits of ELE professional development? Who benefits and in what ways?

### 4. Distinguish between Training and Development

In 2004, a new state-of-the art digital language laboratory was installed in the School that generated necessary discussion about distinctions between *training* and *development*. Katie Head and Pauline Taylor (1997) ask, "How are 'training' and 'development' different?" (p. 8). They respond with the following distinction: "Teacher training essentially concerns knowledge of the topic to be taught, and the methodology for teaching it. It emphasizes classroom skills and techniques" (p. 9). Drawing on the work of Adrian Underhill (1986), Head and Taylor describe teacher development as being "concerned with the learning atmosphere which is created through the effect of the teacher on the learners and their effect on the teacher" (p. 9). They conclude that development has "to do with 'presence' and 'people skills' and being aware of how your attitudes and behavior affect these" (p. 9).

It is important to note here that *training* and *development* are not mutually exclusive dichotomies, any more than language teaching *theory* and *practice* are mutually exclusive. Instead, *training* and *development* represent a continuum. As Head and Taylor put it, rather than emphasizing the differences, "it is more useful to see training and development as two complementary components of a fully rounded teacher education" (p. 9). To return to the new language lab example, learning to use the lab constituted the acquisition of a particular set of skills to complete a specific task, i.e., to operate the lab. This is training because of its "how to" focus, whereas development is often why-focused—for example, why teach this particular language skill in this way when there are many ways to teach it? Language schools should be investing in and supporting both training and development. However, when resources are scarce—as they usually are—and one may need to be prioritized, it becomes important to be able to distinguish between the two.

### 5. Engage Everyone

According to the *New York Times* best-selling author and entrepreneurial expert, Robert Kiyosaki (2005), "the receptionist of a company has one of the most important jobs in the company" (p. 67) because "if the receptionist does his or her job well, the company actually runs smoother," but "if the receptionist delivers a bad *product*, for example, by being rude over the phone, then his/her value to the company goes down" (p. 67). At the School, the receptionist did play a pivotal role, as she was often the first person to have contact with a student, through an initial email inquiry followed by up to a year or more of correspondence regarding visas, travel itineraries, accommodation, etc. The receptionist was also one of the last people to have contact with the student, through follow-up email with the student after he or she had left the program, for example, helping to arrange for certificates to be posted and references letters sent. In spite of occupying such a central position, in this case, as the first and last person at the school to have contact with the student, receptionists are not generally thought of in relation to ongoing professional development in the same way as development is considered important for teachers. This is a common oversight and one that should be avoided. The simplest way to do this is to include everyone in the language teaching organization in the professional development plans.

Mandating and engaging, however, are not the same thing. Mandating simply requires a position of authority. Engaging is a much more subtle and complex process in which the benefits of taking part in a particular activity become clear to those who are being encouraged to take part. Like "lead by example" (see Point 2), the idea of "working smarter, not working harder" has also become something of a cliché in the leadership literature. But if staff can see that, for example, attending a workshop on time management will help them have even a little more time, then they are likely to attend willingly and enthusiastically.

## 6. Fund Your PD Program Properly, Positively, and Proportionally

Here, "properly" refers to adequate funding. People who work in education are tired of being told to "do more with less," especially perhaps those working in English language education. Therefore, if a senior administrator advocates professional development, two questions should be put to them immediately. First, they should be asked how much professional development *they* plan on engaging in, including specific details of what they plan to do, when, and why. They should also be asked what resources, such as time and money, have been budgeted for and dedicated to professional development. Positively and proportionally, here, refer indirectly to the culture of entitlement increasingly common in many older institutions, such as the Canadian university within which the School existed. Within such a culture, some staff expect that they are entitled to certain benefits as a result of seniority, years of service, etc. This was the system in place when I arrived at the school, in which, for example, teaching staff would be funded to attend English language teaching conferences based on their seniority. The system was changed to one based on contributions to each event, so that if a teacher wanted to attend a conference and was giving a presentation at that conference, the school would fully fund them for all expenses. However, only partial funding was approved for attendance alone. The rationale for this funding structure was that teachers who were presenting were sharing their work with the larger English language teaching community and raising the profile of the school in a highly competitive marketplace.

In terms of proportionality, the more conferences a teacher attended and presented at the more professional development funding they received. Also, in order to engage everyone (see Point 5), part-time teaching and full-time administrative staff were also eligible for funding for appropriate professional development opportunities.

## 7. Get Senior-Level Support

Of all the challenges of establishing a professional development program for yourself and others, getting senior level support may be one of the greatest. Unfortunately, a model in which business managers who have no teaching qualifications or teaching experience are put in charge of teaching units does appear to be coming more popular in Canadian universities, and perhaps elsewhere. Consequently, persuading those who control the purse strings of the benefits of investing in professional development can be a considerable challenge, but it is possible. The annual budget for the year before I arrived at the School showed a total professional development expenditure of $87.78 (Cdn), though it was not clear on what this had been spent. Within two years, this figure had been increased to $10,000 per year for professional development. It remained at that level until I left the School, after which time it declined.

One of the reasons this kind of spending on professional development was allowed by the accountant/business manager was the fact that the workplace satisfaction surveys that we instituted showed that the majority of staff were positive and appreciative of the professional development support funded by the school. One of the results of this level of satisfaction was that the rate of turnover of staff was low, which in turn meant that less time and money needed to be spent on advertising, interviewing, and appointing new staff.

Another way to get senior-level support is to encourage and support staff who wish to write up accounts of their professional development activities. These accounts are not for publication in scholarly or academic journals, as these can take years of reviewing and revising before they appear in print, by which time the work may be out of date. There are, however, a great many professional newsletters, such as those published by the TESOL and IATEFL. By helping teachers at the School write articles for such newsletters, based on their professional development work, we were able to show the accountant/business manager that our investment was helping to contribute to the international community of ELEs, which addressed a number of the much-trumpeted missions of the university, i.e., to increase its international profile through teaching, research, and publication.

There are many reasons for ensuring the existence of a professional development program in any English language teaching organization, including: keeping the organization growing; creating communities of language teachers, learners, and administrators; and preventing ELE burnout. There are many principles to bear in mind when creating a professional development program, seven of which are, from A to G:

1. Articulate Your Awareness
2. Be an Example
3. Count the Cost
4. Distinguish between Training and Development
5. Engage Everyone
6. Fund Your PD Program Properly, Positively, and Proportionally
7. Get Senior-Level Support

It will not be possible to successfully attempt all of these steps at the same time or in a short space of time. Creating a sustainable professional development program for yourself and for others can take years to establish, but once it is in place and working effectively, the returns on the investment of time, energy, and other resources will considerably outweigh the costs.

---

**SUGGESTED RESOURCES**

Bailey, K., Curtis, A., & Nunan, D. (2001). *Pursuing professional development: The self as source.* Boston: Heinle & Heinle.
   A comprehensive overview, with an introductory chapter on reasons to engage in professional development.

Diaz-Maggioli, G. H. (2003, August). Professional development for language teachers. *CAL Digest.* (EDO-Fl-03-03).
   Available online at http://www.cal.org/resources/digest/0303diaz.html A comparison of five different approaches to professional development for language teachers.

England, L. ( 1998, April–June). Promoting effective professional development in English Language Teaching. *The English Teaching Forum, 36*(2). Available online at http://exchanges.state.gov/forum/vols/vol36/no2/p18.htm
   An older article but still a useful summary.

Farrell, T. (1998, October–December). Reflective teaching: The principles and practices by Thomas Farrell. The *English Teaching Forum, 36*(4).
   A clear and concise staring point for would-be reflective practitioners. Available online at http://exchanges.state.gov/forum/vols/vol36/no4/p10.htm

> *Discussion Questions*
>
> 1. How would you define professional development in the context of EFL/ESL?
> 2. What do you consider to be some of the key characteristics of a reflective practitioner?
> 3. What are some of the factors in your context that *promote* professional development?
> 4. What are some of the factors in your context that *prevent* professional development?
> 5. What would be some of the main goals of your professional development program?

## REFERENCES

Bailey, K. M., Curtis, A., & Nunan, D. (2001). *Pursuing professional development: The self as source.* Boston: Heinle & Heinle.

Breen, M. P. (2007). Appropriating uncertainty: EFL professional development in the new century. In J. Cummins & C. Davison (Eds.), *International handbook of English Language Teaching* (pp. 1–19). New York: Springer.

Curtis A. (2005). From judgmental to developmental: Creating community through conference. In T. Murphey & K. Sato (Eds.), *Professional development in language education. Vol. Four: Communities of supportive professionals* (pp. 1–12). Alexandria, VA: TESOL.

Curtis, A. (2006). Weighing the why and why nots of professional development. *Essential Teacher, 3*(1), 14–15.

Dewey, J. (1933). *How we think.* Chicago: Henry Regent.

Edge, J. (1992). *Cooperative development: Professional self-development through cooperation with colleagues.* Harlow, UK: Longman.

Glassman, R. B. (2000). A "theory of relativity" for cognitive elasticity of time and modality dimensions supporting constant working memory capacity: Involvement of harmonics among ultradian clocks? *Progress in Neuro-Psychopharmacology and Biological Psychiatry, 24*(2), 163–182.

Head, K., & Taylor, P. (1997). *Readings in teacher development.* Oxford, UK: Heinemann.

Kemmis, S. (1986). Critical reflection. Unpublished manuscript. Deakin University, Geelong, Australia.

Kiyosaki, R., & Lechter, S. L. (2005). *Rich dad's before you quit your job: Ten real-life lessons every entrepreneur should know.* New York: Warner.

Knapp, M. S. (2004). Professional development as a policy pathway. In R. E. Floden (Ed.), *Review of research in education, 27* (pp. 109–157). Washington, DC: AERA.

Lange, D. E. (1990). A blueprint for teacher development. In J. C. Richards & D. Nunan (Eds.), *Second language teacher education* (pp. 245–268). New York: Cambridge University Press.

Larsen-Freeman, D. (1998). Expanding roles of learners and teachers in learner-centered instruction. In W. A. Renandya & G. M. Jacobs (Eds.), *Learners and language learning* (pp. 207–226). Singapore: SEAMEO Regional Language Centre.

Lortie, D. (1975). *Schoolteacher: A sociological study.* Chicago: University of Chicago Press.

Maslach, C. (1982). *Burnout: The cost of caring.* Englewood Cliffs, NJ: Prentice Hall.

Maslach, C., & Jackson, S. E. (1986). *Maslach burnout inventory manual.* Palo Alto, CA: Consulting Psychologists Press.

Miller, G. A. (1956). The magical number seven, plus or minus two: Some limits on our capacity for processing information. *Psychological Review, 63,* 81–97.

National Institutes of Health (NIH). 1999. Cost-Benefit analysis guide for NIH IT projects. Retrieved October 1, 2006, from http://irm.cit.nih.gov/itmra/cbaguide.html

Paley, V. G. (1997). Talking to myself in a daily journal: Reflections of a kindergarten teacher. In C. P. Casanave, & S. R. Schecter (Eds.), *On becoming a language educator* (pp. 115–122). Mahwah, NJ: Lawrence Erlbaum.

Richards, J. C., & Lockhart, C. (1994). *Reflective teaching in second language classrooms.* Cambridge: Cambridge University Press.

Schön, D. A. (1983). *The reflective practitioner: How professionals think in action.* New York: Basic Books.

———. (1987). *Educating the reflective practitioner: Toward a new design for teaching and learning in the professions.* New York: Teachers College Press.

Underhill, A. (1986). Training, development and teacher education. *Teacher Development Newsletter, 4,* 9.

van Lier, L. (1998). The relationship between consciousness, interaction and language awareness. *Language Awareness, 7*(2, 3), 128–145.

Watkins, T. (n.d.). *An introduction to cost-benefit analysis.* Retrieved October 1, 2006, from http://www.sjsu.edu/faculty/watkins/cba.htm

Zeichner, K. M., & Liston, D. P. (1996). *Reflective teaching: An introduction.* Mahwah, NJ: Lawrence Erlbaum.

# Chapter 11

## Strategic Planning for English Language Teachers and Leaders

MaryAnn Christison and Denise Murray

### WHY IS STRATEGIC PLANNING IMPORTANT?

As educational consultants, we have worked with English language programs, institutes, schools, departments, companies, institutions, and organizations[1] in many different contexts all over the world. We have noticed that two qualities are consistent among the entities that we consider successful. Those that are most successful in meeting their educational goals and performing at the highest levels have some type of formalized strategic plan and work consistently to implement it, while those entities that have been least successful have no plan in place. The second quality that we see among these successful entities is that they have identified leaders who understand the process of strategic planning and are skilled in developing a strategic plan and providing the leadership necessary to carry out the plan. We suggest that in order for any English language program, institute, school, department, company, institution, or organization to be successful, there must not only be a plan in place for the future, but there must also be competent leadership in place to both create the plan and oversee its implementation. In this chapter, we will focus on both of these components. We want to help you understand the process of strategic planning so that you can take a leadership role in developing a strategic plan and, in addition, develop specific leadership skills to carry out and implement a strategic plan.

### WHAT IS STRATEGIC PLANNING?

Strategic planning is the process that determines where a program, unit, department, institution, association, organization, or company wants to be in

---

[1]   In reference to English language and teaching the following terms are used consistently and often interchangeably in the literature depending on the contextual reference: *entity, program, institute, academy, school, center, department, company, institution,* and *organization.*

five to seven years and how it is going to get there. In the past, organizations have referred to strategic planning as long-range planning. However, more recently, the term *strategic planning* has been adopted because it captures the idea that the planning process is not only long term, but is also strategic, meaning that the process is comprehensive and purposeful. The term *strategic* is also meant as a reference to the placement of an organization in the future in terms of where it wants to be in relation to other organizations in the field. In other words, the strategic plan is a blueprint for the future.

Strategic planning has been defined in the literature as "the process of determining the mission, major objectives, strategies, and policies that govern the acquisition and allocation of resources to achieve organizational aims" (Pearce, Freeman, & Robinson, 1997, p. 658). As this definition suggests, strategic planning consists of various processes, such as defining objectives and goals, developing strategies, and then delineating the specific tasks that help one reach the objectives. In the business world, the goal of strategic planning is often focused on maintaining or creating a competitive advantage over rivals in order to improve financial performance. With English language programs we are, of course, concerned with the quality of instruction, but we also want to attract students to our programs in order to secure funding and ensure future financial health. Strategic planning takes an approach that attempts to control the future by predicting the future. However, recent research in systems theory shows that open systems such as educational organizations and marketplaces are not predictable; instead, they can be enormously uncertain. Strategic planning in English language programs, then, becomes a much more complicated matter. For this reason, educational leaders need sophisticated skills in strategic planning in order to make relatively accurate, yet flexible, predictions about the future and to determine how to interact with the predictions in terms of resource allocation, both human and material.

## THE ROLE OF STRATEGIC PLANNING IN BUSINESS AND ENGLISH LANGUAGE PROGRAMS

Strategic planning has been used in business and then adopted in education, including in English language program administration, as a means of developing a direction for the organization that is adopted by all employees. Organizations see their strategic plan as a means to (a) ensure that all staff are committed to similar goals and (b) define their work for their clients.

Kanter (1983) notes that leaders use strategic planning to ensure that the organization doesn't drift into new areas or fall back on old ideas without conscious decision-making. The strategic plan guides the everyday activity of an organization. For example, any new, innovative idea or request from outside the organization is measured against the plan. Does this idea or proposal fit the plan? If not, should the plan be modified, or should the organization reject the idea or proposal? The values of the organization can be used in performance management and in hiring. When a new teacher is hired into the organization, he or she can be requested to agree to the values, which are then used as one measure of the teacher's performance. So, for example, if one of the organization's values is a focus on a particular teaching approach, such as cooperative learning or content-based instruction, a new teacher might be asked to exhibit certain types of teaching behaviors that are consistent with this approach.

Strategic planning, although used extensively in education, is largely unresearched in this context. Therefore, practitioners draw on research and often on anecdotal evidence from the business world. While there are some similarities in contexts, such as the need to satisfy customers (i.e., students), a realization that the organization works within a competitive environment, and a desire to provide the best product on the market, there are differences. Education traditionally has been less concerned with the factors that drive businesses because the focus in education has been on the public good and on service. More recently, however, almost every sector of ELT has found that many of the factors that drive businesses are central to an educational organization's survival. While business focuses on strategic planning to ensure better profit margins, educational institutions can adopt these processes to improve their service and thereby improve the educational outcomes for language learners. Some of the research in business has shown that, in turbulent times, an adaptive approach to strategic planning gives an organization the flexibility to respond quickly to a changing environment. This approach comes from the trend in the science to understand emergent systems (for example, Lissack 1999).

The approach we take is that planning helps an organization focus and develop agreed-upon goals; however, to be able to respond to change and also to capture the creativity of staff, the planning process itself must include a commitment to processes that allow for such adaptability.

## THE PROCESS OF STRATEGIC PLANNING

### Determining an Approach to Strategic Planning

In many language education situations, program planning is a regular part of an organization's calendar. We ourselves have been involved in regular five-year program planning exercises. However, often these exercises are perfunctory and only take a limited approach to strategic planning. They often involve program evaluation. But this is often restricted to an internal evaluation of the current program, especially curriculum content, followed by a decision to change the curriculum content, usually based on the intuitions of staff. The approach we present here is a more systematic, objective analysis of the current situation and a decision about the organization's future directions, based on several analyses.

The first step in strategic planning is to determine the approach to take and to consider the advantages and disadvantages of each approach. Strategic planning can be approached top-down, bottom-up, or a combination of both.

In the top-down approach, strategic plans are developed by management or the administrative arm of the entity and presented to other members as a *fait accompli.* The advantage of this approach is speed and efficiency since the plan is often put together by a relatively small group of people who know the most about the organization and, presumably, have the most investment in its success. The disadvantage of this approach is that it is difficult to get commitment and investment from nonmanagement, nonadministrative employees because they have nothing invested in the plan. As a result, the plan is ignored, avoided, sabotaged, or only given lip service.

In the bottom-up approach, each individual has an opportunity to contribute to the process on some level. The disadvantage of this approach is that it is much slower and usually more expensive. Inevitably, there will be widely divergent views among staff about both the goals and the trajectory for accomplishing the goals. In addition, these views may diverge considerably from the management/administrative view. For example, while management may be focusing on profitability and sustainability of the organization, staff members may be more interested in their particular role and how to ensure their own survival through the process. Further, without guidance from management, staff may believe that management is not really committed to strategic planning, but is doing it perfunctorily to meet some external need, such as a program review or a directive from the school's owners or the university president. It takes time and patience to work through these issues. Even when the bottom-up approach is used and the extra time is taken, there is no guarantee that all individuals or groups will support it. Nevertheless, the obvious advantage of the bottom-up approach to strategic planning is that once the plan is in place, there is a better chance of commitment across the board.

Many experts on strategic planning believe that a process that captures features of both the top-down and bottom-up approach is the most effective way to proceed with strategic planning in educational settings (Cope, 1989). This type of approach can be achieved by creating a planning team that is constantly working with management/administration, faculty, and staff. Creating a planning team also demonstrates to everyone that management/administration is committed to the process of strategic planning and its outcomes.

## STEPS IN STRATEGIC PLANNING

There is no perfect way to conduct strategic planning. Different people and groups, especially within different cultures, use different approaches and different names for the activities the planning process involves. However, there are three steps that most experts on strategic planning consider essential in the overall process (for example, Ansoff, 1979; Cope, 1989; Covey, 1990; Klinghammer, 1997; Bennis & Manus, 1997). These are (1) assessing the situation, (2) determining the organization's goals, and (3) deciding on a path for getting from the present to the goal at some point in the future. Exactly how to assess, determine the organization's goals, and decide on a path to follow varies from organization to organization. We will provide a basic template that you can adapt and revise to suit your needs.

## Assessing the Situation

Assessing includes conducting a review of all components of the organization, including its economic, social, political, and technical features. Strategic planners must consider various driving forces in the environment, such as increasing competition and changing demographics. One way to do this is to look at the various strengths, weaknesses, opportunities, and threats within the organization and in the environment through a SWOT Analysis.

The term *strengths* refers to the internal strengths of the organization—the expertise of staff, the school's reputation, or its diversity. Assessing the organization's weaknesses requires an honest appraisal. There is little value in papering over problems as this prevents the organization from developing strategies to improve. Opportunities are externally driven and might derive from an influx of international students or immigrants, for example. Threats refer to external organizations, policies or procedures that could lead to a loss of business. For example, a local university may institute an M.A. TESOL, providing competition for your program.

Figure 1 provides a matrix for developing the SWOT analysis. While this is a very blunt instrument, it provides a starting point for staff discussion about the current situation and therefore where the organization might go in the future.

In order for the SWOT analysis to work well, there must be skilled and competent leadership to guide the individuals involved in the task (see Klinghammer, 1997, for a more detailed account of the SWOT analysis in an IEP). We have both participated in SWOT analyses within our own institutions and within professional organizations, volunteer boards, and associations. The most effective SWOT analyses have included at least the following activities.

*Figure 11.1:* SWOT Analysis Matrix

| Strengths | Opportunities |
|---|---|
| | |
| Weaknesses | Threats |
| | |

*Brainstorming*

The purpose of brainstorming is to get people together to generate ideas. In SWOT analysis, brainstorming must be structured around each of the components of SWOT—strengths, weaknesses, opportunities, and threats. A leader does not have to be the most vocal contributor or the most innovative thinker. A leader's job in a brainstorming session is focused on helping others generate ideas and encouraging creative thinking by creating a safe and supportive atmosphere for sharing. Such brainstorming sessions need to be both focused and open. They need to be focused so that staff do not use them purely as an opportunity to push their own particular issues. They need to be sufficiently open so new ideas can blossom and be discussed rather than dismissed.

*Balance*

We believe that the process must give individuals time to collect their own thoughts and determine what they think and believe before they hear others' comments. We then believe it is important for the group to experience a structured sharing and recording of ideas so that everyone can see the ideas generated. We have used large pieces of butcher paper, flip charts, or a computer with projector for this purpose. Small group sessions, with groups writing up their ideas in one of these ways, allows for nonjudgmental approaches to new ideas that may be comforting to some colleagues.

*Best Ideas*

Since not all ideas can become part of the strategic plan or are even of equal value, the group must next select the best ideas from the list. Some groups may reach consensus easily while others will need to take a majority vote to select the best ideas. All members of the group must feel that they have the right to challenge ideas and discuss them in an environment of mutual respect and trust.

## Determining the Organization's Goals

*Vision Statement*

The assessing process interacts with an organization's vision, mission, and values statement. The next step is the development or refinement of the entity's vision statement. Vision statements are brief written descriptions of the purpose of the organization, used to communicate with individuals external to the organization. For example, the Adult Multicultural Education Services (AMES) in Victoria, Australia, provides a comprehensive range of education for immigrants and international students—from general English to helping students obtain jobs. Their vision statement is, *AMES—Full participation in a cohesive and diverse society.*

*Mission Statement*

A mission statement is an aim for the future, based on the vision. Thus, a mission statement is usually a description of how the organization will or should operate in the future and of how customers or clients will benefit from the organization's products or services. To develop a mission statement, an organization must be able to define exactly what it is aiming to achieve and be able to map out what it needs to do to bridge the gap from the present into the future. Individuals reading an organization's mission statement for the first time should be able to extract a practical understanding of what the organization values. Most mission statements are ones that almost anyone would agree with, and so they often lack a real force or differentiate one organization from another. However, it is in the development of specific objectives that the mission statements become clear and provide accountable, measurable goals. Consider National Centre for English Language Teaching and Research's (NCELTR) mission statement in Column A of Table 11.1. Then, look at the questions this mission statement raises. These are the sorts of questions that need to be asked during the strategic planning sessions in order to move to the next stage of goals and objectives.

*Value Statements*

Value statements list the overall priorities for the organization. Value statements can be focused on moral values (such as acting with integrity, honesty, respect) or how they should behave as professionals (plan lessons carefully, show concern for students, return papers in a timely manner). Value statements can also be focused on organizational values (such as increasing the number of students, improving the quality of instruction at all levels, and creating more opportunities for teacher growth and development. Value statements can also be a combination of both moral and organizational values. Along with the vision and mission statement, the value statements provide guiding principles for all staff and demonstrate for clients how the organization responds to them or to suppliers, and what the organization requires of them. Following is the value statement of the professional organization TESOL:

professionalism in language education
individual language rights
accessible, high-quality education
collaboration in a global community
interaction of research and reflective practice for educational improvement
respect for diversity and multiculturalism

*Table 11.1: Creating Mission Statements*

| Column A Mission Statements | Column B Questions? | Column C Answers to the questions |
|---|---|---|
| NCELTR's mission is to provide leadership to the English language teaching community and promote excellence in English language education through innovative and high-quality programs, services, products, and research. | How will you provide leadership? How will you measure quality and excellence? How will you develop innovative programs? | We will develop a quality assurance plan to measure the effectiveness of our programs, services, products, and research. We will develop processes and commit resources for staff to develop new programs, products, and research. We will publish widely and present in international arenas to model the quality of our programs, products, and research. |

## Determining Goals and Objectives

Determining and laying out the goals that need to be accomplished is the next step in the process of strategic planning. You need to use the information derived from the assessment stage and from your interrogation of your mission statement to determine the goals. Goals are desired end states that a group of individuals decide are important for the success of an organization. They often lack specificity. Therefore, for each goal you need to identify the specific objectives that you must achieve in order to accomplish the goal. Objectives (sometimes also called projects) are lists of activities that help you achieve your goals. Table 11.2 provides examples of three goals for one mission statement and several different objectives that would need to be accomplished in order to achieve the goals.

Establishing goals and objectives is the basis of planning. Articulating goals and objectives should be second nature to anyone who has been in a leadership position, but it is often not the case. Goals should be ambitious in order to stretch the organization. People respond to the promise of high achievement. However, objectives and goals should also be achievable.

## Implementing the Goals and Achieving the Strategic Plan

According to Klinghammer (1997), a strategic plan is ready to be implemented only when certain conditions have been met. Figure 2 outlines the minimum conditions that must be met if the implementation of the strategic plan is to be successful.

*Table 11.2: The Relationship between Mission Statements, Goals, and Objectives*

**Mission Statement:** We have a strong student orientation, and we demonstrate care for every student and teacher.

*Answers to our interrogation of our mission statement:* Our curriculum and classes are centered on the students and how they learn. We conduct a needs analysis with our students each semester to determine what and how they want to learn. We use classroom activities that encourage students to try new things and to talk freely with the teacher and with each other. We also provide positive reinforcement to help students in their efforts.

| **Goal 1:** Conduct a needs analysis for all incoming learners. | **Goal 2:** Use classroom activities that encourage students to try new things and to talk freely with the teacher and with each other. | **Goal 3:** Provide positive reinforcement to students. |
| --- | --- | --- |
| **Objectives** | **Objectives** | **Objectives** |
| • Appoint two individuals to create a needs analysis instrument<br>• Pilot the instrument<br>• Analyze the data<br>• Decide on when to routinely administer the instrument<br>• Decide on how to analyze the data<br>• Determine a process for implementing the feedback from the process | • Create a curriculum development team to develop classroom activities for all teachers to use<br>• Conduct professional development sessions with teaching staff on how to use these activities and develop their own<br>• Develop an evaluation instrument for evaluating language classrooms<br>• Pilot the instrument<br>• Administer on a regular basis<br>• Analyze the data and work with teaching staff on how to improve the activities | • Have teachers conduct action research in their own classrooms about their own responses to students<br>• Conduct a focus group with teachers to discuss the types of positive reinforcement they already use<br>• Have teachers decide which are effective<br>• Have teachers pilot this type of feedback<br>• Have teachers evaluate their pilots and share with colleagues |

If implementation is to be successful, then competent and committed individuals must be identified to oversee the process. If implementation is not successful, then all of the efforts to develop a strategic plan will have been wasted. Heller (1999), Klinghammer (1997), and Tichy and Charan (1995) believe that implementation is the key to successful strategic planning and that people are the key to successful implementation.

## Revising the Strategic Plan

Goals are rarely met without having to overcome some unexpected difficulties or problems. Being able to achieve the goals despite setbacks is the sign of competent and committed leadership. If the strategic plan gets off track, don't panic or start placing blame on others. Come with a solution. Assess the situation and develop

*Figure 2:* Conditions for Successful Implementation

1. Each goal has been clearly articulated and individuals have agreed on how it can be achieved by delineating objectives clearly.
2. The resources necessary to achieve the goals are available.
3. A detailed timeline for achieving each goal has been established.
4. Communication and responsibility networks have been agreed upon. Everyone knows whom to report to and who is taking responsibility for the achievement of each objective.
5. The planning team has determined how they will know that the efforts they are making are successful (Kotter, 1995).
6. The outcomes for each objective are measurable.
7. A person or persons have been identified to take responsibility to see that each goal is completed.
8. Checkpoints have been decided to determine whether the objectives are on track or whether they need to be revised based on new information or challenges.

a plan to get back on track as quickly and efficiently as possible. When you suffer a setback, it is also a good time to reassess the viability of achieving the goal. Do you still believe that it is important? Have the problems that have arisen caused you to rethink the goal? Look for the positive side in any negative situation. Effective leaders always assume that there will be some challenges and setbacks and look at these events as opportunities to improve on the strategic plan and to stimulate a renewed effort and focus on achieving the plan that was agreed upon.

## EVALUATING LEADERSHIP SKILLS IN STRATEGIC PLANNING

The case that we have consistently made throughout this chapter is that successful strategic planning is composed of both a systematic and carefully applied process and the presence of skilled and trained leadership to oversee the process and its implementation. In this chapter we have given you some tools for developing expertise in strategic planning. To see how well-equipped you are to demonstrate your leadership in strategic planning, see how well you can answer the questions in Figure 3. You will want to have the answers to all of these questions at your fingertips if you are to take a leadership role in strategic planning.

In this chapter, we have taken an approach to leadership and management that involves planning for the future development of any ELT organization. We have delineated the way visions, mission statements, and values interact and how they lead to realistic, achievable goals and objectives. Our approach to strategic planning involves both planning and flexibility. While planning is an essential tool for any leader, so, too, is planning for change and the unexpected. Plans that are inflexible prevent talented, creative staff from innovating and prevent

*Figure 3:* Leadership in Strategic Planning

**Strategic Planning Leadership Evaluation**

1. What approach to strategic planning will you take and why?
2. What is a SWOT analysis? What are the three important components of SWOT?
3. What are mission, vision, and values statements? Who is the audience for these statements?
4. What is the difference between goals and objectives? How do goals and objectives interact with mission, vision, and values statements?
5. What important criteria must be considered in setting goals?
6. What are the minimum conditions that must be met in the implementation of a strategic plan?
7. What is the important step that must be taken during and after implementation?

the organization from responding to external or internal challenges. Plans that are not jointly constructed often fail because not all staff take ownership of the goals and objectives. However, we have noted that the culture in which the organization is embedded must be considered when engaging in strategic planning. Planning for the future of any organization requires strong leadership. Many of the qualities and competencies of strong leadership are discussed in other chapters in this volume.

## SUGGESTED RESOURCES

Murray, D., and Christison M. A. (2007). *Leadership in English language education: Theoretical foundations and practical skills for changing times.* Mahwah, NJ: Lawrence Erlbaum.

This volume on leadership in English language education focuses on the roles and characteristics of leaders and the skills needed for leading. Chapter topics include the role of emotional intelligence in ELT leadership, planning strategically, developing leadership IQ, leading from behind, and diversity in leadership.

Christison, M. A., and Stoller, F. (1998). *A handbook for language program administrators.* Burlingame, CA: Alta Book Center Publishers.

Experienced professionals in the field of language program administration wrote this handbook for practicing and prospective administrators and leaders. The volume focuses on the multiple roles that language program administrators must play, including that of strategic planner. In addition, other roles are covered, such as decision-maker; negotiator; innovator; student, faculty, and program advocate; promoter; organizer; and budgeter.

## Associations and Websites

Association for Strategic Planning is a non-profit 5013C professional organization whose mission is to enable people and organizations to succeed through improved strategic thinking, planning, and action. Website: www.strategyplus.org/

The Center for Simplified Strategic Planning has an extensive library of articles and tools for strategic planning. Website: www.managementhelp. org/plan_dec/str_plan/str_plan.htm

Planning for Governmental Agencies is a resource that provides an article for public sector planning by the National Endowment for the Arts. Website: http://arts.endow.gov/resources/Lessons/indes.html

---

### *Discussion Questions*

1. Assume that you are on a strategic planning team and are participating in a SWOT analysis. Make a list of at least five strengths, weaknesses, opportunities, and threats for an English program with which you are familiar.
2. What do you think the greatest challenge is in the strategic planning process? Explain why you chose the challenge you did and why you consider it the greatest challenge.
3. Write a sample mission statement, accompanying goals, and the specific objectives needed to achieve the goal for a program with which you are familiar.
4. Work in groups of three to five. Each person in the group should use the Internet to find at least two mission statements from two different English language or teacher education programs. Discuss each mission statement. Determine whether the mission statements meet the criteria outlined in this chapter. Are they brief, written descriptions of the purpose of the organization? Do you understand the purpose when you read the mission statement? Is the mission statement brief and clearly written? Is the mission statement written for individuals external to the organization, as well as internal to it?
5. If you were in a leadership position and in charge of creating a strategic plan, which approach would you choose and why? If you had to complete the strategic plan quickly, do you think you would select the same approach?

## REFERENCES

Ansoff, H. (1979). *Strategic management.* London: Macmillan.

Bennis, W., & Manus, B. (1997). *Leaders: The strategies for taking charge* (2nd ed.). New York: HarperBusiness.

Cope, R. G. (1989). *High involvement strategic planning: When people and their ideas matter.* London: Basil Blackwell.

Covey, S. R. (1990). *Principle-centered leadership.* Provo, UT: IPCL.

Heller, R. (1999). *Learning to lead.* New York: DK Publishing.

Kanter, R. M. (1983). *The change masters.* New York: Simon & Schuster.

Klinghammer, S. (1997). The strategic planner. In M. A. Christison and F. L. Stoller (Eds.), *A Handbook for Language Program Administrators* (pp. 61–76). Burlingame, CA: Alta Book Center Publishers.

Kotter, J. P. (1995, March–April). Leading change: Why transformation efforts fail. *Harvard Business Review, 73*(2), 59–67.

Lissack, M. R. (1999). Complexity and management: It is more than jargon. In M. R. Lissack & H. P. Gunz (Eds.), *Managing complexity in organizations* (pp. 11–28). Westport, CT: Quorum Books.

Pearce II, J. A., Freeman, E. B., & Robinson Jr., R. B. (1997). The tenuous link between formal strategic planning and financial performance. *Academy of Management Review, 12*(4), 658–675.

Tichy, N. M., & and Charan, R. (1995). The CEO as coach: An interview with Allied Signal's Lawrence A. Bossidy. *Harvard Business Review, 73*(2), 69–78.

# Chapter 12

## Technologies for Leaders in ELT

Claire Bradin Siskin and Emily Reynolds

### THE IMPORTANCE OF TECHNOLOGY TO ELT TEACHERS/LEADERS

Leaders may take different approaches to leadership in technology. They may be interested in and knowledgeable about technology. They may be interested but not knowledgeable, or they may be neither interested nor knowledgeable. Regardless of their own situation or approach, it is important to recognize that a leader sets the tone for technology use among faculty.

The ELT profession is all about communication. We ESOL educators are expert communicators, and we can parlay the ability to communicate that we cherish so much as teachers into a valuable asset in leadership. While the computer is seen by some as a giant calculator or database, it may be useful for us to think of it as a tool to enhance communication. We can enhance our professional skills by mastering it and by learning to use it successfully. The National Educational Standards (NETS) (2007) state: "An underlying assumption of these standards is that administrators should be competent users of information and technology tools common to information-age professionals," and surely the same level of proficiency should be expected of all ELT leaders.

### BACKGROUND LITERATURE

We are unaware of literature that refers specifically to knowledge or use of technology by ELT leaders. However, the National Educational Standards (NETS) project of the International Society for Technology in Education (ISTE) has developed standards for administrators that are highly relevant to our discussion. Helpful guidelines for the competencies required by ESOL educators are provided by Chapelle & Hegelheimer (2004), while Browne and Gerrity (2004) outline the procedures for establishing and operating a CALL facility. Burston (2005) is an essential reference for anyone who wishes to learn about the digital language laboratories that are currently available. Case studies for the implementation of technology are provided by Hanson-Smith (2000).

## COMPUTER LITERACY SKILLS

ELT leaders often have basic computer literacy skills: email, Internet navigation, word processing, presentation software (such as PowerPoint), and spreadsheet software (such as Excel). With knowledge of some of these applications, leaders are poised to acquire further computer skills more efficiently. In this section, we provide recommendations for computer literacy skills and software options that we consider essential to ELT educators. These skills are based on the principles and recommendations of leading CALL experts.

Building computer skills may be an urgent or long-term need for you and your staff in achieving your students' learning goals and facilitating communication among faculty, staff, and students. The desire to take advantage of helpful ELT electronic resources might take the form of integrating stand-alone CALL software into your curriculum and getting students to submit their writing in word-processed form. Or it might consist of moving toward partial or complete use of online instruction to deliver content. There are countless possible variations. The table that follows represents those computer literacy skills that TESOL leaders should consider learning to manage communication and enhance learning within their institutions.

## ACQUIRING COMPUTER SKILLS

How many of these skills do you have already? Many leaders in ELT will already have mastered some items on this list. The software skills—software evaluation, selection, and integration—are often best accomplished by committee, so these can be worked on with others. Members of the committee can learn a lot by working together. Most of the other skills can be tackled alone or with the support of a tech-savvy colleague.

If you are new to technology, however, where do you begin with this long list? Start at the top of the list, and work your way down to the more sophisticated topics. Get some basic help from colleagues, family, and friends. To acquire more of these frequently required skills, make use of local resources to get what you need. Are there free or low-cost courses through schools, community colleges, or continuing education courses at universities? Do you belong to a school district or university that provides tech support and could offer workshops for your instructors? Are you or any of your teachers tech-savvy enough to offer short, one-off workshops on file management or other topics? If not, make your next hire a tech-savvy person. There are also productive online skills courses from TESOL and other providers to get you and your teachers immersed quickly.

### Instant Messaging, Blogs, Wikis, and Webcasts

There are free, real-time options for communication between students and teachers and among groups of students or faculty. A favorite in business and

## Essential Technical Skills for ELT Leaders

| | |
|---|---|
| Email | Send, receive, and open attachments to email for fast communication with faculty, staff, clients, partners, etc. |
| Word Processing | Use word processing software such as Microsoft Word. |
| Internet Navigation | Use a web search engine such as Google™ to surf the web for information, news, media clips and other content. Set browser preferences, manage cookies, download Java. |
| Internet Search Skills | Make skilled choices in using search terms. See Advanced Search Tips at Google™ for guidelines. |
| PowerPoint | Microsoft presentation software. |
| Excel | Microsoft spreadsheet software. |
| File Management | Back up files (make copies) Compress files (StuffIt® for Macs; WinZip™ for PCs) Find files on local computer and network (search function) Create/delete a folder (directory) Copy and paste (keep material in memory for later use) Burn a CD or DVD (copy digital media) |
| Set up a Computer and Projector | Attach computer to a projector so that a roomful of people can see your projected screen. |
| Download and Install an Application | Download an application and follow installation instructions for programs such as Audacity, Quia, or Skype™ from the Internet. |
| Scan and Edit an Image | Use a scanner to copy, save, and print images. Use an image editor such as Photoshop to crop, brighten, or save to different formats such as .gif, .jpeg and .bmp. |
| Download and Read .pdf Files | Use Adobe Acrobat to read (save, edit, print) .pdf files. These files can be written so that the material cannot be edited or printed. |
| Evaluate Websites and Software | Evaluate whether a website or piece of software will add value for your teachers in working with students. |
| Select Software to Meet Goals | Select software for purchase that meets pedagogical goals. This includes the post-purchase process of installing the software and training teachers to use it. |
| Integrate Software into Instruction | Integrate software into the pedagogy of your institution. If technology is carefully integrated, it serves a strong purpose and enhances face-to-face instruction. |
| Course Management | Manage the use of a course management system (CMS) such as Blackboard, WebCT, Desire2Learn, or Moodle. |
| Content Management | Manage the content that is included in online and hybrid or tech-enhanced courses. Provide content guidelines. |
| Communicate with Tech Support Staff | Learn the lingo and facilitate the process of you and your faculty learning from and working with tech support. |
| Trouble-Shoot Tech Difficulties | More likely the responsibility of tech support, but leaders soon discover common difficulties and can advise others. |

among the younger crowd is Instant Messaging (IMing). IMing is very similar to texting on your cell phone and is accomplished at your computer using an application such as Yahoo!® Messenger, MSN Messenger, or Skype™. The first two are best for sending text messages, and although they also have voice and video capability, Skype™ is the clear favorite today for speaking in real time. The sound quality is remarkably clear.

Audacity is a favorite tool to record your voice. Be sure to download the mp3 encoder so that you can compress your sound files into mp3s, which are about ten times smaller than the standard .wav file. Audacity is a top-notch recording application, not a real-time application. Use it to record your voice or have students record themselves and send back and forth as an attachment to an email, for example.

Webcasts and podcasts use the Internet to broadcast live or delayed audio and/ or video, similar to TV or radio. A school might offer online courses in which the instructor webcasts a pre-recorded or live lecture. Webcasts are also used extensively in business for purposes as diverse as broadcasting product information, training, or holding a press conference. A podcast is downloaded automatically.

## Blogs and Wikis

A blog (originally weblog) is a website where journal-style entries are made and displayed in a reverse chronological order. Blogs usually offer comments and discussion on one topic; however, some blogs are more personal. Blogs have become popular for mainstream media as well as the original unconventional group of bloggers.

Wikis are virtual collaborative content creation websites. Visitors to a wiki can edit and make changes to the content provided and comment on or explain their changes. Wikipedia is a well-known example of a wiki. This online encyclopedia is subject to intense peer review, and its reliability has been questioned because of the collaborative nature of a wiki.

## Course Management Systems

In addition to stand-alone CALL software such as CD-ROM programs, ELT leaders need to be aware of course management software options and how they might best serve their student populations. A Course Management System (CMS) is a larger software system housed on a server, which delivers the virtual content. An instructional designer or teacher makes web pages and sets up a virtual classroom environment. The content is then available and accessible at any time to students and teachers alike from the password-protected site. Popular CMSs include Blackboard, WebCT, Moodle, and Desire2Learn.

In addition to presenting content on web pages, a CMS includes a variety of communication and evaluation features. There is usually email and an address book within a CMS. There is also a discussion board where students and teacher exchange ideas and respond to assignments and discussion topics. The designer can also include evaluation tools such as quizzes and exams (true/false, fill-in, multiple choice, short answer, essay), the results of which are neatly assembled in a grades area. Also typical are a real-time text chat room, a links section, a glossary, and extensive tracking of progress for each student.

## ADDITIONAL TECHNOLOGIES FOR ELT EDUCATORS

### Conference Ware

Expensive conference ware, programs such as Elluminate® or WebEx®, are used for presentations, demos, training, and support. They make use of Voice over Internet Protocol (VoIP) or conference calls for voice. With VoIP, participants can talk in real time with their teachers.

### Voice Email and Discussion Boards

Voice email is useful when the teacher does not see students every day or when class is conducted exclusively online. Horizon Wimba can be used alone or integrated into a CMS so that voice emails, voice discussion boards, and voice teacher announcements are included inside a virtual classroom environment such as Blackboard or WebCT. There are also freeware programs for voice email.

### Open-Source Software

It is helpful to gain information and background about open-source software such as Nvu (pronounced N-View), Moodle, and Audacity. Nvu is software that allows one to create web pages without typing html tags. Moodle is an open-source CMS where teachers can create their own virtual classrooms. Audacity is recording software. All are free and accept specific development suggestions from users or allow users to copy the software and modify it for their own purposes.

## PLANNING FOR TECH DECISIONS

One of the areas that leaders in ELT will face is making decisions about technology. As such, we will address technology planning from the perspective of an ESOL administrator who must develop a strategy to provide for the implementation of technology and provide leadership in this area. We will use the acronym CALL (computer-assisted language learning), which is also referred to as ICT (information and communications technology). For CALL to succeed, teachers and learners must have the appropriate hardware, software, and infrastructure. Everything has to work properly, and institutional policies must allow for success. Using computers for language learning involves special needs, and not all administrators and IT managers have an adequate understanding of what the specific requirements are. We second language instructors may have a very clear idea of what our pedagogical objectives are, and if we have training in the use of CALL, we may be aware of how computers can help to meet our objectives. But we still may be unaware of exactly what hardware, software, and technical support is required, and we may be unable to articulate these needs. In those cases where computers are purchased for us, outsiders (those who are not specialists in language pedagogy) may make these decisions for us. The likely result is that the hardware and software provided will not be a good fit for the needs of language learning. In those cases where the configuration is not a good fit, we will not be able to use it to best advantage, and we may not use it at all. If we don't use the technology or if we use it in less than optimal ways, as a profession, we may look bad to outsiders. ELT leaders need to ensure that they are consulted and that their voices are heard with respect to achieving conditions under which CALL can flourish.

## Options in CALL

Language teachers are now faced with an ever-growing list of options when it comes to CALL. CALL succeeds best when teachers have a voice in the decision-making process, but they will be able to make appropriate choices only when they know what the options are. We will summarize some of the options that are currently available.

### Internet and CMC

The Internet has been a major force both in popularizing the general use of computers and in emphasizing their utility in language learning. It gives us and our students access to rich resources in the form of authentic materials, which may include text, pictures, audio, and video. The Internet also offers instructional sites and online courses. Computer-mediated communication (CMC) is facilitated through email, discussion boards, video teleconferences, chat rooms, blogs, and wikis.

### Project-Based Learning

Through constructivist projects, students use the target language to create their own meaning and unique messages. Computers provide powerful tools to enhance these projects through word processing and presentation software. The students' messages may be in the form of multimedia portfolios, including digital audio and video recordings, or they may be published as websites. In any case, the experience of constructing the language while communicating with other language learners may be as important as the final product.

### Tutorial CALL

Although tutorial CALL is sometimes maligned as drill and kill, it is more kindly referred to as language practice software. It has been found useful in many situations and is still alive and well in the form of standalone courseware, instructional websites, and online courses. Programs such as Hot Potatoes have provided user friendly ways for teachers to create tutorial materials and make them available via the Internet.

### Concordances

Concordancing software is a tool for lexical analysis and the study of word usage. Language learners discover patterns of use in the target language as they search corpora for examples of authentic use rather than depending on prescriptive rules of grammar. Students can use concordances to explore collocations and their meaning in context, and instructors can use them to find real-life examples and to create exercises based on authentic language.

### Electronic References

Electronic references, which may be CD-ROM- or DVD-ROM-based or Web-based, are useful tools to facilitate the study of vocabulary and text. These go far beyond the capability of printed text since they may include hypertext links to related text, audio files to serve as pronunciation guides, graphics for clarification, and animated or video clips for further illustration.

### Text Reconstruction

Text reconstruction exercises may be web-based, or they may be created by the teacher with special software. This genre presents students with an opportunity to use prediction skills, recall vocabulary, and apply metalinguistic knowledge of structure as they type in text and receive confirmation (or lack thereof) that it is correct.

### Simulations

Computer-based simulations and games provide opportunities for students to discuss, work through, and solve problems that change constantly just as situations do in real life. These provide endless possibilities for language immersion, recycling of language, and practice of rhetorical strategies.

All of these options involve the use of computers in ways that assist language learning. However, the sheer number of choices can be overwhelming for newcomers in the field.

## ASSESSING THE OPTIONS

As language professionals and leaders, we need to ask hard questions as we decide which options will work best in our particular situation, and we believe that it is essential for the classroom teachers to be involved in the process. Fortunately, experience in language teaching and knowledge of the needs of our own students count far more than experience with computers. Here are some questions that should be asked before adopting any option in CALL:

- What access to computers do we and our students have?
- Do we have the necessary software, browsers, and plug-ins, or can we get them? Will it be possible to have them installed?
- Are the computers powerful enough to handle the software or websites that we would like to use?
- Is our Internet connection fast enough and reliable enough to access the sites that we would like to use?
- Is the computer lab layout conducive to the desired activity?
- Is there a projector in the room? (Can we get a projector? If not, can we do without one?)
- Will we need speakers? (Can we get them? If not, can we do without them?)
- Do we and our students have access to the necessary peripherals and accessories to carry out the activity? The tools might include headsets, microphones, printers, scanners, webcams, and CD burners
- How will files be managed and stored? Some possibilities for distributing files are email, CMSs, servers, thumb (USB) drives, CD burners, and DVD burners.
- Will the policies at our institution permit us to implement this option? Some institutions do not permit the use of the very types of applications that are most facilitative of communicative language practices, such as chat programs, audio, and computer games. If such policies are unnecessarily restrictive, can they be changed?
- Will we have time to learn how to use the software or set up the websites or develop the materials—depending on what is required for the activity in question? If not, who can help us?
- Is there adequate staff to make everything work? Such employees may fill roles such as tech support person, computer lab coordinator, server administrator, instructional technology specialist, multimedia designer, webmaster, or lab assistant.

## RECOMMENDATIONS

With a new awareness of the many tech options and capabilities as outlined above, we now turn to a discussion of recommendations based on wide-ranging issues that our collective experience has shown to be of particular relevance to ELT educators.

### Communicate Effectively

With newer methods of transmitting information such as fax, email, the Internet, and cell phones, we can now communicate in unprecedented ways. It is clear that we can get masses of information very quickly. We readily understand that technology can bring us closer together and that we can use it to learn about other cultures. However, it might be less obvious that electronic communication itself involves a special culture that we must develop special competencies to deal with. Warschauer (2002) enumerates various types of literacy: computer literacy, information literacy, multimedia literacy, and computer-mediated literacy, which he defines as "knowledge of the pragmatics of individual and group online interaction" (p. 454). This last type of literacy involves skills that may be the most difficult to master since they involve social interaction and may appear to be the least clear-cut. We focus here on issues of email since it is currently the most commonly used tool.

## Spotlight on Email

What is different about email in terms of communicating effectively? Since email can be transmitted and received almost instantly, it often takes on the informality of casual conversation. But since it consists of written text, it provides a written record of an interaction. Because email tends to use a less formal style of writing, people may tend to forget they are not engaging in a face-to-face conversation. Since email is often used informally, a sense of intimacy can be created. Paradoxically, it can become public very easily.

### Send Email Messages Only to Those Concerned with the Content

The casual nature of email implies that many of us are inundated with messages. Leaders should keep in mind that they may be taken more seriously if recipients know that all messages are earmarked for them. Likewise, all messages should contain relevant subject lines. This will provide context cues for readers, and it will be easier for both senders and recipients to find them later.

### Keep Your Messages Brief

Try to keep the lines short since not all email software handles text wrapping in the same way. Most email is read directly on-screen rather then printed out, so the text should be divided into shorter paragraphs than usual since scrollbars may mean that it is more difficult to track text visually. If it is necessary to transmit longer documents, consider sending these as attachments to the email. However, attachments should be used cautiously since it is possible that the recipient will not be able to open them; very large attachments should not be sent without checking with the recipient in advance.

### An Awareness of the Common Conventions of Email Is Essential

Do not write in capital letters in email, or use them sparingly. Capital letters are like shouting and are thus considered impolite. They are considered to be the mark of a novice user. If you want to emphasize something, surround it with asterisks instead. For example,

> **Instead of: "If you are late, we WON'T wait for you."**
>
> **Use: "If you are late, we \*\*\*won't\*\*\* wait for you."**

Be aware that not everyone's email software can display styles such as bold face, colors, italics, and diacritical markings; only plain text may be shown.

### Be Polite, and Watch Your Language

The reader cannot see you in person, does not necessarily share your context, and cannot detect cues from your facial expression or body language. Text may be interpreted literally, and jokes may be misunderstood. Be especially careful with sarcasm and irony. If you think there is any doubt that someone might take you seriously, state that you are joking or use a smiley character like this: :-)

### Be Discreet

One of the most important things to remember about email is that anything you write has the potential of becoming public. The content of an email message can easily be forwarded—with or without your knowledge or permission—to anyone. It may even be forwarded to hundreds (or thousands) of people by means of an electronic listserv. The content of an email message may also be posted to a website or blog—again with or without your awareness or authorization. Do not write anything in email that you would not say in public.

### Respect the Privacy of Others

If someone sends you a message, the professional rule of thumb is that it should not be forwarded to someone else without the author's permission. There are some exceptions, of course. Within an organization or group of people who know each other well, by mutual agreement, messages may be forwarded to another person if the information does not contain personal references and if it is quite clear that the forwardee needs the information. Anytime someone asks you not to forward a message, you should respect the request.

The principal advantage of email is that it is very fast. But be aware that the disadvantage of email is that is very fast! If you are not completely sure if you should send an email message, do not send it. Consider it for a while before sending it.

## ADDITIONAL RECOMMENDATIONS

Other essential actions ELT leaders can take to improve their tech understanding and capability are numerous. Taking some time on a daily basis for these strategies will go a long way toward getting ELT leaders up-to-speed on aspects of technology that they need for today's tech-enhanced language learning situations.

• **Improve your tech talk.** An enormous amount of specialized terminology is commonly used by the tech community. Work gradually on this vocabulary to improve your tech talk. Try to acquire enough acronyms and technical jargon so that your conversations are accurate and productive when talking to tech support, staff, or teachers. Consult online resources such as dictionaries and Wikipedia. Find definitions to tech terms easily by googling using the search terms "tech item + definition."

• **Educate yourself.** Educate yourself on your hardware/software and technological options so that you know their capabilities, advantages, and pitfalls. Don't believe all the extravagant claims made by software sales representatives and website developers!

• **Technology in the service of pedagogy, not vice versa.** Don't try to use all of the options or change anyone's way of teaching completely. CALL does not have to take over the learning process; instead, the various options may simply be added to the repertoire of instructional tools already available to us.

• **Don't join every technology stampede.** Add new options gradually, and don't try to do everything at once. New tools are constantly becoming available, but some of the older ones may be just as effective pedagogically and may actually work better in your situation. If you can't get the hardware and software that you want, make effective use of what you have.

• **Involve all stakeholders.** Participate in technology planning committee meetings at your school or campus so that your department will have a voice in how technology is implemented. If technical support staff are scarce or non-existent, consider the possibility of drawing on the students' technical expertise to solve technical problems. With the proper encouragement, students may become eager allies.

• **Provide the necessary resources.** If at all possible, allow release time for a faculty person to serve as CALL Coordinator. Provide professional development opportunities for faculty, not only in terms of learning how to use the technology but in how to integrate technology effectively into language teaching and learning. Recognize that the need for expenditures for new equipment, repairs, and upgrades will be ongoing, and budget accordingly.

- **Learn from the experiences of others.** Talk to your colleagues from other institutions and learn from their experiences. As technology changes, we are all learning how to use new tools. No one has all the answers. You can gain a good deal of hands-on experience through professional conferences such as TESOL and IATEFL, workshops, and face-to-face and online courses. In addition, a wealth of information is available on the Internet and various electronic mailing lists. The road to technological literacy is a challenging one, but you are not alone in this quest.

As we have emphasized and as you have likely experienced for yourself, technology can help us to become better communicators and leaders. Moreover, numerous technological options are available to assist our students in learning English. The challenge is professional development for teachers in these areas of technology so that they too become effective online communicators and can use technology to enhance language learning.

We close with one last thought: It is more important to use what technology we have intelligently than to have the latest ineffective gadget. The choices about how and when to use technology are up to us, and we will make good decisions when we are well informed.

---

**SUGGESTED RESOURCES**

A companion web page with a list of online and printed resources is available at www.edvista.com/leaders.html. This page will be updated on a regular basis.

de Szendeffy, J. (2005). *A Practical Guide to Using Computers in Language Teaching.* Ann Arbor: University of Michigan Press.
This book is a resource for teachers faced with integrating computers into their classrooms.

---

### Discussion Questions

1. In what ways can/should leaders serve as role models as users of technology?
2. How can a leader who doesn't know much about technology manage to make decisions about technology? How can such a leader manage to cope?
3. What can leaders in professional organizations do to ensure that equipment (such as projection) is provided for presenters at conferences?
4. In terms of effective communication, how can leaders cope with inevitable technological change successfully?

## REFERENCES

Browne, C. & S., Gerrity (2004). Setting up and maintaining a CALL laboratory. In S. Fotos & C. Browne (Eds.), *New perspectives in CALL for second language classrooms* (pp. 171–197). Mahwah, NJ: Lawrence Erlbaum.

Burston, J. (Ed.) (2005). *Digital language lab solutions: An evaluation of software-based virtual labs.* Madison, WI: International Association of Language Learning Technologies.

Chapelle, C., & Hegelheimer, V. (2004). The English language teacher in the 21st century. In S. Fotos & C. Browne (Eds.), *New perspectives in CALL for second language classrooms* (pp. 299–316). Mahwah, NJ: Lawrence Erlbaum.

Educational Technology Standards and Performance Indicators for Administrators. Retrieved 29 August 2007, from www.iste.org/inhouse/nets/cnets/administrators/index.html

Hanson-Smith, E. (Ed.). (2000) *Technology-enhanced learning environments.* TESOL practice series. Bloomington, IL: TESOL.

International Society for Technology in Education (ISTE). http://www.iste.org

Warschauer, M. (2002). A developmental perspective on technology in language education. *TESOL Quarterly, 36*(3), 453–475.

# Chapter 13

## Development, a.k.a. Fundraising: A Neglected Element of Professional Development

Brock Brady

While the past decade has emphasized professional development in English language education, relatively little attention has been devoted to fundraising. This should not surprise. Most colleges and universities call their fundraising operations development offices, and regardless of the theoretical justifications involved (Kelly, 1998), they prefer the term *development* because fundraising's connotations are not entirely positive. This is understandable. Fundraising requires asking others to give (Klein, 2004). Yet we know that people are often unable or unwilling to give, and if a giving opportunity is declined, a loss of face results.

Lack of experience with organized giving beyond weekly offerings at our place of worship or annual workplace pledge drives may compound such unease. We may simply have no models of people like us engaging in organized giving (Maxwell, 2003).

Nevertheless, fundraising (through grants and research support) is vital to our personal development as teachers and researchers. Fundraising is one more tool to grow our professional community and institutions, providing services that might not be available otherwise. Finally, fundraising counts because giving goes beyond the gift: Fundraising creates and strengthens relationships that might not exist otherwise, leading to a professional community that is both richer and more dynamic (Kelly, 1998).

Therefore we need to educate ourselves, as potential askers and givers of contributions. In our profession, we cannot neglect to add community-building tools to our repertoire, and to use fundraising wisely and well, we must do it with forethought.

## BACKGROUND LITERATURE

Fundraising has a long history. Mullen (2002, in Tempel, 2003, p. 5), notes the use of subscriptions in fundraising for public projects by Greeks as far back as the 4th century BCE. Philanthropy's longevity is not surprising when viewed in its most simple terms. Philanthropy is "doing good...without requiring something in return" (Hildebrant, 2005, p. 1).

Philanthropy in the United States dates to colonial times and is a potent force today. Tempel (2003) claims that philanthropy plays a larger role in U.S. civil society than in any other country. Certainly we are a nation of contributors. One survey found that three-quarters of all Americans give to philanthropic causes, and they give two percent of their income (Hodgkinson, Weitzman, Abrahams, Centchfield, & Stevenson, 1996, in Kelly, 1998, p. 328). Indeed in 1996, $150.7 billion was given to charity—an increase of 7.3 percent from 1995 (AAFRC Trust for Philanthropy, 1996, in Kelly, 1998, p. 39).

Many see philanthropic nonprofit organizations as essential to a healthy civil society. Tempel (2003) ascribes seven roles to nonprofit entities and philanthropy: (1) reducing human suffering, (2) enhancing human potential, (3) promoting private equity and justice, (4) building community, (5) providing human fulfillment, (6) supporting experimentation and change, and (7) fostering pluralism (pp. 4–5).

Philanthropy occurs through fundraising. Kelly (1998) defines fundraising as "the process and activities related to helping charitable organizations obtain private gifts" (p. 6). In fact, Payton, Rosso, and Tempel (1991, p. 5) propose the following syllogism:

1. Philanthropy is necessary in a democratic society.
2. Fundraising is necessary to philanthropy.
3. Fundraising is necessary to a democratic society.

Despite philanthropy's long history and the key role that nonprofit organizations play, the body of fundraising literature is not extensive (Crowder & Hodgkinson, 1991). In part, this stems from fundraising's recent recognition as a profession. Kelly (1998) claims that fundraising "as an internal organizational function is less than 50 years old," (p. 18), with most theoretical treatments of fundraising dating only from the 1990s.

Accordingly, much available literature lacks general applicability and rigor, being predominantly anecdotal in style. Carbone notes in Kelly, 1998, "fundraising has an enormous body of lore and experience, but limited theoretical knowledge." (p. 4).

## WHAT IS FUNDRAISING?

Here we discuss fundraising in terms of educational institutions or associations for the advancement of education or educators. It will be defined as activities that procure funding (or possibly in-kind contributions) (a) to permit maintenance, expansion, or introduction of projects; (b) to subsidize participant services; or (c) to protect the organization from contingencies. Fundraising is typically used to expand operations that cannot be supported by the existing revenue sources. We consider grants, regardless of their source, as fundraising, for grants provide funds that permit English language educational organizations to engage in activities they could not engage in otherwise.

## WHY RAISE FUNDS?

For individual teachers, grants can finance research, work-related travel, and professional development opportunities. For professional associations, contributions can support such grants to members through activities such as conference raffles, and can subsidize membership costs for students or part-time teachers. Contributions can also support outreach efforts, funding projects in the local community, or sustaining sister relationships with affiliates from other countries. Finally, contributions can create reserve funds to shield organizations from unexpected drops in revenue.

As academic programs and nonprofit institutions, many adult education ESL programs simply would not exist without grants from various entities. Colleges and university programs depend on fundraising for capital improvements and endowments. For public schools, fundraising events and contributions generated based on grocery store purchases may support athletic programs, P.T.A events, physical improvements, and finance travel or field trips for students.

## JUSTIFYING FUNDRAISING

Because most English language educators perceive their profession as a "giving profession," where salary is often not a primary motive, they may legitimately ask, "Don't I already do enough?" It is reasonable to respond.

First, fundraising permits activities and provide services that might otherwise be unavailable. For example, a middle school might raise funds to replace worn athletic equipment or fund the part-time employment of a chorus leader if no district funds are available. Similarly, if a professional association mounts a symposium in a country where the disposable income is limited, international association members might begin a campaign to subsidize the cost of teachers' attendance. Thus, good fundraising:

a.  has specific, defined goals that are unique and interesting to those contributors
b.  benefits a segment of the community in need
c.  is used when existing resources are not sufficient to support important activities.

(Panas, 2006)

The benefit of the gift is not limited to its actual use. The act of giving benefits the donor in terms of self-esteem, reputation, and the enjoyment that comes from participating in an effort that one finds worthy. For those established in their careers, contributing can be a way to give back to the community and extend a helping hand to new members. Many donors make contributions simply to be involved in something distinctive or original (Rosso, 2003b). Such giving represents the essence of Kelly's (1998) "symmetrical approach" to fundraising where fund raisers and donors work together as equals, funding a vision of a more vibrant community.

As such, the act of giving creates a relationship between the donor and the recipient, and may bring new partners into the community or engage existing partners in new, more fulfilling roles. Such relationships deepen and strengthen the existing community, create multiple bonds that add dimensions to established enterprises, provide potential for new projects, and create contexts for building a vision of the community—one shared by both its members and partners.

Such community-building maximizes professional development. Professional development rarely occurs in a vacuum—it occurs when we watch others doing what we are doing; it occurs when we watch others in roles related to our role doing what <u>they</u> do (and seeing how and what they do relates to our activities); it occurs when we as a professional community show how we inform the greater society—and how it informs us. Educational institutions and associations can at times become parochial in vision. Active fundraising operations, especially with a symmetrical orientation, can provide new ways of viewing what we do and its importance to society.

## PRINCIPLES OF SUCCESSFUL FUNDRAISING

### Have a Plan

When launching a fundraising effort, Hildebrant provides the following advice: "begin by creating a plan or strategy...forecast how much money needs to be raised, [determine] who [you] can anticipate to give...and how [you] will ask people to give" (p. 2). Kelly's (1998) more articulated model for fundraising planning captures these basic principles and goes by the acronym ROPES: Research, Objectives, Programming, Evaluation, and Stewardship (where *stewardship* is defined as accepting long-term responsibility for both gifts and donors, so as to maintain and increase goodwill to achieve the organization's long-term aspirations).

Fundraising should be planned as an element of overall financial planning, and both must be contextualized within overall programmatic planning (Seiler, 2003). For example, fundraising planning can be structured to respond to the goals of an organization's strategic plan. Fundraising must not be reactive, but proactive (Rosso, 2003b). Fundraising that is launched to respond to an immediate need will not be an integral element of the organizational operations and will do little to build community. A well-designed fundraising plan will:

- determine the amount of funding needed for programmatic activity
- establish the type of fundraising activities to be undertaken
- identify who will engage in fundraising
- set a time line for the fundraising process
- identify potential donors
- provide means for evaluating the fundraising effort
- develop a system for ensuring that gifts and donors will be treated appropriately.

## Identify your Constituency

An organization's constituency can be defined as "those who care" (Rosso, 2003a). They are those who will be affected by or interested in the organization's activities. Clearly those who are closest to the organization, those who have the strongest belief in its mission, those who have given before will be most likely to give again (Kelly, p. 369).

Effective constituent identification is key to good fundraising. As Kelly (1998) states, we need to "separate prospects from suspects" (p. 350)— that is, distinguish those who could _possibly_ give from those who are more _likely_ to give. Since obtaining a gift usually results from a personal relationship with a donor, which takes time, we want to invest our efforts where they are most likely to succeed.

One way to separate suspects and prospects is to analyze prospects in terms of the _LAI_ principle (i.e., _Linkage_, _Ability_, and _Interest_). _Linkage_ is a question of the human connection between the organization and the individual. _Ability_ considers how financially capable an individual will be to give the type of gift desired, and finally, _Interest_ concerns an individual's willingness to be involved in the organization (Maxwell, 2003, p. 164).

## Develop and Make Your Case

An organization's "case" generally answers the question, "Why do we exist?" (Rosso, 2003a). Case development determines the activities and projects that our organization engages in, with a view to attracting donor support. An organization's mission statement can guide the case development process, defining the kinds of cases that conform to its mission. A good case development matches organizational needs with donor needs (Kelly, 1998). People give money to organizations that they know and care about (Seiler, 2003, p.28).

In general terms, we want to develop cases that emphasize:

- opportunities to participate
- personal benefit to donors
- choice (multiple cases allow multiple ways to participate)

- donor status and recognition
- the worthiness of those who receive the benefits.

## Putting It All Together

Fundraising plans can be evaluated using Rosso's "Six Rights." Rosso claims that fundraising will be successful when the *right* person asks the *right* prospect for the *right* amount of money for the *right* cause in the *right* way at the *right* time (Maxwell, 2003, p. 165). However, determining "right" in each case requires both data and experience. For this reason, Seiler (2003) views fundraising as a cyclical process: with every cycle, our available data becomes richer and more useful.

## COMMON TYPES OF FUNDRAISING

There are a variety of types of fundraising, and they have different appeals for different donors. Some activities may be more appropriate to some types of organizations than others. Those involved in fundraising must have a basic knowledge of these fundraising types, their characteristics, and the factors that ensure their effectiveness.

### Grants

Individuals can obtain grants for research, professional development, or career-related travel. Grants for individuals support new research and provide organizational leadership by supporting professional development. Organizations seek grants to fund major research projects, for large-scale projects to aid others, to enhance their reputation, and to provide complementary support for ongoing projects (for example, "buying out" part of an employee's salary to support grant work).

#### Obtaining Grants

Many texts and programs provide grant-writing instruction (e.g., Foundation Center, 2006). An in-depth analysis of this process is outside the scope of this work; however, some recommendations can be provided.

*1. Be sure the grant is a good fit for your personal needs or the organization's mission.* Grants not directly related to the organization's goals will prove a distraction and may actually draw resources away from primary activities.

*2. Know the granting organization well.* What is the organization's mission? What kinds of projects have been funded in the past? Is the granting agency putting out a call only because of a legal requirement and not actually seeking a new grant recipient?

*3. Read the fine print (and respond to it).* Don't do as I once did and submit a 12-month proposal for an 18-month grant!

*4. Search out past grant recipients.* What were their experiences like? What tips do they have?

*5. Talk to the administrator managing proposal submissions.* Those managing the submission process cannot evaluate your proposal or give advice, but in the process of answering procedural questions they may provide additional context for structuring your application.

*6. If an assessment procedure is required, be realistic in your expectations.* If you receive the grant, you'll need to do the assessment. Make it feasible.

### Annual Funds

Traditionally, annual funds are fundraising campaigns conducted at certain times of the year (Cohen, 2006). Annual funds (or "annual giving") are not directly connected to special events or projects but focus more on regular organizational activities that donors have an interest in supporting. Usually donors are given the opportunity to earmark their gift for an activity or project of particular interest.

Rosso (2003b) sees the annual fund as "the building block for all fundraising." Cohen suggests that interest in annual funds has increased greatly because organizations see them as "hubs" for integrating various fundraising efforts (2006). Benefits of annual funds include

- needing a relatively small body of committed volunteers to launch the effort
- yielding data on prospects (those who might give) and donors (those who do give) for future planning and new projects
- can create "habitual involvement" (those who give once tend to give again)
- create opportunities to reach out to the community and inform members about the good work and interesting initiatives.

### Planned Giving

The TESOL website defines planned gifts as:

"a charitable donation made in conjunction with the donor's financial, tax, and estate planning. Gifts may be immediate or deferred, and are often made by a legacy in a will, a donation from life insurance, or a contribution from a donor's estate" (2006, p. 1).

Planned gifts are a focus of fundraising today due to the accumulation of personal assets since World War II, the aging of the Baby Boom generation, and changes in capital gains and estate tax regulations in the past 20 years (Kelly, 1998). Planned giving was previously referred to as deferred giving, with the bulk of planned gifts received in the future, usually as part of the legacy of the donor (e.g., a bequest in a will). Thus, planned giving becomes a potent tool for long-range financial planning. It embodies the principle that fundraising is less about the gift and more about the relationship: Donors make planned gifts to institutions that become part of their lives (Regenovich, 2003). Consequently, planned giving demands accountability, for donors must trust the organization to use their gift as intended after they are gone.

One advantage to planned giving is that those without extensive current assets (which will include many English teachers!), can make significant deferred gifts now. A classic example is establishing an insurance policy with the recipient organization as beneficiary. Small- to medium-range policies can be had for very little. As an illustration, a quick web search suggests that someone in their 30s could have a 20-year $100,000 policy for as little as $10 a month.Intuitively perhaps, one may sense something exploitive about planned giving (since the organization is asking to be included in the will). However, planned giving is successful because it typically benefits the donor as much as the recipient organization. Donors can save on capital gains, on estate, and on income taxes through properly structured gift packages. As Quinn (1994) states (in Kelly, 1998, p. 517), "if the tax code didn't exist, America's charities would have to invent it."

## Major Gifts

Kelly (1998) notes that "fundraising is incomplete without a major gifts program" (p. 475). Such gifts are important elements of fundraising because wealth is not distributed proportionally in our society, and some individuals, corporations, and foundations are capable of making large gifts. Hodge notes, "the truly wealthy have the advantage of satisfying all their comfort needs in life...they can explore ways their resources can have a meaningful impact on the world" (2003, p. 91).

Major gifts, as those in planned giving, can come in many forms, cash, securities, in-kind gifts such as art, tangible personal property, or real estate. Major giving differs from planned giving in that it is outright and immediate, not deferred (Kelly, 1998).

One type of major gift of particular interest is that of an endowment contribution. Endowments are significant gifts (of at least $10,000, Kelly, 1998, p. 482) that are established in perpetuity. The principle of the endowment is left untouched, and only a percentage of the interest income is considered "spendable income" each year. In this way, an institution's reserves grow, giving it resources for when unexpected needs arise.

### Sponsorships and Branding

Sponsorship, especially by publishers, is an important source of funds raised by many language teaching organizations, which is becoming increasingly more common in public schools. Burlingame (2003) lists eight reasons why companies engage in sponsorship:

- to create greater public trust in the company
- to enhance the company's image or reputation
- to build "brand awareness"
- to create goodwill
- to increase profits for the company
- to attract investors
- to increase employee morale and attract and retain employees
- to provide a competitive advantage.

The benefits of sponsorship to the organization are funding sources for certain activities and introducing participants to useful goods or services. However, sponsorship has costs. For example, the organization must provide commercialism; participants or donors may opt out.

### Special Events

Special events run the gamut from school bake sales to high-end charity auctions (Wendroff, 2003). An obvious benefit of special events is their potential for raising an organization's visibility and creating excitement about its initiatives. They establish opportunities to involve volunteers and to acknowledge donors. They also may attract donors who don't desire a long-term involvement with the organization.

However, mounting special events requires special effort. The type of event proposed must be concordant with the organization's mission and goals. The event must be well promoted to ensure sufficient participation. Volunteer staff must be recruited and trained to appropriately represent the organization. A budget must be established, and since the point of the special event is to raise (not use) funds, overhead must be monitored.

## FUNDRAISING PRINCIPLES AND TECHNIQUES

Fundraising is not for those who need regular positive reinforcement. When you ask, people will often say no and do so for good reasons. Our anxieties about fundraising come from anxieties about money. To overcome them, your belief in the cause must be greater than your anxiety (Klein, 2004). However, one must ask. An axiom in fundraising is that, "People do not give to people. They give to people with causes." Even then, "they only give to people who *ask* on behalf of causes" (Rosso, 2003b, p. 73).

Just as introducing students to new classroom routines requires *learner training*, fundraising involves giver training. Often prospects must be solicited many times (possibly over years) before they give, so that even a declined gift request may result in a successful request <u>next</u> time. Also, once someone gives a first time, they are typically more inclined to give again (and possibly give even more), and having given to one good cause, they may be more ready to contribute to other causes. Thus, over time, giving becomes an established routine and an element of the giver's identity.

Even if we are not wealthy (and few language educators are), being able to contribute to causes we care about makes us feel that we have "come into our own." We see ourselves as responsible people participating in society in the ways that conform to our internal, idealized images of what successful people do.

For those with sufficient assets to itemize their tax returns, contributions to certain types of organizations are tax deductible, so that the contributions cost the donors no more than they would already be paying in taxes, plus donors have the benefit of directing these funds to a cause that they support.

An organization must apply to the government for tax exempt status, and while there are many categories of tax-exempt entities, almost all nonprofit charitable organizations are categorized as 501(c)(3) organizations (Kelly, 1998, p. 53). If you give to a 501(c)(3), you may deduct the amount of your contribution minus the value of any premium (e.g., a shirt, mug, or calendar) you received when you made your contribution (McAllister, 1998). You can generally contribute up to 50 percent of your gross income on federal tax returns to charitable giving (Network for the Good, 2006).

## How to Ask

People give for specific needs and programs. Rarely will donors feel moved to contribute for general operational support. When asking for a gift, some key points to emphasize include:

- how the donor will benefit (e.g., better services, a cleaner planet)
- how the donor can help others
- how being able to participate signifies the donor's success.
- that the amount asked is not a burden

(Panas, 2006)

In fundraising, despite reluctance we may feel about asking for money, we must stress the positive. As Klein observes, "People [tend to] avoid people who make them feel bad" (p. 12). Rosso similarly advocates "never apologize" (2003a, p. 18). If your cause is worthy, you honor prospects by asking them to participate. If they decline to participate, you still respected them sufficiently to ask. Keep in mind that while people will refuse, the refusal typically has little to do with you (Klein, 2003).

Therefore, be straight-forward: When asking for a gift one should specify the amount to give (e.g., "Alyson, I'd like you to consider giving $200 this year"). An established rule of thumb suggests that a request should never be less than $25. Small gifts should be avoided because they may actually cost the organization in terms of processing costs (Kelly, 1998).

The closer the contact you or your organization has with the prospect, the more the likelihood of receiving a gift. Accordingly, those who have given before are most likely to give again. Those very involved with the organization are good prospects because in a sense, their involvement means they are helping themselves. Other stakeholders—family, friends, close business associates—will also be more inclined to give than those with no direct contact.

The nature of solicitation also matters. Obviously, face-to-face contact, however anxiety producing, will more likely succeed than an anonymous letter. Also follow-up is very important. One common technique is to send a letter announcing your intention to make contact, then following up with a phone call seeking an appointment two weeks later (Rosso, 2003b).

Follow up is also important for acknowledgement and accountability. Any gift, regardless of size, must receive an expression of gratitude. This seems obvious, but if much effort is being put into asking, the thanking may be forgotten. Consequently, Klein (2003) has coined the phrase "thank before you bank" (p. 11).

Equally important is showing how gifts have been used (indeed, this can be thought of as another part of the gift's acknowledgment). As Klein (2003) notes, "Donors are not ATMs" (p. 11). Without evidence that their gifts are wisely used, donors may not give again.

Giving to organizations that represent one's profession may be thought of as the third leg of professional engagement. The first leg is membership. The second is participation—participation as a writer or presenter sharing your research; participation as a volunteer filling roles the organization needs to fulfill. Giving to your organization is the third leg of professional engagement: acknowledging, through giving back, that your personal success has been furthered by the organization, and providing the financial support to activities that you have benefited from. When we give, we signify that we have arrived in our profession, and by giving, we signify that our profession is worthy.

---

**SUGGESTED RESOURCES**

*The Center on Philanthropy at Indiana University.* One of the most respected fundraising institutions, this site provides many downloadable primary sources and other reference materials. Access it at: www.philanthropy.iupui.edu/index.html

*Foundation Center.* Another highly respected center for fundraising research with resources for grant writing and for fundraising directed toward individuals. Access it at: http://foundationcenter.org/

*The Grantsmanship Center.* An online resource to learn more about the grant application processes and engage in grant-writing programs. Access it at: www.tgci.com/

*Grassroots Fundraising Journal.* An accessible, user-friendly resource for fundraising, including Kim Klein's article, "The Ten Most Important Things You Can Know about Fundraising." Access it at: www.grassrootsfundraising. org/howto/links.html

---

### Discussion Questions

1. What are some reasons people hesitate to get involved in fundraising? If your organization or institution asked you to engage in a fundraising activity, what would you do to "make the cause greater than your anxiety" about asking for a gift?
2. How does the benefit of giving go beyond the use of the gift itself? How does this relate to enhancing professional development?
3. If your organization or institution asked you to draft a fundraising plan, what are some elements that you would include in your outline?
4. What are some characteristics of the five fundraising types discussed in this chapter? Which are most relevant to the kind of fundraising that you might do?
5. If you had to ask an individual for a charitable contribution, what are some basic principles you would keep in mind?

---

## REFERENCES

Burlingame, D. (2003). Corporate giving and fund raising. In E. Tempel (Ed.), *Henry Rosso's achieving excellence in fund raising* (2nd ed.) (pp. 177–187). San Francisco: Jossey-Bass.

Cohen, T. (2006). Annual giving: Heart of strategic shift. *The Philanthropy Journal.* Retrieved September 17, 2006, from http://philanthropyjournal. org/lu.cfm?lu=9309

Crowder, L., & Hodgkinson. (1991). *Compendium of resources for teaching about the nonprofit sectors, voluntarism and philanthropy* (2nd ed). Washington, DC: Independent Sector.

Foundation Center. (2006). *Proposal Writing Short Course.* Retrieved October 3, 2006, from the Foundation Center website, http://foundationcenterorg/ getstarted/tutorials/ shortcourse/index.html

Hildebrant, C. (2005). *Philanthropic fundraising.* Retrieved October 3, 2006, from the Learning to Give website, http://www.learningtogive.org/ papers/index.asp?bpid=43

Hodge, J. (2003). Gifts of significance. In E. Tempel (Ed.), *Henry Rosso's achieving excellence in fund raising* (2nd ed.) (pp. 89–102). San Francisco: Jossey-Bass.

Hodgkinson, V. A., Weitzman, M. S., Abrahams, J. A., Centchfield, E. A., Stevenson, D. R. (1996). *Nonprofit almanac 1996–1997: Dimensions of the independent sector.* San Francisco: Jossey-Bass.

Kelly, K. (1998*). Effective fundraising management.* Mahwah, NJ: Lawrence Erlbaum.

Klein, K. (2004, January/February). The ten most important things you can know about fundraising. *Grassroots Fundraising Journal,* 23 August 2007, 11–14. Retrieved from http://www.grassrootsfundraising.org/howto/v23_n1_art03.pdf

Maxwell, M. (2003). Individuals as donors. In E. Tempel (Ed.). *Henry Rosso's achieving excellence in fund raising* (2nd ed.) (pp. 161–176). San Francisco: Jossey-Bass.

McAllister, P. (1998). *Contributions and premiums.* Retrieved Oct. 3, 2006, from the Grantsmanship Center website, http://www.tgci.com/magazine/Contributions%20and%20Premiums.pdf

Network for the Good. (2006). How much to give. Retrieved October 3, 2006, from the Network for the Good website, http://www.networkforgood.org/donate/calculator/ ?source=GOOG&cmpgn=CALC#5

Panas, J. (2006). *Asking: A 59-minute guide to everything board members, volunteers, and staff must know to secure the gift.* Medfield, MA: Emerson & Church.

Payton, R., Rosso, H., & Tempel, E. (1991). Towards a philosophy of fundraising: Taking fund raising seriously: An agenda. In D. Burlingame & L. Hulse (Eds.), *Taking fundraising seriously: Advancing the profession and practice of raising money.* (pp. 3–17). San Francisco: Jossey-Bass.

Regenovich, D. (2003). Establishing a planned giving program. In E. Tempel (Ed.), *Henry Rosso's achieving excellence in fund raising* (2nd ed.) (pp. 139–158). San Francisco: Jossey-Bass.

Rosso, H. (2003a). A philosophy of fund raising. In E. Tempel (Ed.), *Henry Rosso's achieving excellence in fund raising* (2nd ed.) (pp. 3–13). San Francisco: Jossey-Bass.

———. (2003b). The annual fund. In E. Tempel (Ed.), *Henry Rosso's achieving excellence in fund raising* (2nd ed.) (pp. 71–88). San Francisco: Jossey-Bass.

Seiler, T. (2003). Plan to succeed. In E. Tempel (Ed.), *Henry Rosso's achieving excellence in fund raising* (2nd ed.) (pp. 23–29). San Francisco: Jossey-Bass.

Tempel, E. (2003a). Contemporary dynamics of fund raising. In E. Tempel (Ed.), *Henry Rosso's achieving excellence in fund raising* (2nd ed.) (pp. 3–13). San Francisco: Jossey Bass.

TESOL. (2006). *Planned giving.* Retrieved September 17, 2006, from http://www.tesol.org/s_tesol/sec_document.asp?CID=418&DID+2

Wendroff, A. (2003) Special events for the twenty-first century. In E. Tempel (Ed.), *Henry Rosso's achieving excellence in fund raising* (2nd ed.) (pp. 273–288). San Francisco: Jossey Bass.

# Chapter 14

## Taking the Lead: Recruiting for Success

Ross Currie and Bryan Gilroy

The effective management of an educational institution or unit thereof is a complex task. It requires a diverse array of management skills ranging from financial understanding to managing interpersonal relationships to strategic planning. Understanding the role and value of education is no longer the only requirement for success. Unfortunately, the TESOL profession has yet to get fully behind this movement toward requiring or demanding professional management. The clearest indication that we are still upgrading the profession is our attitude toward recruitment.

Traditionally many TESOL leaders have arrived at their positions with little formal management training, especially in the area of recruitment. Furthermore, many managers have had little practical experience of recruitment and selection beyond their own personal job quests. This lack of professionally trained recruiters is a key issue facing the profession. This is because if an institution has gaps in its instructional skill areas, there are basically two main options. The institution must either (a) train faculty, which is usually time-consuming and probably expensive, or (b) buy in the missing expertise from outside the institution. As it is cheaper and quicker, Option B is frequently the most preferred one. However, the need for leadership skills in recruitment is vital

As indicated, effective recruitment is a key factor in achieving success in the education sector. TESOL leaders, no matter how good they are, will not be able to bring about successful and sustained change and improvements to their institutions without having faculty with the relevant skills and experience and above all the wish to support changes. Beaumont (1993) noted three crucial factors for organizations in their selection decisions. Organizations, he notes, are looking for more diversity in their employees, more flexible multi-skilled employees who work well in teams and who have good interpersonal skills and attitudes toward successful teamwork. This, then, is the first recruitment challenge TESOL leaders face: recruiting faculty who may be more skilled or experienced in a particular area than the leader himself or herself. Successful leaders need to be self-confident and secure. A leader who does not exhibit these characteristics will be unwilling to recruit faculty who have expertise that they do not. Weak leaders will try very hard to keep all the power, knowledge, and experience within their personal domain, at the expense of the institution. On the other hand, good leaders will recruit faculty with the required experience and not to the lowest common denominator. Smart leaders are aware that poor performance in their department is a threat to their leadership. Leaders should not always be the ones who "do"; effective leaders should set the direction and act as facilitators to enable those with the skills and abilities to achieve what needs to be done.

Poor recruitment through failed leadership will have significant financial and human costs for both the organization and the students it serves. A key goal for recruiters is to focus on attracting applicants with the targeted profile. Appointing people who do not have the right knowledge, skills, experience, and professional attitude can be costly in terms of money, outcomes, and department morale. However, the world of TESOL is still not fully cognizant of this. The absence of any significant body of research on recruitment issues and patterns in educational and more specifically TESOL and TEFL contexts is an indication that this is a neglected area in terms of TESOL leadership. Most of the research and guiding principles in terms of recruitment for the TESOL field come from generic contexts (Middlewood, 1997). This sets the obvious end goal for TESOL leaders, but the processes and strategies to achieve this goal need to be clearly in place.

Whatever the process or strategy taken, one thing is absolutely essential: recruitment must be done in a systematic way. Dowling and Schuler (1990, p. 204) have identified questions that point to key stages that should be part of such a systematic approach: Who do we want? How can we attract them? How can we identify them? How do we know we have succeeded in getting it right?

Clearly, like all processes, there is a beginning and an end. In actuality there is even a pre-recruitment stage that cannot be ignored. A preliminary stage to recruitment could be identifying aspects of the organization that are likely to attract or not attract potential candidates. Identifying the strengths and weaknesses and the competitive advantages and disadvantages can help an organization to ensure that it creates interest in the positions but at the same time avoids overselling the job and the institution (Armstrong, 1997).

All leaders need to ask, "What recruitment skills and knowledge do I need in order to attract the best teachers and tomorrow's leaders to my team and to my organization?" This chapter will help guide TESOL leaders as they build their skills and knowledge to become more effective recruiters of quality English language teachers, and future teacher leaders. It will also examine how leaders can collaborate with the wider Human Resources Department (HR) in their system so that all people involved with recruitment are working toward the same goals. In contexts where there are no formal HR structures, suggestions will be made as to how TESOL leaders can draw from sound HR principles.

Intrinsic to the recruitment process are five key principles for TESOL leaders.

## PRINCIPLE 1: RECRUITMENT IS A TEAM EFFORT

Recruitment should involve the organization as a whole. There is a tendency to believe that recruitment is an administrative affair, and in extreme cases the administration may even be unwilling to let others get involved. This approach is very detrimental to the goal of quality recruitment. A prospective new teacher has to be the right "fit" for the organization. In many ways, the candidate's peers are the best judge of whether a candidate is a good fit. It is therefore always a positive move to involve full-time teaching faculty in the recruitment process. Current faculty should not be looked at only in terms of what they can deliver in the classroom. Faculty-to-faculty relations are just as important as student-to-faculty relations (and certainly consume a great deal of management time). For example, a major cause of problems is when members of a team do not pull their weight, causing resentment from those who do. Faculty members involved at the interview stage have a greater insight into whether a candidate is likely to be a team player than perhaps the administration does.

A whole team effort in recruitment can help to ensure that poor recruiting does not take place. Inappropriate recruiting is very costly for the institution. It can result in lost hours of work due to poor team work and dysfunctional work relationships. Further costs can be incurred with replacing personnel. These include the management time involved, the readvertising, the interview costs, possible candidate travel costs, and simply the psychological wear on the organization. Terminating someone from the organization can create camps among teachers with knock-on effects in terms of team morale, productivity, the reputation of the institution, and dissatisfaction from students and community stakeholders.

As previously mentioned, recruitment is a team effort. However, it is also important to remember who the team is. While the TESOL Department may focus on its specific needs and requirements, thought needs to be given to the fact that the TESOL unit is part of a wider organization. Poor recruitment will have a negative impact on the reputation and the marketability of the wider organization. Remember, the organization, personnel, and the unit itself are also assessed and evaluated by the candidate. Poorly executed recruitment will not reflect well on the institution and will make subsequent recruitment targets harder to achieve. It is therefore also advisable to have a member from HR (or the legal department) involved at the interview stage.

## PRINCIPLE 2: RECRUIT FOR TOMORROW

Education, like most other white collar work contexts, is undergoing rapid change. The integration of IT into the learning-teaching mix is a prime example of such change. Consequently, TESOL recruiters should not be looking for people who match their current skills requirements. Although meeting current needs is important, not targeting future needs shows a lack of forward planning by the leadership team that ultimately will hurt the organization in the future. The TESOL recruitment team should ideally be looking ahead to see what skill requirements will be needed in the future and assessing applicants against future need/wishes. In other words, recruitment should be aligned with strategic planning of the unit.

An organization with effective leadership will aim to recruit for tomorrow's needs while still covering today's immediate wants. Recruitment should be used as a method for constantly upgrading the quality of faculty and the program itself. Being a good teacher is no longer sufficient, that is now a given. A good teacher must also have other skills and abilities. Again, the use of technology is a good example. Recruiters are now looking to recruit teachers who are able to surf the Internet and integrate websites, blogs, and podcasts into their teaching and their classrooms. A further example would be the change taking place in student enrollments. Changes due to global, political, and financial developments are changing student enrollment, and this is changing recruitment profiles. For example, any Australian educational organization that does not target the recruitment of TEFL teachers with Middle East experience will be doing themselves a great disservice. Middle East students in the thousands are turning to Australia as their preferred country of study.

## PRINCIPLE 3: RECRUIT SYSTEMATICALLY

Interviewing is only one step in the selection process. To be effective it must build on the previous steps (as well as be related to post-selection activities). Furthermore, interviews are less likely to lead to faculty appointment if the initial recruitment stages have not been done effectively. For example, at Zayed University in the UAE, all stages of recruitment are handled by HR with ongoing cooperation and input from the academic units. In this way all applicants are systematically and fairly treated. Furthermore, every applicant can be identified and traced no matter where she or he is in the recruitment process.

A TESOL leader can maximize the benefits of recruitment by being systematic at all stages of the process. At the very outset this requires that all steps in the recruitment process should be defined and complementary. Marketing, for example, needs to be aligned with targeted applicant profiles, the key points of contact with the applicant should be clear, and the criteria for selection and interview should be aligned. Effective outcomes are more likely if all steps of the recruitment process are working toward the same goals. There are five basic steps in the recruitment process:

*Stage 1: Get the facts.*
Prior to any external activity related to recruitment, the unit leader needs to confirm there is a position opening (and with flexible budget and changes

to student enrollment patterns, this is never a foregone conclusion) and that TACOS (terms and conditions of service, such as contract length, salary, and benefits) have been officially agreed on and that this information can be used to attract the right candidates.

Leaders must know that:

- there are confirmed vacancies (and, if appropriate, at what grade in the organizational hierarchy)
- there is a need to fill the vacant positions
- TACOS have been defined/agreed
- the recruitment is compliant with the institution's legal requirements such as external regulations that address issues of race, age, or disability

*Stage 2:  Focus on the job.*

In the contemporary workplace few teachers can expect to have only one function or role within institution. Certainly from the TEFL leader's position, faculty with good interpersonal skills and who can perform a number of roles and responsibilities are highly desirable. In short, TESOL leaders are recruiting more than just a classroom teacher. The chart that follows indicates some of the key requirements often considered in teacher recruitment with a focus on recruiting teachers who have a wide variety of skills and abilities. However, these roles and functions should be clearly articulated in the recruitment criteria. Failure to do so will result in inappropriate applicants being interviewed and a great deal of management and faculty time being wasted.

---

**Skills/Abilities:**
- able to work as an effective member of a team
- able to work to a timeframe independently
- able to effectively use IT to promote learning
- able to work in a changeable context

**Qualifications:**
- university degree
- recognized teaching certification
- EFL/ESL diploma

**Experience: Must have**
- some overseas experience
- 5 years teaching adult education
- taught non-native speakers of English

---

*Stage 3: Ensure your institution attracts and is attractive.*

Few organizations are able to recruit passively (i.e., by word of mouth). Recruitment takes place in a competitive environment. It is therefore incumbent on the recruitment team to advertise their institution in the best light possible and in doing so attract appropriate candidates.

Advertising clearly depends on a budget, but the more strategic the approach, the greater the chances of achieving successful outcomes. Recruitment teams should aim to attract sufficient applicants to ensure enough choice but not so many applicants that the system is overloaded. Successful recruitment is not based on the number of applications or the number of interviews but on the number of successful applicants. As McKenna and Beech (2002) point out, recruitment can be costly and labor intensive. The recruitment team needs to avoid recruitment fatigue caused by too many interviews.

These key questions need to be asked in order to establish an advertising strategy:

- Who are you targeting?
- Where are these people?
- What online sources do they access?
- What professional resources will they read?
- Is there a particular time of year these people could be available?
- If we spend money on advertisements in hard copy, what is the profile of the readership?

Successful advertising is not only about creating an effective (not to be confused with attractive looking) ad, it is also about advertising in the right place, using appropriate media. The TEFL world still has a large number of relatively transient workers (many stay in a position for only one to two contracts). As a result, a large proportion of today's job-seekers use the Internet, which, unlike newspapers, is accessible from most locations. It is essential that an institution has a website and that it can be used for recruitment (which includes the receiving of applications). This can easily become the cheapest and most effective advertising and marketing medium.

In addition to advertising on the institution's website, alternative websites can be used. A very successful site for advertising is, of course, Dave's ESL Café, which has a section dedicated to recruitment (and is very modestly priced for the recruiting institution).

The next step is deciding what information to post. Remember, you need to attract candidates, and they need to be attracted to you. Perhaps the best approach for a TESOL leader is to imagine what kind of information the targeted applicants will be looking for and step into their shoes. Applicants usually have a predictable range of key questions they need to answer prior to applying. What is this job? What kind of institution is this? When do they want people to start? Do I have enough experience? Am I qualified? Where would I be working? Would this job help me with future career prospects? What kind of students will I be teaching? What professional opportunities will there be with this organization? How do I apply? Am I a good fit for this organization? Will I have the support of my current and previous employer for this application?

Decisions need to be made as to what is essential for the position advertisement and what other information the applicants can source, usually from the website. Don't forget the principle: *Effective outcomes are more likely if all steps of the recruitment process are working toward the same goals.*

Applicants need a great deal of information before they take the next step of applying, and the recruiting organization needs to ensure that different sources of information are complementary and cohesive.

*Stage 4: Screening the applicants: To proceed or not to proceed?*

The recruitment team needs to obtain the right information from applicants in order to decide whether to shortlist and proceed to interview. If the application consists of simply forwarding a cover letter and curriculum vitae, employers run the risk of either not getting sufficient key information to make an informed decision or being victims of slightly abbreviated life histories.

The solution to avoiding such extremes is to take control and have a specially designed application form, which preferably is accessible online and enables applications to be made electronically. In this way the recruitment team controls the information being supplied (but not the validity of it—hence the need for interviews). In addition to the specific application form, applicants will also need to supply an up-to-date resume or CV.

At this stage of the employment process, leaders need to be looking for the basic requirements as well as getting a feel for the wider qualities of the applicant. The Higher Colleges of Technology in the UAE, for example, asks applicants to describe themselves "in the words of a fair and impartial critic" and to describe their greatest achievement. Descriptions enable the recruiters to start to get a picture of the applicant as they move from the factual to the more reflective, evaluative, and personal domain.

*Stage 5. Interview and select and offer.*

A formal job interview is a two-way information exchange process. This is where the institution, represented by the interviewing team, decides if they feel the candidate is suitable for the position and where the candidate decides if he or she would like to work for the institution.

The purpose of the interview is for the interviewer to systematically collect evidence of a candidate's fit for the position. Past performance is always a strong indicator of future performance, so obtaining previous work references is essential. Remember, there are no best candidates, simply those who are more suitable. For the interview to go well, the interviewing team needs to create a series of questions that focus on addressing the points identified as the recruitment criteria for that institution. In this way not only does the interview appear coherent and effective, but the interviewing team gains a greater understanding of the candidate's skills, abilities, and qualities.

Remember, the interview creates a lasting image of your organization in the mind of the person being interviewed. Candidates, whether successful or otherwise, need to leave the interview knowing they were treated professionally and respectfully, and that they were given multiple opportunities to give evidence of their suitability for the job.

*Principle 4: Nature versus nurture: What makes a leader?*

As humans grow and develop, so do their personal traits and characteristics. Clearly, there are some characteristics that appear to be inherited (nature), and there are others that seem to develop as a result of the environment (nurture). The same is true of leaders. Leaders are not born; they develop as a result of nature and nurture. In essence there is no "leadership DNA." However, some people are more suitable for a leadership role than others. Nevertheless, even personnel suitable for leadership need training and professional nurturing. This is very true in the case of recruitment. No one was born a great interviewer. He or she becomes one through practice and training.

Professional development in recruitment for TESOL leaders needs to be an early priority when leaders are appointed. There is little benefit to be gained by waiting for the recruitment period to arrive and then beginning some form of professional development. This approach may lead to disaster. The best approach is to initiate training prior to the main recruitment period. The best way to do this is to work with another unit and perhaps attend or sit in on their interviews (and subsequently review the interview). In this way, the interview outcome is not affected by the observer.

TESOL leaders need to develop extensive recruitment skills and knowledge and be involved in all aspects of the recruitment process, including marketing, evaluating and screening applications; interviewing, and in effective, strategic communication at all stages of the process.

*Principle 5: The recruitment process takes a year.*

Successfully recruiting an employee is really only the front end of a long relationship. Selection subsequently needs to be followed by orientation to the new organization; this needs to be a well organized and seamless event as it will be the first major and long-lasting impression the new employee will receive.

Once selection is completed and the new TESOL teacher arrives, a structured induction and mentoring period is necessary. Induction that is focused, well organized, and reflective can assist the new teacher to quickly become a valued, fully effective, and participative member of a team. It is crucial that new teachers are introduced early into the culture of the TESOL department through a formal and informal process of induction and mentoring. Institutions invest considerable time and a large sum of money in recruiting a successful applicant and inducting him or her into the department. There are vested interests for both the employer and the employee for long-term employment. A leader cannot be effective, long term, if there is constant change of personnel within a unit. It is in the interest of the organization and the leader to maximize staff retention.

To help with retention, and as part of the probationary period, the leader should ensure that there are a series of post-orientation/induction meetings that regularly check on the settling-in progress made by the employee. In addition to supporting the new team member, this will provide an ideal opportunity for the leader to gain input from the new employee regarding orientation. Is there something else that should have been included (or not included) in the orientation?

---

**Elements to Consider as Part of an Induction/Orientation**

**Job-Specific Elements**
• organizational vision—outline the organization's goal
• identify and explain the organizational culture—how things are achieved
• a "who's who/who does what" chart
• IT training if required
• map of the building outlining who is where

**Social Support Elements**
• Language training (if working abroad)
• Cultural training (if working abroad or recruiting foreigners)
• Some form of social gathering enabling new and current staff to mix

---

Following the orientation/induction period, the new teacher begins work and begins the probationary period. This is a very sensitive period and needs to be handled with care and consideration. The probationary period is a time of adjustment, and a leader's attitude toward probation is very central to the way probation is undertaken. Ideally, probation should be viewed as a two-way process. Both the employee and the employer can use this time to reflect on whether the decision to join the organization was the correct one. Probation should be seen as a process that confirms recruitment was successful and not as the last chance to remove someone without major legal or ethical ramifications.

At the beginning of the probationary period, the new teacher should receive some form of an employee handbook. This handbooks needs to include information on the purpose of probation, what is needed in order to meet the probationary requirements, information on how the probationary period is evaluated, who will be supporting the probationary teacher, and, of course, a timeframe in which to meet the requirements.

Finally, it is advisable to create a probation timeframe that allows for an extension if needed. Having gone through the expense and work of employing a new teacher, the worst thing that can happen is to have someone fail the probation (which should not happen if selection was done well). Since probation should be regarded as an adjustment period, people may need slightly different times to adjust (often this will depend on personal circumstances, i.e., does the teacher have a family who are also adjusting?). Consequently, there needs to be time available to extend probation if necessary. Therefore, it is recommended that probation be no shorter than the duration of one course (usually 8–20 weeks) and no longer than a semester (frequently 16–20 weeks). This suggested timeframe allows successful teachers to effectively and quickly exit the probationary period but more importantly allows extra time and support for those few who experience difficulty in adjusting to the new work context. This timeframe provides an opportunity for the probation process to be repeated. Furthermore, in the unlikely event that the probation period is not successfully completed (which has a negative effect on the individual as well as the organization—she or he will have made friends in the organization), time will be available to (a) recruit a replacement for the next academic year and (b) smoothly and professionally ease out the probationary teacher who has not been able to meet expectations.

Effective recruitment skills and the appropriate knowledge are neglected but crucial elements in the skills set and qualities of TESOL leaders. Management recruitment and retention training and professional development for managers are essential as we strive to continue to upgrade the TESOL profession. TESOL leaders need to be aware of the processes that lead to effective recruitment and to identify what aspects of these processes need to be improved or in some cases actually established. Effective recruitment should be a team effort in any institution (and involving not just the top administration), and the processes outlined in this chapter indicate it needs time, well-defined processes, and clear roles and functions. The staffing needs may be immediate, but effective organizations recruit for the future and their interview and selection strategies are aligned with these future needs. To be successful, and sustainable, institutions must look to the future even when dealing with the here and now. No leader, no matter how hardworking or gifted, can achieve targeted goals unless there is a team that is prepared and able to work toward these goals.

> ### Discussion Questions
>
> 1. Define the qualities that are needed in managers for effective recruitment and retention.
> 2. Examine your current job descriptions. What areas/points need to be clarified in order to achieve better targeted recruitment?
> 3. What challenges does your organization face now or in the future? How can recruitment help meet or overcome some of these challenges?
> 4. What challenges do you personally face as a manager in the recruitment process?
> 5. Think of your recruitment needs for the coming years. Work with a colleague to create a recruitment plan. This should include all key dates and activities ranging from identifying recruitment needs through to requesting permission to recruit through to end of orientation.
> 6. What evidence and information do you need before you appoint an English teacher to your department?

## REFERENCES

Armstrong, M. (1997). *A handbook of personnel management.* London: Kogan Page.

Beaumont, P. (1993) *Human resource management: Key concepts and skills.* London: Sage.

Bush, T., & Middlewood, D. (Eds). (1997). *Managing people in education.* London: Paul Chapman Publishing, Ltd.

Dowling, P., & Schuler, R. (1990). *International dimensions of human resource management.* Boston: PWS-Kent.

McKenna, E., & Beech, N. (2002). *Human resource management: A concise analysis.* Harlow, UK: Financial Times Prentice Hall.

Middlewood, D. (1997). Managing recruitment and selection. In T. Bush, & D. Middlewood (Eds.), *Managing people in education* (pp. 139–154). London: Paul Chapman Publishing, Ltd.

# Chapter 15

## Promoting Intensive ESL Programs: Taking Charge of a Market

Suzanne Panferov

### THE IMPORTANCE OF PROGRAM PROMOTION

Becoming a leader in English language program administration is filled with accomplishments and challenges. Trained mostly in Applied Linguistics and TESOL, many English language program leaders face program promotion issues with little or no prior training. Questions we face include: How do I recruit more students? Where should I advertise the program? What are the best types of advertising agencies for my program? How do I promote my program and still maintain its academic integrity? Depending on how a given pedagogical institute organizes and funds language programs, the English language program administrator may find that he or she alone is responsible for both the academic oversight of a department as well as the financial well-being. Bringing in resources whether via grants, university/corporate budget allocations, or tuition may be among the most daunting tasks an administrator faces, as both teacher salaries and overall program viability may depend on this funding. Recruiting students and bringing in tuition monies are fundamental to sustainability.

Despite the importance of program promotion, in a recent survey of English language program administrators, I found that program leaders ranked marketing as the third most important issue in their daily operations. However, more than 65 percent reported that they did not have any training in program promotion prior to starting their first administrative positions and that training in marketing continued to be the most desirable training area identified by these "on the job" leaders. Clearly there exists a gap in our professional training about program promotion. Paradoxically, while our field has recently asserted the need for professional credentialing among English teachers, we are often lax in the professional training in program promotion that we require of program leaders in our field.

In this chapter, I introduce some current methods of promotion and suggest steps for establishing a promotional plan for a typical intensive university English as a Second Language program. Even though attracting students may be more critical in IEP contexts, particularly in North America, the recommendations provided here are transferable to promoting other types of educational programs and events. In times of economic fluctuations and shrinking school budgets, the marketing of all educational programs becomes imperative. As program leaders, it is beneficial to have a fundamental understanding of the promotional process.

## BACKGROUND LITERATURE ON PROGRAM PROMOTION

At first, English language program leaders may fall into two traps if they avoid active promotion. The first trap is that they do not want to be tainted by considering the "selling" of any product, and the second trap is the misnomer that no promotion is required of a quality English course or service. To mitigate this hesitation, I find it helpful to consider two similar terms: *marketing* and *selling*. Marketing includes the analysis of the needs of any given market and then the decision whether filling the niche needs of the market is both feasible in terms of program strengths and profitability. For instance, there may be a need to offer English training for nursing students in a given university. The English department may find that it can offer affordable convenient classes for the students and may choose then to promote that program. *Selling*, on the other hand, refers more to creating a product and then going out and selling it to consumers (White, Martin, Stimson, & Hodge, 1991). In fact, the marketing research that an English language professional might do is quite similar to an academic needs analysis of a single student in one's class but merely expanded to a group of potential students. Taken this way, the marketing of a given program may be more familiar to an English language professional. *Promotion* can then be viewed as the direct or indirect advertising of any given program or event. This can be as minimal as reminding a student to register for class or as advanced as a major advertising campaign.

Once a decision has been made to market and promote a program, the choice of promotional approach falls into two categories: *direct* or *indirect*. Direct promotion is more commonly thought of as advertising via brochures, posters, print advertisements, commercials, videos, and increasingly electronic campaigns via email or webpage listings. Both Miller (1997) and Jenks (1991) review various direct promotional tools and give suggestions for tools created in-house. Numerous professional advertising agencies now specialize in creating direct promotional tools to recruit English language and international students as well. Active recruitment of students via educational fairs and tours with direct contact with potential students is another common direct form of promotion.

Indirect promotion relies more on *viral* advertising, where an idea is spread person to person or via a relationship that in turn benefits a given program. Often "word of mouth" recommendations might fill this role for a program.

Educational consultants or agents, usually abroad in the students' home country, are recruiters paid to bring students to a program or course. The English program has no contact with the student prior to arriving and generally upon registration the agent is paid a finder's fee. The benefit here is that no money is paid out until a student has actually materialized in a program. Risks, of course, include improper advertising of your program or even fleecing of potential students by the agents. Professional organizations like the Association of International Educators (formerly NAFSA, the National Association of Foreign Student Advisors) and UCIEP (a consortium of university and college intensive English programs) offer guidelines on and ethics of working with agents. A less costly indirect option often available to English language programs is to collaborate with university recruiters by piggy-backing on their recruitment efforts at university fairs, as potential visitors may lack appropriate-level English skills prior to matriculating into the university and properly versed university recruiters can promote the English program on the spot. Agreements such as conditional admission with university programs may also indirectly bring students to an English program as affiliation and leadership presentations will reflect positively on the home institution. Additionally, White et al. (1991) describe numerous academic events such as conference presentations or publications as indirect means of promoting a program. Finally, membership in professional standard-bearing organizations such as TESOL, IATEFL, NAFSA, UCIEP, or AAIEP (American Association of Intensive English Programs) may indirectly promote a program as potential students may first check these organizational membership lists for program references. Program evaluation and accreditation through agencies such as the Commission on English Language (CEA) Programs offer an indirect plug for a program as well. Both accreditation and membership in standard-bearing organizations attract students, as discerning students quickly learn to screen for programs touting these select qualifiers.

## PRINCIPLES AND RECOMMENDATIONS

We are surrounded by a world of advertising and marketing. Use this commercialism to spark your own creativity and as an opportunity to watch for ideas that might transfer to your own program contexts. Pay attention to how various advertising programs affect you as a consumer, and watch for innovative marketing tools you might transfer to your own context. For example, you might see a catchy TV commercial and be able to take that idea and use it for a web broadcast ad for a new course that you are offering. To find ideas specific to English language program promotion, participate in professional workshops, such as those run by NAFSA or UCIEP. Enrolling in university courses in introductory marketing may also increase your professional knowledge in marketing. Some may even offer student interns who might adopt your own program's marketing needs as a course project. Certain commercial marketing vendors targeted at international students also offer professional consultation.

The key out of all of the commercial chaos is to create a solid logical plan to most effectively market your program and to keep the promotion fresh. Creating a promotional plan is basically a four-step cyclical process. This process is actually quite similar to a course development process where research is conducted initially via a needs analysis and diagnosis, creation and implementation of the course, and then review and evaluation of educational goals met. When preparing to launch a promotional campaign for a new program, the entire cycle is completed. Many program leaders land mid-cycle and circle continuously through the process in existing programs. It is important that you especially pay attention to the Research and Evaluation steps, as often these steps will give you the best data to make the best decisions about future promotions. Unfortunately, one must approach this whole process with the idea that this is not an exact science. Approach your own promotional campaign with great hope for success of meeting your goals but acknowledge that this may not happen. Keep a financial cushion to guard your budget and data to guide your judgments.

Before launching a promotion to bring in new students, if your promotion will be for an existing program, turn your attention to your current students to find out what suggestions for improvements they have in terms of services and course offerings. Regular ongoing surveys about the program as well as focus group discussions are helpful for gathering data. Comb through the data to sort out the immediate changes that can (and should) be made and establish procedures to follow through on longer-range suggestions. Current students and alumni are vital as they already feed your program, and "word of mouth" advertising is very powerful (Jenks, 1991). You might even consider a special discount for current students who refer new recruits.

It is helpful when beginning a promotional campaign to return to and to review your program's mission statement. Take time to reflect on the current expertise of your program, as well as to inventory the skills that can be expanded when given proper resources. A common management tool to evaluate a program is to conduct a "SWOT" analysis—**S**trengths, **W**eaknesses, **O**pportunities, and **T**hreats. When starting up a new program or course, the SWOT analysis is particularly important for anticipating management issues that may come down the pike. This research should define your target audience and the parameters of any course that might be marketed.

Program promotion is an on-going task. Consider the WWW to begin your promotion—the **W**hy, the **W**hen, and the **W**here. Drops in enrollment, the launch of a new course, changes in community needs, or even shifts in world political climates might be a time when you should consider program promotion. If program enrollments are stable but heavy in one native language background, this is a reason why you should consider diversification. Diversifying student demographics in a program requires the attraction of students from varied language backgrounds or countries. This will help teachers by creating more diverse classroom demographics. This too may protect a program financially so that revenue streams from varied origins—a take on the adage to "not put too many eggs in one basket."

Deciding where to market a program requires a bit of socio-economic-political acrobatics. An excellent resource for global statistics on enrollment trends is the annual Open Doors report compiled by the Institute for International Education. This document shows economic data trends both for students coming into a country as well as going abroad to study. External issues affecting student enrollment trends vary greatly, but trends have shown that foreign policy, visa procedures, currency fluctuation, costs, and geographic location of a program may positively or negatively affect enrollments. For instance, after the 9/11 tragedy in the United States, student visa regulations became stricter, discouraging many students from applying to study English; as a result, the students sought to study English in other countries where the visa policies were more lax. Economic variations across the world may naturally encourage or prohibit students from coming to a particular program. Sudden economic changes will affect enrollments, such as the Asian economic crisis in the late 1990s that reduced the pool of students leaving Asia to study, since it was cheaper for them to study English at home rather than expend resources to travel around the globe to study.

When deciding where to market, consider the adage, "One hundred dollars spent in Europe will bring one dollar. One dollar spent in Asia will bring one hundred dollars." Geographic factors such as weather, climate, and proximity to major urban centers may draw students in or similarly repel them. Marketing programs tuned into seasonal variations may encourage program growth. A final dilemma about where to market a program is whether to market in stable and well-established markets or to risk marketing in potential new up-and-coming markets. A possible benefit of being one of the earliest programs to recruit in an emerging market is a definite plus in initial branding of a program in a new arena.

Once you have established that it is time to promote a program, five distinct issues need to be addressed: (1) What is your budget for marketing? (2) How will you promote? (3) Will translations need to be used? (4) What will your procedures be for managing leads that evolve out of the promotion? (5) How will you evaluate the effectiveness of your campaign?

We began this chapter recognizing that financial resources secure the fiscal health of a program. All promotion involves the risk that resources may be pumped into a campaign and absolutely no leads will result. As such, a margin of cushion should be built into any new program budget to promote the program. Miller (1997) recommends allotting 10 to 20 percent of a program's operational budget toward promotional tools. Determine the absolute minimal number of registrations that must be completed in order to break even in a program. Cost proposals from outside vendors as well as totals for internal promotional costs (such as postage, paper, copying, overhead, salaries, etc.) will help you determine the cost range you can apply toward the promotional campaign.

When selecting how your program will be promoted, include a combination of direct and indirect promotional tools as well as a mix of cost and no- or low-cost options. Much like investing in the stock or bond market, a diverse portfolio will best position your program to endure marketing gains and losses.

Direct marketing tools might include brochures, posters, pens, t-shirts, bookmarks, key chains, etc. Quantity and cost of production should be considered with these items. The advantage of buying products in bulk means that obviously the cost per item is lower; however, avoid trendy items as well as date or year indicators that may make a product appear outdated in the future. Jenks (1991) suggests that large programs might expect to distribute around 200,000 promotional pieces a year, while smaller operations might average around 4,000 to 5,000. However, programs enduring numerous changes might consider producing in-house any items that frequently change to allow for updates so as to not be left with large quantities of defunct promo pieces.

Professional vendors offer numerous marketing outlets both in print and electronic format. U.S. Journal, Study in the USA, Hobsons, and Apply ESL are marketing agencies that offer all sorts of services to promote a program abroad. Review your program's history of working with professional vendors, and clarify legal contracting procedures before engaging a professional contract. Colleagues in organizations such as UCIEP and AAIEP are often ready and willing to offer feedback about success in working with certain professional promoters and agents.

Consider a combination of both print and electronic formats depending on where the marketing materials are headed. Certain countries are already more experienced and reliant on Internet information, while others rely still on print magazines, newspapers, and brochures. An informal survey of current students from the areas of the world where you would like to recruit students may help determine which format to use and occasionally even which press or publisher to use. Consider also publications or websites that are referenced time and again for information about English programs such as the annual Intensive English Directory published by IIE. These references are essential for advising centers around the world in selecting programs for students. Omission from a directory may spell repeated missed opportunities for a program to be promoted.

Depending on where you market your programs, you may need to consider the option of whether to use translations in your promotional materials. One school of thought expects all "sales" to be in the language of the customer; another expects that if students are to succeed in a program abroad, they must already have some English skills and thus marketing in English is acceptable. Consider the audience for the marketing tools as sponsors or parents of potential students, who themselves may have weak English language skills yet need to access the information about your program in their native language(s) in order to decide whether they want their child or benefactor to study in your program. At the same time, translating documents will limit where they can be distributed as well. Given the various dialects and stylistic issues in advertising, when working with translations, consider using professional translators to encourage best market value of the product.

Once a promotional product is launched, especially advertisements and professional Internet campaigns, procedures need to be in place to handle leads from a given promotional tool. The key is to turn cool leads into hot leads who eventually enroll and pay for your program. Establish mechanisms to collect data both for electronic and postal mail communications. Marketing experts suggest five or more communications with a potential customer before he or she applies or registers in a given program. Create a system to frequently communicate with a lead to convert that inquiry into a sale. Be sure your program database allows for tracking by country so that data subsets can be collected for targeted campaigns and future site visits.

Finally, no promotional campaign is complete without evaluation of the effectiveness of the marketing efforts. The main idea is to determine a mechanism to sort out how many student sales have resulted from a promotional tool and whether the expenses of the marketing outweigh the gains from enrollments. A common way to do this is to have the student bring or mail in the actual advertisement that drew them to the program. Similarly, a student being referred by another or an agent might list that person on his or her application. Some electronic campaigns will direct students to email addresses or websites created specifically for that promotional tool so that leads can be tallied in that manner. Promotional codes are another similar and simpler option assuming that students actively select or list on applications. Jenks (1991) suggests even low-tech tricks like marking applications with colored dots to track applications. Simpler still is to survey arriving students about where they learned about your program. Periodically stop during your fiscal year and tally and compare the leads that have come in for each advertising tool and determine whether you have reached a return on your investment. Analyze whether you have surpassed the cost expended with positive income flow for each tool. Return regularly to the beginning of the promotional process to review fresh needs in the program and opportunities for program growth. Re-balance the promotional campaign accordingly.

Promoting a language program takes a combination of research, creativity, funding, and insight into future sales. Eventually, with regular practice and involvement, program promotion becomes less mysterious and more manageable. Surround yourself with supportive colleagues and professional marketers to exchange experiences and glean wisdom from their successes and failures. Smart adherence to a regular marketing plan will make the experience more manageable and profitable in the end. And that next time a telemarketer calls, you might even feel obliged to listen—if only to fish for new ideas.

**SUGGESTED RESOURCES**

Christison, M. A., & Stoller, F. L. (Eds.). *A handbook for language program administrators.* (1997). Burlingame, CA: Alta.

Workshops presented at annual meetings of TESOL, NAFSA, IATEFL, and UCIEP. Information available on www.tesol.org, www.nafsa.org, www.iatefl. org, and www.uciep.org, and on each association's electronic listservs.

Pennington, M.C. (Ed.). (1991). *Building better English language programs.* Washington, DC: NAFSA.

White, R., Martin, M., Stimson, M., & Hodge, R. (1991). *Management in English language teaching.* Cambridge, UK: Cambridge University Press.

---

### Discussion Questions

1. Consider your own English language program. What are the current direct and indirect promotional strategies used in marketing today?
2. How do the stages of creating a promotional plan mirror those in an academic classroom setting?
3. Tracking the effectiveness of a promotional plan is important for considering future financial investments in marketing. How might you track the effectiveness of indirect promotion?
4. Program promotion is logically engrained in ESL contexts. Discuss situations in EFL environments when promotion is vital as well.

---

**REFERENCES**

Jenks, F. (1991). Designing and assessing the efficacy of ESL promotional materials. In M. C. Pennington (Ed.), *Building better English language programs* (pp. 172–188). Washington DC: NAFSA.
Miller, B. (1997). Marketing principles for the language program administrator. In M. A. Christison & F. L. Stoller (Eds.), *A handbook for language program administrators* (pp. 309–312). Burlingame, CA: Alta Book Center Publishers.
White, R., Martin, M., Stimson, M., & Hodge, R. (1991). *Management in English language teaching.* Cambridge, UK: Cambridge University Press.

# Chapter 16

## DREAM Management:
## Involving and Motivating Teachers

Phil Quirke and Steve Allison

All too often in educational management we see quality teaching struggle against administrative and paperwork constraints. This chapter looks at a management policy that keeps teaching and learning processes at the core of the institution. We believe that students and learning are at the heart of everything we do in ELT, and therefore teachers, those closest to both students and learning, must be the engine of educational management.

The authors claim that the DREAM model they have developed over the last five years ensures the engagement of teachers in the leadership of their institution and thereby maintains a primary focus on students and learning. DREAM management is a series of principles that keeps teaching and learning at the heart of education. It reflects the beliefs and values we attempt to live and work by in our day-to-day management life, and this chapter attempts to capture how we promote the principles among our colleagues.

### BACKGROUND LITERATURE

The DREAM Management concept is self-initiated by the authors. It has been developed over five years of experience in the professional environment. We have found over the last year several sources in the literature that support this principled and practical description of our management approach, and we have used the works of Covey (1989) and Maslow (1970) to clarify our time management and motivation techniques.

Covey (1989) has provided a method of focus through his use of the Time Management Matrix that has led to a further refinement of the DREAM aims to include elements of leadership in balance with management skills. The conclusions have led to the understanding that by developing our management practices into more effective processes, we are able to lend more time to issues of leadership.

Maslow (1970) has also provided the main framework for the focus on motivation through the utilization of his hierarchy of needs. Besides these two references there are various sources available on the Internet that are listed at the end of this chapter.

We have often been asked to name the literature that has influenced the development of this model, but the truth is this model has been developed in practice during our educational management careers and is a description of an experiential approach to leading teachers and an academic team. However, we have recently discovered the literature that supports our approach from a theoretical standpoint. The works of Fullan (2004) and Senge (1992) in particular ring true to our approach, and we would encourage you to read these authors.

The influence of other authors is evident in the principles below. Scriven's work (1973, 1981, 1994) has greatly influenced the formation of our approach to the appraisal of teachers. The use of action research and learning in the development of teachers, which draws heavily on Quirke (2001a), was largely informed by Kemmis and McTaggart (1988), Wallace (1998) and Burns (1999). Underlying the whole approach is a belief in the power of cooperative (Edge, 2002) and reflective learning (Richards & Lockhart, 1994).

## PRINCIPLES AND RECOMMENDATIONS

DREAM is a simple acronym that provides us with a powerful set of educational leadership principles. The principles have been developed over the last five years by the authors, who have 20 years of leadership experience in ELT between them. The model is a tried and tested formula that has been successfully implemented by both authors that should give educational leaders more time to lead effectively.

The acronym of DREAM stands for:

- **D**elegate and Develop
- **R**ecruit and Respect
- **E**nhance and Enjoy
- **A**ppraise and Attend
- **M**otivate and Mimic

We **delegate** responsibility to staff so that they can do their job. This means avoiding a top-down approach, involving teachers in every aspect of the institution's work, allowing and encouraging them to take responsibility for the areas they are interested in, for example through Action Learning and Research Groups.

We **develop** staff by promoting research and reflective working practices.

We **recruit** staff that fit our team's ethos and approach.

We **respect** staff as professionals by allowing them to do the job we have recruited them for. This refers to how we, as managers, appreciate the professional standing of our employees and rely fully on their input in their areas of expertise. By doing so, we demonstrate an understanding that each new recruit enhances the existing talent pool already available within our faculty ranks. In addition, we recognize that new recruits also bring new skills to the team that can prove to be advantageous for all team members (Quirke, 1999).

We **enhance** staff skills based on their annual appraisals that rely on a portfolio system that allows teachers to drive their development.

We **enjoy** working with those around us and show it. This is the central letter of DREAM and the central theme of DREAM management. It emphasizes the belief that a happy staff creates the environment that is most conducive to effective learning for our staff and students.

We **appraise** staff, not evaluate them. This focuses on the development of our staff. Don't criticize every move but appraise through constructive and formative approaches.

We **attend** to the details that affect the day-to-day jobs of the teacher. Managers should manage. This means that a manager's role is to act as a buffer zone to filter out the various issues that faculty need not be concerned with to perform their teaching duties effectively.

We **motivate** staff by supporting them professionally in every way we can.

We **mimic** staff by never asking them to do something we wouldn't do ourselves, and we demonstrate this continually. Educational managers should teach alongside their faculty, provide cover as they expect their teachers to cover, and be available at the same hours that they expect teachers to be on-site.

In effect the philosophy reads most coherently when we read it as follows in the form of a virtuous circle:

*Figure 16.1:* The Cycle of Application

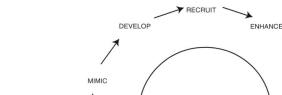
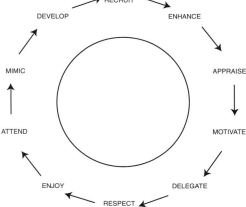

This chapter describes each of the ten principles and how they have been applied in practice.

## RECRUIT

As we recruit to our team of teachers, the essential steps in the recruitment process become the clarity of the job description, the accuracy of the application screening, and, most importantly, the humanity of the interview and reference checks. It is the latter two that ensure that the faculty hired is not simply qualified for the position but is also an ideal fit for the character composition of the existing team. To do this effectively, we must be honest and frank with potential recruits so they too know what to expect on arrival at the new workplace. We not only look for specific characteristics in the new-hire, but also allow them to explore our institution's ethos and character. In addition, we have to be strong enough to reject applicants when necessary in order for (a) the current team to remain effective and (b) the candidate to find a better-suited position.

## ENHANCE

The enhancement of faculty is essential in the DREAM model. The approach is detailed in the section on appraisal, but it is introduced in the first weeks of a new faculty's arrival at the institute. Once they have familiarized themselves with the mission and goals of the institution and department, they are asked to draw up their own personal and professional development plan in consultation with their line Chair. These goals will be directly aligned to the departmental goals, and the Chair ensures that the teacher has institutional support to attain these. A sample layout would look something like Table 1.

These goals can then be developed into a firm action plan with a focus on the short-term goals using Table 2.

This approach to goal-setting is, in effect, the first stage and foundation for the next principle.

## APPRAISE

An effective appraisal system, like the Performance Enhancement Programme (PEP) at the Higher Colleges of Technology, is one that is standard and coherent and adheres to best practice and principles.

*Table 16.1:  Template for Planning Goals*

| # | Role | Short-term goal | Mid-term goal | Long-term goal |
|---|------|-----------------|---------------|----------------|
| 1 | Teacher | Understand new Emirati students | Develop online delivery skills | Publish my teaching work |
| 2 | Materials Writer | Develop my existing materials for new students | Develop these materials for online delivery | Launch WebCT teaching site |
| 3 | Team Worker | Settle into department | Take on assistant team-leading role | Take on a team-leading role |

*Table 16.2:  Sample Action Plan*

| Teacher | | | | |
|---|---|---|---|---|
| **Activities** | **Support Group** | **Completion** | **Output Indicators** | **Achievement Level** |
| 1. | | | | |
| 2. | | | | |
| Materials Writer | | | | |
| 1. | | | | |
| 2. | | | | |
| Team Worker | | | | |
| 1. | | | | |
| 2. | | | | |

It is a process that:

- is fair to all
- is based on sound principles
- allows problems to be detected early and therefore acted upon quickly
- ensures both consistency in approach and documentation when applied correctly

Such a system ensures that teachers realize they are respected and valued, and the institution transparently communicates its principles clearly. Ongoing feedback to support and enhance performance is a key element of the appraisal programme and the whole DREAM management philosophy. Effective two-way feedback should not only enhance performance and morale, it should contribute to more fruitful subsequent discussions and ongoing work.

*Figure 16.2:* The Seven Stages of Appraisal

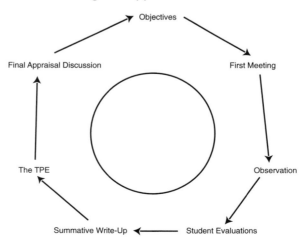

There are seven stages of the appraisal process.

### 1. Objectives
Teachers draw up their objectives based on the previous year's final appraisal meeting and include the following:

1. Classroom teaching
2. Professional development
3. Departmental duty
4. College duty
5. Other—follow-up from last year's final discussion record

### 2. First Meeting
The teacher and chair discuss the following and ensure that classroom, department, and college objectives are covered.

1. Objectives
2. Observations—when they should take place, with which class, and who will observe
3. What format the observation should take
4. Student evaluations

The teacher then sends a final electronic copy to the chair. These can be updated during the year as objectives change.

### 3. Observation
There should be at least one observation every year. Every observation must have a pre-observation discussion and a feedback hour (as well as a write-up if the teacher wishes) or it is NOT an observation. The pre-observation meeting sets the focus for the observer and allows the observer to brief the teacher on how the observation will be conducted. Preferably the observer should know the class and even teach it beforehand. We like to offer teachers the choice of:

- straight 45-minute observation
- short 20-minute observation with each section
- blitz observation of every class in a given week
- unseen observation (Quirke, 1996)
- peer observation (with chair present at pre-observation and feedback meeting)

During the observation the chair takes notes with questions throughout the lesson. After the observation, the teacher receives the notes and uses the questions to reflect upon the lesson. At the feedback session, which should be at least a couple of hours later, the teacher leads the discussion using their answers to the questions posed in the notes. An observation write up is not required by the process but it is encouraged as it does give the teacher support in compiling their extract. Teacher and chair can decide if they want one at all or who should write it up—chair, teacher, peer, or students.

### 4. Student Evaluations

Every teacher should have a minimum of four class sections evaluating them during the academic year. If this is not possible—e.g., the teacher is teaching only one section all year—then two evaluations at different times should be done. If a teacher is teaching more than four sections over the year, they can decide to have them all do evaluations.

Student evaluations should be conducted at a time that is appropriate to teachers, students, and the institution. Chairs can insist on student evaluations from any given section if they wish. Teachers should also be encouraged to collect their own informal student feedback to support their classroom objectives. When the results are available, the chair and teacher should discuss them and how they will be referred to in the portfolio extract. The chair must know the class and the circumstances of the student evaluation—e.g., was it done just after a testing week?

### 5. Summative Write-Up

This is not required by many appraisal programmes, but it does give teachers some meat to include in their Portfolio Extract. We recommend writing a one-page review of how we feel the teacher has fulfilled his or her objectives.

### 6. The Teaching Portfolio Extract (TPE)

This is the teacher's four- to six-page summary of his or her portfolio. It must be noted that the portfolio is private and can take any form the teacher is comfortable with. It is not a public document. It is simply where the teacher stores the material he or she refers to in the extract and which the teacher can access quickly if required to do so. The extract must include a self-evaluation with reflection on teaching, reference to student evaluations, and reference to line chair's comments. It must adhere to the honesty principle in that anything stated in the TPE can be supported by documentation in the portfolio.

### 7. The Final Appraisal Discussion Meeting and Record

This meeting is held between the chair and the teacher, and the record is completed during the meeting with both present. The power of this meeting is that it not only looks back and reviews the last year but also draws on that review to look forward and set goals for the coming year (see Point 1) that we feel results in a truly cyclical process.

## MOTIVATE

The most important element in motivating teachers is involving them in every aspect of the day-to-day life of the institution, while listening to them and understanding their needs and the motivational factors that drive them. Reading from the foot of Maslow's hierarchy, the levels relate to the following needs:

1. Biological and Physiological needs—air, food, drink, shelter, warmth, sleep, etc.
2. Safety needs—protection from elements, security, order, law, limits, stability, etc.
3. Belongingness and Love needs—work group, family, affection, relationships, etc.
4. Esteem needs—self-esteem, achievement, mastery, independence, status, dominance, prestige, managerial responsibility, etc.
5. Self-Actualization needs—realizing personal potential, self-fulfillment, seeking personal growth, and peak experiences.

Translated into the DREAM model through the label of MOTIVATE, the highest level (5) is self-actualization or the need for self-fulfillment, a sense that one's potential has been fully realized. It is suggested that this is a stage that one needs to work on continuously throughout a lifetime, and we must therefore continually address this need through daily praise and demonstration that we appreciate the work of our teachers. The fourth level in Maslow's hierarchy refers to the need to develop self-esteem through personal achievement, as well as social esteem through the recognition and respect we get from others. Therefore, we must support teachers in the setting of attainable goals and publicly recognize their attainment of these goals. Maslow's third need is the sense of belonging that refers to an individual's need for love, affection, and interaction with other people. By focusing on an institutional ethos of enjoyment as the central tenet of our DREAM philosophy, we can ensure that teachers have a strong sense of belonging. The lower two elements of Maslow's hierarchy are safety and physiological and involve the need for a secure and stable environment with basic biological needs such as food, clean air and water, and adequate shelter. These needs should be satisfied by the terms of the contract, but DREAM managers must always demonstrate to their teachers that they are concerned for the basic welfare of their staff and responsive to any concerns that teachers voice.

We should promote teacher leadership in addressing these needs by encouraging faculty initiatives. A few examples we have supported in the last few years include the development of a spouse's social club, a college family day, staff gym hours, college support for conference presentations abroad, teacher activity exchanges over college funded lunches, and rewards for long-serving faculty. These are simple ideas but we would expect your teachers to come up with ideas that are as motivating and innovative as these.

## DELEGATE

We all use many excuses for not delegating, and most of these are usually unfounded. We can get far more done through delegation if we assume that the opposite of the following statements is true:

- I could do it better myself.
- I don't know if I can trust her to do it.
- He isn't qualified to do it.
- She doesn't want any added responsibilities.
- I don't have the time to show anyone how to do it.
- I don't want to give up this task because I like doing it.
- I'm the only person who knows how to do this.
- She messed up last time, so I'm not giving her anything else to do.

So, we have to assume that most people want added responsibilities, as we ourselves do. We assume our teachers are keen to learn and recognize that any short-term training investment always pays off in the long term. In our experience, teachers are always ready to help you if you approach them in the right way. It is also indicated through the recruitment and interview where candidates are invited to:

- indicate what professional development paths they would like to follow
- suggest how they can see themselves fitting into a team
- express future preferences about further responsibilities
- mention specific skills they may want to bring to the team

However, remember that there are some things you can't delegate such as performance reviews and disciplinary incidents.

The most effective way to delegate is to plan the delegation using your teachers' goals and development plans (see Tables 16.1 and 16.2) to inform your decisions. It is also essential that you, as chair, remain responsible for the completion of the tasks you have delegated and that you use the personal and professional development plans to manage the process with clearly stated outcomes and performance indicators. In this way, we can use delegation to generate trust and an ethos of combined responsibility among everyone in the institution.

## RESPECT

We should respect all our staff as professionals by allowing them to do the job we have recruited them for. This refers to how we, as managers, appreciate the professional standing of our employees and how we, as managers, rely fully on their input in their areas of expertise. This means that we allow our teachers to do what they do best—TEACH.

We believe, in our DREAM philosophy, that there are eleven keys to demonstrating our respect of staff in all our communications with them (Quirke, 2006; Quirke, 2001b). In every communication, be it verbal or written, we should:

1. be decisive
2. be appreciative
3. be clear
4. smile ☺—we cannot emphasize enough how important this is
5. empathize, respecting the personal situation of each and every one of our staff
6. pose questions—and listen to the responses
7. praise
8. delegate
9. share
10. support
11. give thanks

It may seem a tall order to do this in every communication, but start trying it in your daily email exchanges and you will be surprised just how many of these keys you are able to accomplish in one short message. In this way, we can demonstrate continually the deep respect we have for our teachers.

## ENJOY

In the introduction to this chapter, we noted that we enjoy working with those around us and show it. E for ENJOY is the central letter of DREAM and the central theme of DREAM management. This emphasizes the belief that a happy staff creates the environment that is most conducive to effective learning for staff and students. Most of us would agree that happiness comes from the inside and is generated by ourselves as individuals. Therefore, individuals control their happiness. If this is true, we must give our staff control if they are to be truly happy.

So, we must use our personal and professional development plans to set clear goals for teachers that allow them to take control of their classes and teaching as well as other tasks we delegate to them. We must appraise them with daily motivational recognition and allow them to take control of their professional lives. In this way we can create the environment for staff to be happy, and we can emphasise this every morning with simple greetings and the smile that shows we too enjoy coming to work.

## ATTEND

We attend to our teachers by ensuring we create the time to work on the day-to-day issues that make a difference to their working lives. This means we must know our teachers well and understand what makes a difference to them. This can be as simple as ensuring they can find a parking place easily or that they know you are available to cover the first five minutes of a period when they have been held up in traffic when dropping the kids at school. To do this is far easier said than done, and it does require very good time management. We promote the use of a good calendar system and a weekly check that you have spent time with each of those teachers or staff under your direct line management. This simple attendance to minor details can make a huge impact on teachers and create an environment of caring and sharing that is at the core of DREAM management.

## MIMIC

The motto of this principle is: "Never ask anyone to do something you would not do yourself." So, if teachers are in class until nine o'clock at night, ensure that there is also a management presence and that you are there yourself at least a couple of times a month as teachers leave their rooms. We are ardent believers that educational managers and leaders should be seen to teach, and both of us have always done a few hours teaching every week. This ensures we have first-hand experience of our students and classrooms and can react knowledgably to teacher issues. This is especially true in areas such as technology in the classroom and student discipline. Having a first-hand experience allows for the manager to approach the relevant support teams with the correct information and get issues resolved without teachers having to take up more of their own time dealing with such issues. Teachers appreciate not only the fact that management is in the classroom the same as everyone else, but also that management is willing to go the extra mile to make life easier for all concerned.

## DEVELOP

This principle is attained by ensuring the institution has a clear and supportive approach to professional development. In our institution we have focused on a programme of Action Learning and Research Groups.

The goal of this approach is to develop a self-managing program, which operates under the control of the teachers themselves. It encourages teachers to define the issues and problems they encounter in the classroom and to address them collaboratively through a process of Action Learning Research. Teachers who share similar classroom and professional interests engage in critical reflection on their teaching practices, which leads to the formation of an action learning project. One of the most evident outcomes of this approach to professional development has been the enthusiasm of the teachers to share their findings with the wider ELT community through both publications and conference presentations (Quirke, 2003).

DREAM management was conceived as the realization dawned on us that there ought to be some way of defining what we believe to be best ELT leadership practices employed at our institution. By focusing on the issues and feedback received from our college community, it was evident that there was a clear need for us to implement a recognized approach to teacher development and involvement at all levels of the college community. The formulation of DREAM has allowed this process to take place, but it is by no means complete. It is an iterative process due to the changing nature of the education sector, and specifically within our own institution, which is constantly looking to update its policies, practices, and technology. The principles of DREAM are available to all in our community and have been recognized as a successful approach to teacher development to the point that we have now started delivering courses to other educational establishments. Through a constant dialogue with our staff and colleagues, we are continuously refining and improving the model. This is not so that it becomes a model to fit all circumstances, rather it is so that there is a practiced model in place that other practitioners can refer to and adapt for their own institutions.

## SUGGESTED RESOURCES

www.philseflsupport.com/management.htm. This is the management section of the website maintained by Phil Quirke.

www.getmoredone.com. An interesting site that inspired the section on delegation.

www.thewisdommeme.com/Articles1/happystaff.htm. A good site focusing on the importance of happiness at the workplace.

Edge, J. (Ed.). (2001). *Action research: Case studies in TESOL practice.* Alexandria, VA: TESOL. An excellent book to introduce the reader to Action Learning and Research, including a chapter by Quirke (2001a) that demonstrates the influence of this approach to Professional Development on the DREAM management model.

Organizational principles & standards: Consistency and alignment between organizational values and individual behaviors is vital. Retrieved October 14, 2004, from www.umich.edu/~busfin/docs/BF_Values_with_Behaviors_Fi.pdf. A good example of a site that reflects the respect principle of the DREAM model.

Quirke, P. (2007). A coherent approach to faculty appraisal. In Coombe, C. M., Al-Hamly, P. Davidson, & S. Troudi (Eds.), *Evaluating teacher effectiveness in EFL/ESL contexts.* Ann Arbor: University of Michigan Press.

---

### Discussion Questions

1. Looking at your institution, you probably already have some of the principles of DREAM in place. With a group of colleagues, articulate how these principles are applied in your institution.

2. If you were to prioritize the DREAM principles, what order would you put them in and why?

3. Looking specifically at the principle of delegation, how do you decide when to delegate and to whom? Is this successful? If not, would you consider implementing the DREAM delegation principle as an alternative?

4. What barriers do you see to the implementation of DREAM management at your institution? How could you overcome these barriers?

5. After one presentation on DREAM management, an audience member suggested that teachers as well as managers should have DREAM principles they should follow to complement the DREAM principles their management is following. The audience then brainstormed what these could be. What would your five DREAM principles for teachers be? Why have you chosen these?

---

## REFERENCES

Burns, A. (1999). *Collaborative action research for English language teachers.* Cambridge, UK: Cambridge University Press.

Covey, S. (1989). *The 7 habits of highly effective people.* London: Simon & Schuster.

Edge, J. (2002). *Continuing cooperative development: A discourse framework for individuals as colleagues* (2nd ed.). Ann Arbor: University of Michigan Press.

Edge, J. (Ed.). (2001). *Action research: Case studies in TESOL practice.* Alexandria, VA: TESOL.

Fullan, M. (2004). *Leading schools in a culture of change.* Jossey-Bass: San Francisco.

Kemmis, S., & McTaggart, R. (Eds.) (1988). *The action research planner* (3rd ed.). Geelong, Victoria: Deakin University Press.

Maslow, A. H. (1970). *Motivation and personality* (2nd ed). New York: Harper & Row.

Quirke, P. (1996). Using unseen observations for an IST development programme. *The Teacher Trainer, 10*(1), 18–20.

———. (1999). Material creation and sharing. *The Higher Colleges of Technology Journal, 3*(2), 2.

————. (2001a). Hearing voices: A reliable and flexible framework for gathering and using student feedback. In J. Edge. (Ed.), *Action research: Case studies in TESOL practice* (pp. 81–92). Alexandria, VA: TESOL.

————. (2001b). Maximizing student writing and minimizing teacher correction. In J. Burton & M. Carroll. (Eds.), *Journal writing: Case studies in TESOL practice* (pp. 11–22). Alexandria, VA: TESOL.

————. (2003). What is out of the box? *The Essential Teacher, 1*(1), 44–47.

————. (2006). *How EFL teachers taking further qualifications through distance learning can best be supported via a web-based medium.* Unpublished doctoral dissertation, Aston University: Birmingham, UK.

————. (2007). A coherent approach to faculty appraisal. In C. Coombe, M. Al-Hamly, P. Davidson, & S. Troudi. (Eds.), *Evaluating teacher effectiveness in EFL/ESL contexts.* Ann Arbor: University of Michigan Press.

Richards, J., & Lockhart, C. (1994). *Reflective teaching in second language classrooms.* Cambridge, UK: Cambridge University Press.

Scriven, M. (1973). *Handbook for model training program in qualitative educational evaluation.* Berkeley: University of California Press.

————. (1981). Summative teacher evaluation. In J. Millman & L. Darling-Hammond (Eds.), *The new handbook of teacher evaluation: Assessing elementary and secondary school teachers* (pp. 244–271). Newbury Park, CA: Sage.

————. (1994). Using student ratings in teacher evaluation. *Evaluation perspectives, 4*(1), 1–6.

Senge, P. M. (1992). *The fifth discipline: The art and practice of the learning organisation.* Milsons Point, NSW: Random House Australia.

Wallace, M. (1998). *Action research for language teachers.* Cambridge, UK: Cambridge University Press.

# Part 5

## ELT Leadership Issues in U.S. Public Schools

This section presents two case studies of leadership in the U.S. public schools. **Carnuccio, Huffman, O'Loughlin, and Rosenthal** provide information and guidelines to see that the ESOL leaders in rural communities are well prepared to deal with the influx of immigrant populations. **Arnow and Webbert's** article describes the successes of the Gwinnett County Public Schools system, which focuses on how superintendents use their positions to improve the instructional practices at their schools.

# Chapter 17

## Leadership in Addressing Linguistic and Cultural Diversity in Low-Incidence Public School Settings

Lynore M. Carnuccio, Cheryl Leever Huffman,
Judith O'Loughlin, and Roger Rosenthal

### THE NEED FOR TEACHER LEADERSHIP IN SETTINGS WITH SMALL POPULATIONS OF ELLs

With more than 5 million English Language learners (ELLs) in schools through-out the United States (National Clearinghouse for English Language Acquisition, 2004), the needs of students whose first language is not English cannot be ignored in any school district. In the last five to ten years, there have been dramatic changes in the demographic patterns in schools in the United States. Jobs in such industries as poultry processing, meat packing, traditional agricultural fieldwork, the service industry, and construction, to name a few, have attracted new immigrant populations to areas that have never seen these populations before. Such new and dramatic shifts in the location of ELLs create special challenges for school systems unfamiliar with and unaccustomed to this population and this type of diversity. Especially affected by these changes are districts in rural areas enrolling small numbers of ELLs, whether from one or from multiple language groups, as well as individual school sites with small multilingual ELL populations in larger urban or suburban districts. These environments, generally described as "low-incidence," are frequently the least likely to have thoughtfully developed programs for meeting the unique needs of ELLs or to have teachers with professional backgrounds or training in ESL, bilingual, or multicultural education (Huffman, Carnuccio, O'Loughlin, & Rosenthal, 2003).

In addition to these changing demographics, educational legislation, especially the No Child Left Behind Act of 2001 (NCLB) (Public Law 107-110), has increased awareness of ELLs in school accountability systems. Low-incidence schools or districts now find themselves propelled to address the needs of students about whom current staff members frequently lack both knowledge and training. The inclusion of a qualified ESL teacher in an existing staff is often interpreted as the solution to the problem. However, existing educational hierarchies often do not empower ESL teachers to become leaders in addressing the needs of ELL populations in their settings. ESL teachers in low-incidence settings are usually very low in the school "hierarchy," even though they may be the most knowledgeable in areas related to the education of ELLs. Their challenge is to find ways to become empowered in this situation so they can guide educational institutions in appropriate program design, standards and assessment, and compliance issues.

ESL teachers in low-incidence settings must often fight an uphill battle with teachers and administrators who are older, more experienced, generally satisfied with the status quo, and in denial that this new population will be a permanent one. There may also be staff members who exhibit animosity toward students who have created new challenges or "discord" as well as the teacher who advocates for those students. In these cases, ESL teachers need all the leadership skills they can muster to guide educational institutions in appropriate program design, standards and assessment, and compliance issues regarding ELL students.

## BACKGROUND LITERATURE ON LOW-INCIDENCE ELL SETTINGS

The presence of English language learners in K–12 classrooms across the United States has produced a considerable body of literature. From Krashen to Cummins, Chamot to Short, the past decades have seen a strong foundation laid of both scientific and experiential data. However, the focus of this body of literature has most often been directed toward high-incidence settings—areas where larger numbers of ELLs have driven school personnel to revamp their delivery of services to focus on these students. Literature specifically designed to target low incidence settings is unfortunately still minimal. One volume that does address the issues of low numbers is Berube's (2000) *Managing ESL Programs in Rural and Small Urban Schools.*

If resources on the topic of low-incidence populations are limited, literature specifically addressing leadership in such situations is even scarcer. Articles such as Ackerman & Mackenzie (2006) inform and empower mainstream educational leaders in generic school settings. However, the very nature of the environment in which educators of ELLs in low-incidence settings find themselves often precludes them from being able to take advantage of such models to become recognized as leaders among their colleagues. The whole area of low-incidence is an opportunity and a high-need area for future research, and the issue of leadership in low-incidence situations presents an even greater need for research, reflection, and publication.

## The Foundation of Leadership in Low-Incidence Situations: Understanding and Acting on Legal Principles

Understanding the rights of English Language Learners (ELLs) and the legal principles that require the establishment of services for this population is critically important to the delivery of quality programs. In fact, as is the case in many areas, knowledge is power. Knowing what the law requires allows ESL teachers, school site or school system administrators (and others involved in the development and implementation of an ESL program) to design, implement, and evaluate a program effectively. In the end, an effective ESL program often serves both the group of enrolled ELLs and the entire school community, given the need for schools and districts to meet the standards set for ELLs and others by federal and state legislation or court decisions. In situations where there is a low incidence of ELLs or a low incidence of ELLs who speak a certain language, understanding key legal principles is especially important. The specifics that follow pertain to the United States and are offered as examples. ESL teachers in other countries will need to research legal principles governing their particular area.

First, U.S.-based ESL teachers must become familiar with basic legal principles in this area. Certainly, reading the landmark U. S. Supreme Court case of *Lau v. Nichols*, 414 U.S. 563 (1974) is a start. From that case one learns that Title VI of the Civil Rights Act of 1964 is the legal springboard from which the requirement for ESL programs derives. Understanding how to evaluate the legal sufficiency of an ESL program using the three-prong test of *Castaneda v. Pickard*, 648 F.2d 989 (5th Cir. 1981), will also assist in developing understanding and leadership in this area. In addition, federal regulations for implementing the current authorization of the Elementary and Secondary Education Act (ESEA) of 1965, the No Child Left Behind Act with respect to Adequate Yearly Progress (AYP), which pertain to ELLs and regulations issued by the U. S Department of Education's Office of English Language Acquisition (OELA) that must be followed when Title III grant funds are involved (see http://ecfr.gpoaccess.gov/).

But, it is also important to do other reading in this area, if possible. Unfortunately, there are currently few clear and accurate sources that precisely set forth the specific legal reasoning and justifications for the establishment and implementation of an ESL program. Most deal with the history of ESL, but they do not give someone who needs to be a leader clear and succinct justifications for why ESL must be implemented and how. Basic information is provided by the U. S. Department of Education Office of Civil Rights.

It is also very important to seek out experts in the field in your state and in the nation for advice, guidance, and even mentoring, especially since a low-incidence situation presents issues that are not always apparent to those who run large programs. A good starting place for locating experts is your state department of education. Important as well is attendance at state and regional meetings that deal with ESL issues. Many states hold annual conferences that include ESL issues or are focused solely on ESL. And there are several national groups, such as the National Association for Bilingual Education (NABE) and Teachers of English to Speakers of Other Languages, Inc. (TESOL) that hold very large national/international conferences. At these conferences, during certain workshops, legal issues are discussed and questions may be posed in order to obtain answers to thorny problems.

All ESL personnel who find themselves in a leadership position, whether formal or informal, should keep the following very basic legal principles in mind.

•      There is an obligation on the part of the local school district to establish an ESL program even when there is only one child who is not fluent in English in the school or school system. The right to an effective ESL program is an individual right.

•      Parents who do not speak English are entitled to communication from the school in a language they can understand. It is the district's obligation to provide such translation/interpretation; it is not appropriate or legally sufficient to ask the parent to bring someone to translate, and it is not appropriate or legally sufficient to use minors to do the translation.

•      Many ELLs are immigrants or are from immigrant families. Immigration status and ELL status are often intertwined educationally and legally. It is important to understand that these children have certain legal rights that derive from their immigrant status as well as from their ELL status. For example, the Supreme Court has ruled that even undocumented children have a right to attend free public school where they live, regardless of their undocumented immigration status (*Plyler v. Doe*, 457 U.S.202 [1982]).

The more ESL teachers understand the law, the more effective they can be as leaders in both the school and the wider community, assisting in both fashioning and implementing a district's ESL program. If one is clear as to what is required with respect to the education of ELLs, it is easier to conduct these programs effectively and provide leadership to the entire school community, even in the face of misunderstanding about, or hostility toward, an ESL program.

### The Challenges of Establishing a Leadership Role in a Low-Incidence Situation

In districts with large numbers of English language learners, the sheer weight of this population usually forces the established administrative hierarchy to have structures and personnel in place to address ELL needs. This impetus of numbers does not exist in low-incidence districts. ESL teachers in these situations are also often new to the existing school staff and usually have no formal status in the administrative leadership hierarchy.

Standard school hierarchies traditionally follow a top-down leadership model. In more progressive schools, there is a movement toward shared leadership among instructional staff. However few, if any, of these models allow for ESL teachers, particularly those who are itinerant (e.g., travel from site to site to serve students' instructional needs), to assume a formal position of leadership in guiding an educational institution to appropriately address the needs of ELLs, while guaranteeing that the program appropriately addresses criteria set by state and federal governments. Low-incidence situations where ESL teachers are not in a formally recognized leadership capacity often require the exercise of less direct, more informal methods of influencing behavior and practices.

## Leading through Sharing and Influence

What does this mean on an operational level for ESL teachers in low-incidence situations? It means that even though ESL teachers are not considered leaders in the traditional hierarchy, they must be prepared to advise all school staff and personnel on all issues related to the education of ELLs. This role differs from the role of ESL teachers in a district or school with high ELL counts where administrators are most likely familiar with the legal requirements of educating ELLs and central office specialists provide technical assistance to site-based teachers. In these larger districts, the role of ESL teachers is to teach. However, low-incidence situations require a more expansive role for ESL teachers, who must be seen as a reliable resource in all facets of ELL programming including state and federal cases, judgments, and mandates.

Unfortunately, ESL teachers are not always seen as a potential resource. They may be isolated from school staff due to the frequently itinerant nature of their position, which may not afford them the opportunity for regular interaction with educational colleagues or staff. If current structures do not encourage ESL teachers to expand their instructional role to also serve as a resource for staff and the school community at large, it falls to these teachers to develop a plan to break the traditions of the existing system and become change agents for the institution.

In the early stages of this plan, ESL teachers usually assume roles as facilitators, assuring existing staff and administration that the dissemination of knowledge and the professional development they are proposing will build capacity within the institution rather than challenge the existing hierarchy. It is also critical at this point that ELL teachers work to secure the support and participation of the administration to provide "protected" meeting time on a regular basis to meet with teachers to discuss instructional and assessment needs, plan for instruction, and plan for ongoing professional development. Whereas ESL teachers in low-incidence settings serve as single resources by sharing information and providing quality professional development, additional staff members also become knowledgeable.

Building capacity in this way requires basic leadership skills, especially the ability to influence others. It is important for ESL teachers to share knowledge in a nonthreatening manner with as many school staff members as possible. A good way to begin this process is by providing small amounts of information on critical ELL issues via emails or hard copy in staff members' mailboxes. ESL teachers should be well prepared for these first steps and provide documentation, including pedagogical and legal support, for shared materials.

ESL teachers in low-incidence arenas may find that school staff will make the first move and call on them to inform or respond to issues having to do with one student or with the ELL population as a whole. Counselors, support staff (e.g., secretaries, lunchroom and playground aides, crossing guards, cafeteria workers, etc.), as well as teachers and administrators frequently find themselves facing situations they have never encountered due to their limited exposure to students from language and cultural groups that differ from the school's historic student population. As staff members prepare to address the needs of this new student group, ESL teachers may be called upon to provide information on any variety of subjects dealing with ELL students. ESL teachers will need to be aware that their plans for professional development will need to include training in cultural sensitivity, respecting differences, creating community for all students in noninstructional settings, and building support for parents and providing open lines of communication between parents and the school, as well as the more traditional classroom-based instructional and assessment topics. Figure 17.1 shows some of these possible situations.

One of the most critical areas where ESL teachers can exert influence, and thus leadership, is the area of professional development for mainstream teachers and administrators. The majority of teacher preparation programs do not prepare general educators to adequately address the needs of ELLs. Initial knowledge

**Figure 17.1:** Knowledge and Leadership Responsibilities of ESL Teachers to Various Staff Members in a Low-density Setting

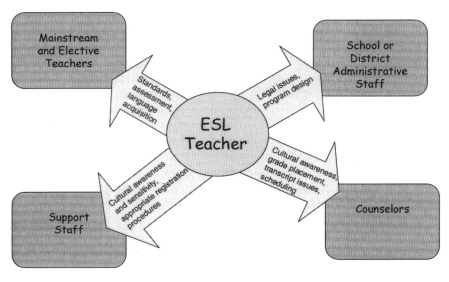

about the second language acquisition process is primary in the education of ESL/bilingual teachers and should provide a good jumping-off point for ESL teachers when working with classroom teachers who are experiencing ELLs in their classes.

A recent study by The Center for the Future of Teaching and Learning and The Linguistic Minority Research Institute (Gándara, Maxwell-Jolly, & Driscoll, 2005) identified a variety of issues and challenges that teachers face when trying to implement highly effective education programs for ELLs. Among these were lack of support from administrators and district and school policy, lack of appropriate instructional materials and assessment instruments, lack of time and support to collaborate for instruction, and lack of appropriate and applicable professional development opportunities. Paramount among the recommendations of the study was the need for tools to facilitate the development and evaluation of programming for ELLs.

Recent research has also shown the critical relationship between high-quality, sustained professional development of teachers and increased student achievement, including the value of peer coaching, the creation of "learning communities," and the development of "critical friends" groups within schools to promote collaboration among colleagues (The National Commission on Teaching and America's Future, Dade [2003], The Annenberg Initiative for School Reform at Brown University, Bambino (2002). ESL teachers can take advantage of these research-based initiatives to establish leadership in delivering information on ELL student rights and legal requirements for serving them, and encouraging staff to adopt best practices in instruction and assessment of ELLs.

ESL teachers in low-incidence situations frequently find themselves clearing up misconceptions regarding what ELLs know in their first language. Many mainstream teachers who are unfamiliar with the process of language acquisition confuse linguistic ability and academic knowledge. Content teachers, particularly those at the secondary level, are often unaware of the concept of interrupted education. In addition, ESL teachers can bring knowledge of standards and assessment, as well as curriculum and instruction, to the table when working in collaborative and /or "critical friends" situations with mainstream teachers. *TESOL's PreK-12 English Language Proficiency Standards* (Gottlieb, Carnuccio, Ernst-Slavit, & Katz, 2006) provides a good starting point and reference for such a discussion. This document not only addresses social and academic language across a developmental continuum, but also addresses national content standards with which most mainstream teachers are familiar. As a tool, these English Language Proficiency Standards can assist ESL teachers who are collaborating or advising mainstream teachers in developing lessons appropriate to the linguistic skills and abilities of ELLs while taking into consideration the academic knowledge these students may bring to the classroom.

In addition to addressing professional development, ESL teachers must also take a leadership role in evaluating the effectiveness of their school's programming for ELL students. Recent federal legislation (specifically the No Child Left

Behind Act of 2001, Titles I and III) has resulted in greater accountability for, and monitoring of, ELL student achievement for all schools, regardless of the number of ELLs enrolled. All schools are required to have specific plans in place for serving ELL students and for training staff. ESL teachers in low-incidence settings are particularly suited, as possibly the only true "experts" on ELLs in their schools, to provide guidance in developing and facilitating the implementation of their district plan, as well as overseeing its evaluation.

Ensuring that their district ELL plan has clear and measurable objectives for student instruction, staff development and community/parent involvement are the first steps in providing leadership in this area. Once focused and specific expectations have been set, ESL teachers will need to guide administrators and teachers in choosing valid and reliable assessments to measure progress toward those expectations. Most states have mandated assessments and have supplied their districts with reporting forms for basic information. However, districts that are serious in their desire for quality ELL programs generally go beyond addressing only the minimum requirements. ESL teachers can find a good resource for evaluating the effectiveness of their program on the U.S. Department of Education's website under the Office for Civil Rights. In addition, the National Study for School Evaluation (NSSE) has published a comprehensive standards-based guide to evaluating ESL Programs (*Program Evaluation*, 2002). For information on purchasing this guide consult the NSSE website at www.nsse.org/.

ESL teachers in low-incidence situations play a key role in ensuring that their students receive an equitable and effective education that meets state and federal mandates, while staying appropriate to their linguistic and academic abilities. To accomplish this, ESL teachers must become change agents, often in situations very resistant to change, and assume leadership roles without any official mantle of authority. ESL teachers in low-incidence settings must be willing and able to impact decisions regarding ELLs, as well as provide a constant stream of information and suggestions to all levels of staff. They can accomplish this by the judicious use of their status as expert, by the persistent dissemination of relevant information, by coordinating effective professional development, and by encouraging collaboration between themselves and school staff. They must learn to use all the basic skills of leadership but then go beyond to practice the fine art of "leading through vision and influence."

## Suggested Resources

Berube, B. (2000). *Managing ESL programs in rural and small urban schools*, Alexandria, VA: TESOL.

This book provides suggestions for managing ESL programs in rural and small urban schools. Its topics cover instruction, student assessment, program evaluation, parent and community involvement, and multimedia resources. Its statutory information predates NCLB.

Hudec, J., & Short, D. (Producers). *Helping English learners succeed: An overview of the SIOP model.* Center for Applied Linguistics (CAL), 2002.

This resource, available in VHS or DVD format, is designed for administrators, policymakers, and teachers as an introduction to sheltered content instruction and for teachers of education as a tool for use in methodology classes. Filmed in a documentary style, this video features six exemplary teachers who are seen following the SIOP Model and employing a wide range of teaching strategies that integrate language and content learning.

National Association for Bilingual Education (NABE) (www.nabe.org)

Located in Washington, DC, the National Association for Bilingual Education (NABE) is a professional organization representing both English language learners and bilingual education professionals. With affiliate organizations in 23 states, NABE has a combined membership of more than 20,000 bilingual and ESL professionals and parents. Its website includes information on research, advocacy, publications, its annual conference, and job openings.

National Clearinghouse on English Language Acquisition (NCELA) at George Washington University, Washington, DC (www.ncela.gwu.edu)

OELA's National Clearinghouse for English Language Acquisition and Language Instruction Educational Programs (NCELA) collects, analyzes, synthesizes, and disseminates information about language instruction educational programs for English language learners and related programs. It is funded by the U.S. Department of Education's Office of English Language Acquisition, Language Enhancement & Academic Achievement for Limited English Proficient Students (OELA) under Title III of the No Child Left Behind (NCLB) Act of 2001.

The National Study of School Evaluation (NSSE) (www.nsse.org)

The National Study of School Evaluation, located in Schaumburg, IL, is a nonprofit educational research and development organization founded in 1933 by the six regional school accreditation commissions in the United States. NSSE works with more than 30,000 schools—public and private and kindergarten through grade 12—across the United States and abroad. Through its resources, tools, and professional development, the NSSE supports school evaluation and the development of school improvement plans and system-wide improvement plans.

*Programs for English Language Learners: Resource materials for planning and self-assessments.*

Retrieved September 15, 2006, from the U.S. Department of Education, Office for Civil Rights website, http://www.ed.gov/about/offices/list/ocr/ell/index.html

The U.S. Department of Education Office of English Language Acquisition (OELA) (http://ed.gov/oela)

OELA administers Title III of the No Child Left Behind Act (2001). Website resources include statues and regulations and a link to the National Clearinghouse for English Language Acquisition & Language Instruction Educational Programs (NCELA).

The U.S. Department of Education Office of Civil Rights (OCR) (www.ed.gov/ocr)

The OCR mission is to ensure equal access to education and to promote educational excellence throughout the nation through vigorous enforcement of civil rights. Numerous resources are posted in the areas of race, national origin (language), and gender.

---

### Discussion Questions

1. Discuss three key legal requirements that underlie the establishment and implementation of an ESL program. Discuss the source of each requirement.
2. As a traveling teacher covering several sites in a low-incidence district, how can an ESL teacher assume a leadership role with limited presence in several buildings?
3. How could you develop a leadership model that included collaboration of all "stakeholders" in the education of ELLs in your school/district? How would you create a set of guidelines to help avoid the top-down traditional model of both leadership and professional development that usually occurs within Pre–K-12 school districts?
4. As the first and only teacher in a low-incidence school district, which topics would you propose to the administration as part of an initial professional development plan for teachers and staff? How would you convince the administrators this was necessary?
5. Using one of the suggested resources for evaluating the effectiveness of a program for serving ELLs, outline the steps you would take to develop a plan for your site or district.

## REFERENCES

Ackerman, R., & Mackenzie, S. V. (2006, May). Uncovering teacher leadership. *Educational Leadership, 63*(8), 66–70.

Bambino, D. (2002). Critical friends. *Educational Leadership, 59*(6), 25–27.

Berube, B. (2000). *Managing ESL programs in rural and small urban schools.* Alexandria, VA: TESOL.

Dade, C. (2003) *A call to action for the National Commission on Teaching and America's Future: Enabling distributed-learning communities for educators via emerging technologies.* Retrieved September 10, 2006, from http://www. nctaf.org/strategies/creat/21st_c_teaching/index.htm

Gándara, P., Maxwell-Jolly, J., & Driscoll, A. (2005) *Listening to teachers of English language learners: A survey of California teachers' challenges, experiences, and professional development needs.* Santa Cruz, CA: The Center for the Future of Teaching and Learning. Overview and summary of the full report available at http://www.cftl.org/centerviews/july05.html

Gottlieb, M., Carnuccio, L., Ernst-Slavit, G., & Katz, A. (2006). *PreK–12 English language proficiency standards.* Alexandria, VA: TESOL.

Huffman, C. L., Carnuccio, L., O'Loughlin, J., & Rosenthal, R. (2003). Small numbers—big challenges: Designing and delivering programs for low-incidence English language learners. *NABE News, 27*(1), 16–19.

National Clearinghouse for English Language Acquisition. (2004). Retrieved August 30, 2007, http://www.ncela.gwu.edu/stats/2_nation.htm

National Study of School Evaluation. (2002). *Program evaluation: English as a Second Language (A comprehensive guide for standards-based program evaluation for schools committed to continuous improvement.)* Schaumburg, IL.

*Plyler v. Doe,* 457 U.S.202 [1982]).

Policy and Programs. (2006). In C. J. Ovando, M. C. Combs, & V. P. Collier (Eds.). *In bilingual and ESL classrooms: Teaching in multicultural contexts* (4th ed.). (pp. 47–84). Boston: McGraw-Hill Higher Education.

# Chapter 18

## Leadership Responding to Linguistic and Cultural Diversity: A Systemic Approach

Beth Arnow and Victoria Vazquez Webbert

U.S. public schools are experiencing significant growth in student diversity that mirrors the increasing cultural and linguistic multiplicity of our communities at large and the country. Thousands of English language teaching educators and leaders involved in Pre-K to grade 12 education must consider the leadership skills they use on a daily basis and how those skills affect the ability of their organizations to respond to the growing diversity.

The U.S. Department of Education (USDOE) through the Office of English Language Acquisition (OELA) and The National Clearinghouse for English Language Acquisition (NCELA) reports that the growth of English Language Learners (ELLs) has been about 400 percent in the last five years in classrooms across America. Based on state-reported data, it is estimated that 5,112,081 ELLs were enrolled in public schools (Pre-K through Grade 12) for the 2003–2004 school year. Also according to NCELA, Georgia's limited English proficient (LEP) population grew 291.6 percent in the ten-year period between 1994–1995 and 2004–2005 ("Georgia Rate of LEP Growth 1994/1995 and 2004/2005"). The ELL numbers do not include students who have a primary or home language other than English and whose skill in English has allowed them to be re-classified as fluent English language proficient. The resulting impact of a growing linguistically and culturally diverse population in grades kindergarten through grade 12 is profound and systemic, with significant ramifications for the teaching and learning process of all students.

These demographic changes come at a time when schools' accountability for *all students* to reach high levels of academic achievement is under intense focus due to mandates of the Elementary and Secondary Education Act reauthorization, known as the No Child Left Behind (NCLB) Act of 2001. The desegregation of achievement data required by NCLB identifies significant discrepancies between results for students of poverty and students of means; between white students and students of color; between able students and students with disabilities; and between students who speak English and those still learning the language.

As Douglas-Hall and Koball (2004, p. 4) point out, 65 percent of the children of recent immigrants are low income. The economically disadvantaged Latino student, who does not yet speak English well enough to learn academic content, will fall into three categorical desegregations that affect whether or not a school can achieve Adequate Yearly Progress (AYP). Schools and school systems must pay attention to these students. School systems can no longer claim success with overall gains in schools if students of all sub-populations are not making the same strides toward achievement.

## ONE SCHOOL SYSTEM

A February 2004 report from the Brookings Institution defined metropolitan Atlanta as an "emerging gateway" for immigrants in the past 20 years (Singer, 2004, p. 1). The term *emerging gateways* was used to distinguish areas from traditional immigrant gateway cities such as New York, San Francisco, Chicago, and others that have been first-stops for the waves of migration from outside our borders. The "emerging gateways" had a very low percentage of foreign-born until 1970 and then experienced high proportions of immigrant growth post-1980.

Gwinnett County Public Schools (GCPS) is a system that has experienced the demographic changes of metropolitan Atlanta acutely. Located in the northeast suburbs of Atlanta, GCPS has experienced tremendous growth in diversity the last decade, much of it fueled by an influx of students from other countries along with the U.S.-born children of immigrant parents. In the 1996–1997 school year, the system enrolled 88,831 students; ten years later, in the 2005–2006 school year, the figure of enrollees was 144,364 students, a 62 percent increase. A comparison of the ethnic breakdowns during that period is shown in Figure 18.1.

*Figure 18.1:* A Comparison of the Ethnic Breakdowns from 1996–2006

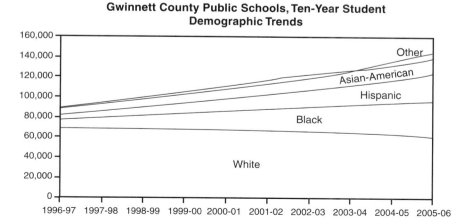

Within those demographic changes, the numbers of students speaking ESL has grown from a small percentage of the student population to almost one in every three students. One student in eleven is currently identified as an LEP ELL in accordance with state-mandated criteria. However, one in four students has a primary or home language other than English (PHLOTE.) Figure 18.2 illustrates the growth of the PHLOTE and LEP populations over the same ten-year period.

The sub-group of students for whom Spanish is the primary or home language is the largest and most rapidly growing group. These students come from a variety of national origins. Significant numbers of speakers of Korean, Vietnamese, Serbo-Croatian, and other languages have similar academic needs. Figure 18.3 illustrates some of the language breakdowns of PHLOTE students in the 2005–2006 school year. Due to the mix of language groups within the system and within individual schools, the instructional focus in GCPS has been an English language development program within the academic context and the provision of specialized language assistance in the ESOL classroom.

One of every seven students (20,391) in the system was born outside the United States. Students come from 178 different countries, from Afghanistan to Zimbabwe. Several years back, the ELLs were largely recent immigrants, but as the linguistic-minority communities have grown larger and more stable, increasingly ELLs in the lower grades are U.S.-born of immigrant parents.

**Figure 18.2:** The Growth of the PHLOTE and LEP Populations from 1996–2006

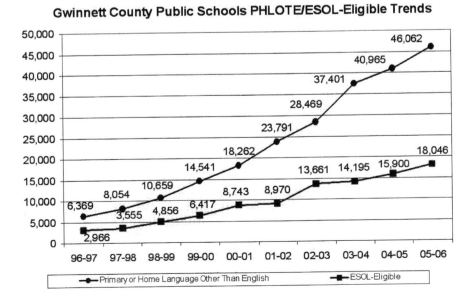

***Figure 18.3:*** Some of the Language Breakdowns of PHLOTE Students in the
2005–2006 School Year

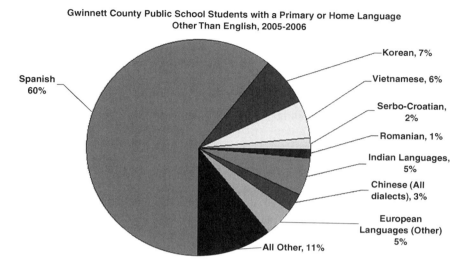

Gwinnett County Public School Students with a Primary or Home Language
Other Than English, 2005-2006

## A SYSTEMIC APPROACH

The changing demographics require a re-thinking of schools and a *systems*
approach to responding to the change. The changes are beyond curriculum content alone and require the examination of our new students, especially Latinos,
and what they bring to the learning process. The dimensions of language and
culture affect how teachers organize instruction and how educational leaders
organize schools and work within communities. In taking a systems view of the
demographic changes, we considered the following components: training for
language development (ESOL) teachers; training for regular classroom teachers; engaging linguistically and culturally diverse parents in children's academic
achievement; developing culturally proficient school and system leadership; and
capitalizing on our diversity to enrich the lives of our communities. Each of these
efforts is ongoing and grows as the demographics change.

## INTENSIVE TRAINING FOR ENGLISH LANGUAGE DEVELOPMENT TEACHERS

Training for ESOL teachers must be rigorous and focus on the characteristics and
needs of diverse learners and the ways those characteristics and needs inform
what we do as teachers. For our Latino and other culturally and linguistically
diverse students, the differences lie largely in the domains of language and culture. Teachers must understand the deep elements of culture related to social
interaction and the learning process. The understanding of culture must give

teachers tools to partner with parents on their own terms (López, 2001, p. 434). ESOL teachers must understand the structural elements of languages, the process of language acquisition, and the literacy process for bilingual learners. They must understand that first language (L1) literacy is a powerful tool in the learning of second language literacy and how to encourage L1 literacy in an English immersion curriculum. ESOL teacher training must provide a firm theoretical foundation with solid practical application and opportunities to reflect professionally. ESOL teachers must have a firm grounding in the content of regular education classrooms to understand the academic and content demands that are placed upon students. The ESOL teacher becomes a consultant to regular classroom teachers in providing them with strategies for incorporating language teaching and for making content instruction comprehensible.

To meet this critical need, GCPS provides a year-long ESOL endorsement training program. The program operates as a four-course sequence. The four courses taught in the ESOL Endorsement program are Cross-Cultural Issues for the ESOL Teacher, Applied Linguistics for the ESOL Teacher, Methods and Materials for the ESOL Teacher, and a 30-hour practicum component. The program balances between the necessary theoretical foundations and practical application. Course requirements include extensive professional readings, and several required field-based projects in which endorsement candidates analyze the culture, linguistic development, or academic needs of selected students in their classrooms and develop instructional units that integrate language objectives with other content area objectives. With the state's adoption of the WIDA/ACCESS™, the WIDA framework for instruction and the Assessing Comprehension and Content from State to State for ELLs has been incorporated into the training program. Supported by local professional development funds, the program has evolved over the past seven years.

## EXTENSIVE EDUCATION FOR REGULAR CLASSROOM TEACHERS AND OTHER SCHOOL STAFF

Across the country, schools are seeking new ways of developing the professional skills of all teachers who work with ELLs (August & Hakuta, 1997, p. 250). High levels of academic achievement occur only if there is strong, ongoing collaboration between the ESOL teacher and other instructional staff working with the same ELLs to plan for congruent instruction for the students throughout the school day. Instruction for ELLs must be made as comprehensible as possible (Cummins, 2000) both in the ELD setting and in the regular classroom setting. As ELLs transition from ESOL programs, they often need instructional interventions to continue their English language development during their two years of monitoring. School systems must educate non-ESOL professionals to understand the cultural and linguistic dimensions of learning and enhance their skills in using strategies to make content instruction comprehensible for ELLs. Regular classroom teachers must also have background knowledge of the process of language acquisition and how this impacts learning. With knowledge about the learner, teachers can apply the strategies that are appropriate at each stage of language acquisition, are culturally responsive, and that spiral from students' prior knowledge to ensure linguistic and academic expectations are within the student's zone of proximal development (Vygotsky in Kozulin, 1986). Comprehensible content instruction in the regular classroom coupled with language instruction that incorporates academic language can be powerful in propelling students to high levels of academic achievement.

To meet the professional development needs of regular classroom teachers, GCPS has developed a 30-hour staff development program titled "Teaching Academic Language and Content to ELLs," which is open to all educators in the system. Using a "trainer-of-trainers model" enables a small central staff to reach larger numbers of teachers and to customize the course delivery to a specific group of teachers (e.g., math/science teachers) or to a specific school setting. Topics of the 30-hour program include: the stages of language acquisition, the effect of culture and prior experiences of learning, classroom cultural responsiveness, assessment strategies, ELL student identification, research-based strategies for ELL instruction, technology resources to support ELL instruction, and system policies for the instruction of ELLs.

Training for regular classroom teachers from across the system began in 1999 as a one-week summer staff development program. Quickly, the need to customize the staff development sequence for different groups of teachers became apparent. With collaboration from content area experts, the planning team adapted the program for middle school and high school teachers and developed content-specific training, such as "Teaching Science (Math/Social Studies, etc.), Academic Language, and Content to ELLs". The program has expanded to other areas such as health/physical education, Title I, gifted, and technology education.

As No Child Left Behind focused on accountability, the "Teaching Academic Language and Content" program has evolved once again to be a school-focused option during the regular school term. The focus on school-based delivery allows for the program to be offered in shorter segments and over a longer period of time, such as three-hour after-school sessions for ten weeks. The longer-term delivery allows participants time to implement suggested strategies and reflect on them. The school-focused option involves school leadership and increased integration into other improvement efforts of the school (National Staff Development Council, 2001, p. 8.). Developing a cadre of 20–25 teachers trained in a school can cause a change in conversation about teaching and learning in the school as teachers develop a common language about ELLs and their instructional needs. This professional learning program has also been a "feeder" program for teachers becoming interested in obtaining their ESOL endorsement. To date, more than 1,400 teachers have completed the 30-hour program. The effort has been supported by local professional learning funds and extended with funding under Title III of No Child Left Behind.

## COLLABORATIVE PLANNING FOR INDIVIDUAL ELL STUDENTS

GCPS's curriculum for grades K–12 is called the Academic Knowledge and Skills (AKS). The AKS for each grade level and subject area define the essential knowledge and academic skills that students are expected to know. The AKS offers a solid base on which teachers build rich curricular experiences. Teachers use curriculum guides, textbooks, technology, and other materials to teach the AKS curriculum and ensure every student is learning to his or her potential.

The instructional day of learners with various special needs can lack congruence if the various professionals working with a student do not plan collaboratively. The challenge is to bring the adults who work with a student together to plan instruction that is cohesive rather than fragmented. Seeing the potential difficulties with supplemental services, GCPS developed a process for planning and assessing for ELLs on an ongoing basis. Based on the system-defined standards, the process is the "AKS Modification and Intervention Plan for ELLs." As the state adopted WIDA/ACCESS, it became very apparent that the new assessment framework fit in very well with what the system was trying to accomplish through the joint planning.

At its inception, the "AKS Modification Plan" was a paper document used by the ESOL teacher and the student's regular classroom teacher to identify the specific AKS that were most critical for the ELL and how that academic material could be made as comprehensible as possible for the learner at his or her current level of language proficiency. The distinction between a "modification" and an "intervention" is important in developing a plan. A "modification" is an alteration of the learning objective (AKS) itself. In contrast, "interventions" are those strategies that a teacher may use with any student. Interventions can include the following: rewording questions/assignments for linguistic comprehensibility; using partners for following directions and explaining assignments; pre-teaching key vocabulary and grammatical structures, especially those used in novel ways; making concepts concrete by the use of visuals, gestures, and realia that provide comprehensible input; providing bilingual resources for reference; and organizing information graphically to make concepts more concrete.

Formative assessment accommodations include allowing more time for task completion, accepting buddy-assisted notes and assignments, permitting the use of class notes during testing, allowing students to perform tasks that reflect their learning, or other alternative assessment strategies.

By way of an example, a very low-proficiency newcomer fourth grader may have as his or her performance objective for a unit on photosynthesis to label the parts of the plant. A student with more proficiency may evidence knowledge of the material by illustrating and labeling the process of photosynthesis. As the student's language proficiency increases, the content and linguistic expectations grow, until they eventually reach the same expectations as those of native English speaking students. As WIDA/ACCESS was implemented, it supported the system's previous instructional direction in integrating language and content into student performance indicators. In all instructional settings, the student must be engaged in academic and language learning within their zones of proximal development (Vygotsky, 1978 p. 86).

As the AKS Modification and Intervention Plan for ELLs has been refined, it has been set up in an online database format. It is now aligned with the WIDA standards and proficiency levels. A collaborative plan is developed at the beginning of the year for each student. As performance indicators are met by the student, progress is noted and additional AKSs are added to the student's plan. In the collaborative process, the ESOL teacher can suggest appropriate strategies for the regular classroom teacher to make the content more comprehensible. In the process of collaborating, the ESOL teacher becomes more aware of which content stems to incorporate into language instruction. Instruction becomes more congruent as content and teaching strategies become more aligned across instructional settings.

Successful implementation of the AKS Modification and Intervention Plan requires that all educators be trained in the concept and in the strategies. The ESOL endorsement program supports this goal by requiring ESOL teacher candidates to develop lesson plans that are WIDA- and AKS-based. The professional learning program for regular classroom teachers supports the effort by giving classroom teachers background knowledge on the stages of language acquisition and linking specific instructional strategies with each of those stages. Teachers often comment that the strategies recommended for ELLs will also help many of their other struggling learners. Indeed, many struggling learners have difficulty with academic language use. The key is for the regular classroom teacher to understand the linguistic and cultural differences of ELLs so they know which strategies to use and when to use them.

## COMMUNICATING WITH AND ENGAGING PARENTS IN THEIR CHILDREN'S ACADEMIC PROGRESS

In high-performing schools with language minority students, parents are engaged in their children's achievement and feel respected and part of a collaborative team (Reyes, Scribner, & Scribner, 1999, p. 38). Parents of English language learners value their children's education, but there is frequently a communication and an expectation gap between language minority parents and schools. When there is an apparent gap in parent involvement, schools must consider the ways in which they reach out to parents and communicate with them in a language they understand. Multiple languages of parents are complicating factors and GCPS is reaching out to the four largest language groups: Spanish-, Korean-, Vietnamese-, and Bosnian-speaking families. This is being accomplished through a two-fold effort at the central office and school level.

To support the schools in communicating with parents, the system has five interpreter/translators for the largest language groups. The interpreter/translators are available to schools for group meetings such as PTAs and orientations, as well as for high-stakes communication concerns such as meetings with parents for Student Support Teams, Individualized Education Programs, and disciplinary panels. The interpreter/translators also support schools for other parent-teacher meetings that may be less formal. Many formal parent-school communications are written and the interpreter/translators translate important parent information documents that are then loaded onto an intranet online database available on every computer in the school system. School staff can access and print out official school documents related to school registration, immunization requirements, welcome books, health forms, testing information, special education information, disciplinary procedures, graduation requirements, parent education, school nutrition, community services, academic achievement, gang prevention, etc. The database contains more than 1,500 locally translated documents and web links to other sources such as the U.S. Department of Education, the U. S. Department of Agriculture, the National P.T.A., and the National Clearinghouse on Education and Language Acquisition. Multilingual school system staff outside the major four languages are contracted to translate other documents as the need arises.

School-based communication with parents is also a priority. Through Title III NCLB funds, elementary schools with larger concentrations of limited English proficient students have been staffed with Title III Parent Outreach Liaisons. The number of these positions has increased to 21 in 2006–2007. The linkage with community support service organizations includes information about community education opportunities, English language instruction, health systems, public libraries, mental health organizations, ethnic community organizations, etc. The parent outreach liaisons provide important communication to the parents regarding school expectations and the importance of academic achievement and the communication is two-way. They also provide school faculties with more information about the families, their expectations for their children's achievement, and any barriers that the families have for supporting their children's success. To expand resources, the Title III-funded staff positions coordinate closely with Title I-funded parent involvement staff. In many schools, the Title III staff positions are only a part of the multilingual school network. Principals have recruited multilingual staff in all areas of the school operation from front office to cafeteria to maintenance and classroom. Many schools have developed their own local "language banks" of bilingual parents and community members who can help out with more casual communication needs, such as newsletters, etc.

## SCHOOL AND SYSTEM LEADERSHIP

Recognizing the fact that the school system was moving toward having a majority-minority student population and that soon Latinos would be the largest non-White minority, the superintendent in the 2001–2002 school year contracted with a local Hispanic-owned marketing company to assess needs of the Latino community vis-à-vis education and recommend steps that the school system could initiate to engage Latino parents in their children's education and promote higher academic achievement for minority students. Findings were presented to the instructional leaders in the system. As a result, professional development for school and central office leaders focused on three specific areas: parent outreach and engagement; effective instructional practices; and recruiting and hiring minority staff. The importance of these areas is reinforced by the superintendent's and the board of education's commitment. That commitment has been evidenced by continued funding of professional learning activities and the funding of interpreter/translator positions. The system's vision recognizes that changing demographics and leadership will continue to evolve to maintain a high level of student academic achievement.

## THE RESULTS

In the face of rapidly changing demographics, achievement levels have remained high and the system has seen "achievement rise to an all-time high at each grade level" (Loe, 2004 p. 29). The system has a high proportion of students taking the SAT and has average scores 19 points above the national average. Elementary and middle school students met or exceeded the state averages at all grade levels on the state Criterion Referenced Tests. The challenges remain, and the system continues to apply concepts of Continuous Quality Improvement to narrow the achievement gap.

The leadership and instructional staff of GCPS remains focused on the direction research-based instructional strategies offer and continuously renews its commitment to become highly effective in promoting student academic achievement regardless of students' language and cultural backgrounds. There is strong conviction that schools that are highly effective produce results that almost entirely overcome the effects of student background (Marzano, 2003, p. 7).

## LOOKING TO THE PAST AND FORWARD AND CAPITALIZING ON DIVERSITY

The education of immigrant children to the United States of America was not even a postscript in the minds of the founding fathers of this nation and it still is a strained concept in the conceptual framework of leaders of the nation these days. "History inevitably entails interpretation" (Kliebard, 2004, p. ix). Joel Spring's (2000, p. 2) opening statement, in *The American School—1642–2000*, assures us that there is no "right interpretation of history." The absence of curriculum efforts addressing the needs of immigrant students is evident in the absence of historical accounts of early curriculum or educational reform efforts to improve the education of immigrants. In this light, the history of the American curriculum becomes the delineation of the struggle between the ideological positions of the various groups present during the inception of America and the way they complemented or contradicted each other (Spring, 2000, p. xix).

The initiatives toward reforming education for the members of various groups must be seen against the backdrop of the political and socioeconomic conditions of the time (Spring, 2000, p. xx). Our classroom diversity is and will be reflected in the workplaces of today and tomorrow. The tools we provide learners in tolerance and how to appreciate the benefits of that diversity will serve them well for the rest of their lives. The key is to support these changes systemically, systematically, and continuously through an organizational quality management process. GCPS has undertaken a proactive, long-term approach in all dimensions of the system operation.

Instructional leadership is key in educational reform. Research indicates that superintendents use their positions in the formal organization to improve instruction through staff selection, principal supervision, instructional goal-setting and monitoring, financial planning, and consultative management practices. Responding to this call for instructional leadership the Office of the Superintendent in GCPS has progressively set the pace for instructional excellence as the result of transformational leadership. With an emphasis on the three things that good principals do: understand the context, understand themselves, and focus on what is best for students (Marzano, 2003, p. 174–178), the school system plows ahead and charts a course for success for all. The results will enrich the lives of the entire community.

---

**SUGGESTED RESOURCES**

---

Douglas-Hall, A., & Koball, H. (2004). *Children of recent immigrants: National and regional trends.* New York: Columbia University, National Center for Children in Poverty. Available from: http://www.nccp.org/media/cri04-text.pdf

National Clearinghouse on English Language Acquisition. (2006). *Georgia rate of LEP growth 1994/95-2004/05* [online]. Washington DC: George Washington University. Available from www.ncela.gwu.edu/policy/states/reports/statedata/2004LEP/Georgia-G-05.pdf

WIDA Consortium. Retrieved September 25, 2006, from www.wida.us/

---

### Discussion Questions

1. What role can teacher/leaders take in providing professional learning opportunities?
2. How can teacher/leaders build the capacity of an organization through collegial networking?
3. In what ways can school leaders promote parental engagement?
4. How can school leaders help set high expectations for *all* learners?

## REFERENCES

August, D., & Hakuta, K. (1997). *Improving schooling for language-minority children: A research agenda.* Washington, DC: National Academy Press.

Cummins, J. (2000). *Language, power, and pedagogy: Bilingual children in the crossfire.* Tonawonda, NY: Multilingual Matters.

Douglas-Hall, A., & Koball, H. (2004). *Children of recent immigrants: National and regional trends.* New York: Columbia University, National Center for Children in Poverty. [online] cited September 25, 2006. http://www.nccp. org/publications/pdf/text_476.pdf

Kliebard, H. (2004). *The struggle for the American curriculum.* New York: Routledge Falmer.

Kozulin, A. (1998). *Psychological tools: A sociocultural approach to education.* Cambridge, MA: Harvard University Press.

Loe, C., (2004, June). Gateways to the future. *American School Board Journal,* 28–31.

López, G., (2001). The value of hard work. *Harvard Educational Review, 71*(3), 416–437.

Marzano, R. J. (2003). *What works in schools: Translating research into action.* Alexandria, VA: ASCD.

National Clearinghouse on English Language Acquisition. (2006). Georgia Rate of LEP Growth 1994/95-2004/05 [online]. Washington, DC: George Washington University, 2006 [Retrieved September 25, 2006]. Available at http://www.ncela.gwu.edu/policy/states/reports/statedata/2004LEP/Georgia-G-05.pdf

National Staff Development Council (2001). *Standards for staff development.* Oxford, OH: National Staff Development Council.

Reyes, P., Scribner, J. D., & Paredes Scribner, A. (1999). *Lessons from high-performing Hispanic schools.* New York: Teachers College Press.

Singer, A. (2004). *The rise of new immigrant gateways.* Washington, DC: The Brookings Institution, Center on Urban and Metropolitan Policy. Available from www.brookings.edu/urban/pubs/20040301_gateways.pdf#search=%22%22the%20rise%20of%20new%20immigrant%20gateways%22%22

Spring, J. (2000). *The American school—1642–2000.* New York: McGraw Hill.

Vygotsky, L. (1978). *Mind in society: The development of higher psychological processes.* Cambridge, MA: Harvard University Press.

# CONTRIBUTORS

**Mark Algren** is an IEP teacher and administrator at the Applied English Center at the University of Kansas. He has extensive experience in the Middle East. He was the TESOL, Inc., conference chair in 2003 (Baltimore), and co-chaired the 2006 TESOL Arabia conference (Dubai, UAE).

**Mashael Al-Hamly** is the head of the Department of English Language and Literature at Kuwait University. She is an Associate Professor of Applied Linguistics, teaching English Language and Linguistics to undergraduate and postgraduate students. Her research interests are in Computer-Assisted Language Learning, testing, as well as translation studies.

**Steve Allison** is the chair of Academic Programmes at the Centre of Excellence for Applied Research and Training (CERT), which is an arm of the Higher Colleges of Technology (HCT) in Abu Dhabi, UAE. Steve has worked with the HCT for the last 9 years and has been in the Gulf for 15 years in total. He is also currently enrolled as a doctoral student with Glasgow University where his interest is in analyzing the effectiveness of training for those clients served by CERT.

**Neil J. Anderson** is a humanities professor of Linguistics and English Language at Brigham Young University. He also serves as the Coordinator of the English Language Center. He is the author of a teacher education text in the TeacherSource series entitled *Exploring Second Language Reading: Issues and Strategies* (Thomson ELT, 1999) and an EFL reading series *ACTIVE Skills for Reading* (Thomson ELT, 2007/2008). Professor Anderson served as President of the international association of Teachers of English to Speakers of Other Languages, Inc., 2001–2002.

**Beth Arnow** is director of ESOL Programs in Gwinnett County Public Schools. Prior to joining GCPS in 1998, she was Georgia state coordinator of ESOL and Migrant Education. She holds an M.S. in Bilingual Education and ESL from State University of New York at Albany.

**Kathleen M. Bailey** served as TESOL President (1998–1999). She is a professor of Applied Linguistics at the Monterey Institute of International Studies, where she directed the TESOL M.A. Program for six years and the Intensive ESL Program for three years. She also directed the 1986 TESOL Summer Institute.

**Brock Brady** is coordinator of American University's TESOL Program where he teaches a variety of teacher education courses. Brady is currently Chair of the Development Committee for the TESOL Board of Directors. A former Fulbright Scholar and Peace Corps volunteer, Brady has taught in various countries around the world.

**Jim Brogan** was a part-time teacher when writing his chapter. He has since become the English Program Coordinator for the Economics faculty at Dokkyo University. A student of Chinese and Japanese, as well as an engineer and professional performing acrobat, Jim has taught for ten years in Taiwan and Japan.

**Lynore Carnuccio** is an educational consultant working with states and districts to develop standards and standards-based programs for English language learners. She was the Lead Developer/Consultant for the Pennsylvania English Language Proficiency Standards and a member of the team that developed the TESOL PreK-12 English Language Proficiency Standards (2006).

**MaryAnn Christison** is a professor and director of graduate studies in the Department of Linguistics at the University of Utah. She is author of 80 refereed and published articles and 16 books. She has been President of TESOL and is now on the Board of Trustees for the International Research Foundation for English Language Education (TIRF).

**Christine Coombe** is a faculty member at Dubai Men's College and an Assessment Leader for the Higher Colleges of Technology in the UAE. During her 14 years in the Arabian Gulf, she has served as President of TESOL Arabia and chaired the annual conference five times. Most recently, she was elected to serve on the TESOL Board of Directors as the Convention Chair for the TESOL 2006 Convention in Tampa.

**Ross Currie** is chair of the Teacher Education programme at Dubai Women's College, the Higher Colleges of Technology (HCT) in the United Arab Emirates. He has worked for more than 30 years as a teacher, teacher educator, and manager in New Zealand, Australia, China, Spain, England, and Japan. He currently chairs the English Recruitment Team for the 14 Colleges in the HCT.

**Andy Curtis** received his M.A. in Applied Linguistics and his Ph.D. in International Education from the University of York, England. He is currently the Director of the English Language Teaching Unit at the Chinese University of Hong Kong. His main teaching and research interests are professional development and program development.

**Luciana C. de Oliveira** is assistant professor of literacy and language education in the Department of Curriculum and Instruction, College of Education, at Purdue University. She is TESOL's Nonnnative English Speakers in TESOL Caucus Chair (2007–2008). Her research interests include the development of academic literacy in content areas in secondary school, second language writing, and nonnative English-speaking professionals.

**Eric Dwyer** is an associate professor in Foreign Language Education at Florida International University. His work includes serving as TESOL 2004 (Long Beach) conference chair on the TESOL Board of Directors.

**William Eggington** is a professor of Linguistics at Brigham Young University. He served on the TESOL Board of Directors as conference chair for the TESOL 2005 Conference in San Antonio.

**Liz England** is professor, TESOL and ESL, Shenandoah University, has presented at international and affiliate TESOL conferences and other organizational conferences for more than 20 years in as many countries. In addition, she has been a featured presenter on the topic of making presentations at professional conferences. She also helps graduate students develop their skills and abilities in public speaking.

**Bryan Gilroy** has held senior management positions at tertiary institutions for more than 17 years. He has an M.A. (USA) and an M.B.A (UK) in Education Management. He has taught courses in Education Management and has presented widely on the management of education. He has worked in Egypt, Colombia, Kuwait, the United States, Saudi Arabia, Turkey, and the UAE. He is currently the Director of the English Language Center, Zayed University.

**Cheryl Leever Huffman** has more than 25 years of instructional and administrative experience in multicultural and bilingual education, ESL, grant writing, and program evaluation. Currently a private consultant and program evaluator, she is incoming chair of TESOL's P-12 ESL Teacher Education Program Standards Committee.

**Lía D. Kamhi-Stein** is professor in the Charter College of Education at California State University, Los Angeles, where she coordinates the TESOL M.A. Program. She is editor of *Learning and Teaching from Experience: Perspectives on Nonnative English-Speaking Professionals* (University of Michigan Press, 2004) and the co-editor (with Marguerite Ann Snow) of *Designing a New Course for Adults* (TESOL). She served on the TESOL Board of Directors (2004–2007). She is recipient of the 2003–2004 Outstanding Professor Award at California State University, Los Angeles.

**Mary Lou McCloskey**, 2002–2003 TESOL president, is Director of Teacher Development and Curriculum Design for Educo in Atlanta, Georgia. She is a global consultant on teaching ESOL to school-age learners and author of professional texts, program reviews, and instructional programs in the ELT field.

**Tim Murphey** is a professor at Kanda University of International Studies and an affiliate professor at Hawaii Pacific University and Teachers College, Tokyo. He is series editor of TESOL's Professional Development in Language Education series and has published books with OUP, CUP, Longman, Peter Lang, and Helbling Languages. He also juggles while skiing.

**Denise Murray** is emeritus professor at Macquarie University, Australia. She has been Chair of Linguistics and Language Development at San Jose State University, Director of NCELTR, and TESOL president. Her research interests and publications are in CALL, cross-cultural literacy, leadership, use of L1, and language education policy.

**Judith B. O'Loughlin,** a former elementary ESL and Special Education teacher, currently teaches graduate certification courses online for New Jersey City University; conducts teacher trainings for classroom and ESL teachers; and collaborates on standards curriculum development projects for school districts, universities, and state departments of education.

**Suzanne Panferov** is the director of the Center for English as a Second Language at the University of Arizona in Tucson, Arizona, in the United States. She markets her IEP and part-time programs with several advertising agencies around the world. In 2006–2007 she served on the TESOL Board of Directors as the annual convention program chair, when she promoted the TESOL 2007 annual conference in Seattle.

**Phil Quirke** is director of the Madinat Zayed College of the Higher Colleges of Technology in the UAE. He has been in ELT Leadership positions for more than a decade and is now implementing DREAM management at his new college. His doctorate focused on supporting teacher development via the web—research that informed the section of his chapter on respect. He has published articles and chapters on areas as diverse as face in the classroom, action research, faculty appraisal, and journal writing.

**Emily Reynolds** directs online programs at BizEnglish and trains teachers in TESOL's Online Certificate Program. She has taught at U.S. universities and lectured in Paris, Hanoi, Seoul, and Dubai. Author of nine ELT textbooks and content for award-winning software programs, she was recently honored with TESOL's Materials Development Award.

**Roger Rosenthal,** an attorney, is executive director of the Migrant Legal Action Program, a non-governmental, non-profit support and advocacy center located in Washington, DC. Mr. Rosenthal is a nationally recognized expert and frequent presenter on the legal rights of immigrant students and English Language Learners in public schools.

**John Schmidt,** academic coordinator of the Texas Intensive English Program, Texas International Education Consortium, has trained EFL instructors on five continents. Active in Toastmasters International, he has taught public speaking to EFL teachers, IEP students, and international M.B.A students. Having given scores of presentations at TESOL and TESOL-affiliate conferences and in other professional forums for 25 years, he has also conducted educational lectures shipboard on the high seas.

**Claire Bradin Siskin** directs the Robert Henderson Language Media Center at the University of Pittsburgh, where she is a lecturer in the Linguistics Department. Her principal interests are faculty development and computer-assisted research in language acquisition.

**Donna Sobel** is an associate professor in the Initial Professional Teacher Education program at the University of Colorado at Denver & Health Sciences Center. She is Chair of the Inclusive Education Program in the School of Education and Human Development. Currently, Dr. Sobel serves as Site Professor at one of UCD & HSC's urban professional development schools, where she spends a minimum of one day per week providing on-site professional development for pre-service and inservice teachers.

**Lauren Stephenson** is the director of graduate programs and the former director of the Center for Professional Development of UAE Educators. She holds a Ph.D. in Educational Leadership and a Master's in Applied Linguistics (TESOL). She has held teaching and leadership positions in ELT and teacher education for the past 18 years in a variety of countries. Her research interests include professional learning, educational leadership, action research and ELT methodology and materials design.

**Sheryl V. Taylor** is an associate professor at the University of Colorado at Denver & Health Sciences Center. She is Chair of the Literacy, Language, and Culturally Responsive Teaching Program in the School of Education & Human Development, where she teaches language acquisition and literacy development, multicultural/bilingual education. She regularly coaches Denver area teachers to support English language learners. Her research examines teachers' cognition and practice about addressing the needs of students from diverse backgrounds and abilities.

**Victoria Vazquez Webbert** is the lead program facilitator for the International Newcomers Center of Gwinnett County Public Schools in the state of Georgia and a doctoral student at Georgia Southern University. She holds a Bachelor's Degree from University of Puerto Rico, a Master's Degree from University of Miami, and a Specialist Degree from Georgia State University.

**Beth Witt** has chaired several conferences, including TESOL 1994 (Baltimore) and TESOL 2002 (Salt Lake City). She serves on the Arizona TESOL board, is Title I school improvement coordinator at Chinle Elementary School on the Navajo Nation in Chinle, Arizona, and is an adjunct instructor for Arizona State University's Diné Teacher Education Program.

# SUBJECT INDEX

# AUTHOR INDEX